Empire of Analogies

Empire of Analogies

Kipling, India and Ireland

KAORI NAGAI

CORK UNIVERSITY PRESS

First published in 2006 by
Cork University Press
Youngline Industrial Estate
Pouladuff Road, Togher
Cork
Ireland

British Library Cataloguing in Publication Data
A CIP catalogue record for this book is available from the British Library
A CIP record for this publication is available from the Library of Congress

ISBN–10: 1–85918–408–1
ISBN–13: 978–185918–408–0
Typeset by Tower Books, Ballincollig, Co. Cork
Printed by ColourBooks Ltd, Baldoyle, Co. Dublin

www.corkuniversitypress.com

Contents

Acknowledgements

I wish to thank Professor Lyn Innes for her supervision and invaluable support over the years, without which this book would have never been written. I was also fortunate to have guidance from Dr Janet Montefiore, who kindly commented on my work and generously shared with me her profound knowledge of Kipling. I also wish to thank Professor Elleke Boehmer, whose input was of great help to me. I am grateful to those at Cork University Press, especially Professor Tom Dunne and Ms Caroline Somers, for all their help in bringing this book to the world.

I am greatly indebted to the intellectual and emotional support given to me by my colleagues and teachers. I would like especially to thank Dr Sarah Wood, Dr Caroline Rooney and Professor Rod Edmond in the University of Kent, and Professor Kenji Nakamura, Professor Kazuhisa Takahashi and Professor Shoichi Kawai, who taught me while I was a graduate student in the University of Tokyo. My friends were always a great source of inspiration to me, and I would like to thank them for all the joy they have brought into my life.

My final thanks go to my family, especially to my parents, whose emotional and practical support has always given me much strength. Ben Grant patiently read numerous drafts and gave me detailed comments, and I am very grateful for his love and encouragement.

An earlier version of Chapter 1 was published in *The Atlantic Literary Review*, 4:3 (2003), and part of Chapter 6 was originally presented in India and Ireland: Fourth Galway Conference on Colonialism, which took place in the University of Galway in 2004.

Introduction

'You have been in *Be* – England?'[1] Kim asks a drummer-boy in the Irish regiment who comes from Liverpool. He pauses, though only for a moment, before articulating the word 'England', a slight break in speech which the drummer-boy probably does not even take any notice of. It is unlike Kim, who is quick-witted and has a singular talent for making himself understood by using whatever vocabulary available, to leave a word unfinished, although it is true that Kim's English is not so good at this stage, that he sometimes has to tap 'his foot impatiently' as he translates 'in his own mind from the vernacular to his clumsy English'.[2] What is Kim trying to say when he says '*Be* –'? Could it be Bexley, Berkshire or even Belfast? Maybe, but quite unlikely, for he does not know anything about European geography yet. Or perhaps Kim tries to ask the boy if he has been to Benares, eager to speak of his dear lama and their quest, but changes his mind in the middle of the word? We will never be sure. However, the certain thing is that this is a significant moment in *Kim*, when 'England' first slips into Kim's world.

The most plausible interpretation of this enigmatic rupture is that Kim was about to pronounce the word '*Belait*'. According to *Hobson-Jobson*, a contemporary glossary of Anglo-Indian words, *Belait*, a vernacular word originally meaning 'kingdom' or 'province', came to mean 'Europe' in India.[3] If Kim's unfinished 'Be –' is indeed '*Belait*', he is here trying to find an English equivalent for the word. This translation proves to be problematic, for Kim goes on to say, 'Tell me something about England. My father he came from there'.[4] That Kipling might deliberately let Kim choose 'England' as a translation is underlined by the fact that Kipling himself translates the same word '*Belait*' as 'Europe' for the reader somewhere else in the text.[5] Kim, without knowing it, erases Ireland, his land of origin, and replaces it with England. '*Eye*-rishti', for Kim, remains the name of the regiment of his father,[6] but will never be associated with an Ireland which longed to free herself from the Union with England. This erasure of Ireland is underlined further by the fact that the conversation takes place with a drummer-boy in the Irish regiment who 'spoke about the Liverpool suburb which was his England'.[7] Liverpool, a great Atlantic port which 'connected Ireland to both Britain and America',[8] was 'the most Irish of British Cities'[9] with 'its flourishing Catholic Church and its republican conspirators and other leaders and moulders of the large working-class Irish Catholic community'.[10] In this scene, therefore, two Irish boys who met in India both looked to England, not Ireland, as their country of origin.

The momentary rupture in translating *Belait* to England reveals that there is more than one 'England' both inside and outside the text. Kipling, by letting Kim choose the word 'England' among other possible translations (for example Britain, Ireland or Europe), creates for the Irish boy an 'England' where neither tension nor division between England and Ireland exists: it is an imaginary place, somewhere far away, which nevertheless guarantees his status as a sahib. It is then interesting to note that throughout the novel Kim does not comment on his own Irishness nor identify himself as Irish. It is the narrator and the sahibs in charge of Kim who know him to be Irish and treat him as such. The narrator occasionally explains Kim's behaviour by referring to his Irishness, and the sahibs, finding out that Kim is the son of an Irish soldier, give him a proper education as an Irish boy in a Catholic School, 'St Xavier's in Partibus at Lucknow',[11] with financial help from the lama. The rupture in translating the word to England is nothing but the rupture between Kim's England of which Ireland is part and the other England which governs its closest colony, Ireland.

* * *

A central purpose of this book is to examine the implications of Rudyard Kipling's representation of the Irish in India. The most famous example of this is, of course, the eponymous hero of *Kim*, but he is by no means the only Irish character in India which Kipling created. There is the Irish soldier Terence Mulvaney, whose life in the Irish regiment is vividly depicted in Kipling's earlier Indian stories. The Mavericks, the Irish regiment, crush an Irish Mutiny plot in India, and Namgay Doola, the son of an Irish soldier who served the East India Company, is found rebelling high up in the Himalayas. Kim, as an Irish character featuring in India, has many predecessors, including his own father, who served and died in India. Indeed, *Kim* is not only the last Indian story which Kipling wrote, but is also the last of his stories in which this curious combination of India and Ireland occurs. Kipling's India is the *home* of his Irish characters, and its appearance as well as disappearance in Kipling's world needs a little explaining. The recurrence of the Irish characters in Kipling's Indian stories also raises an important question regarding the place of Ireland in the Empire, namely, 'Why does Kim, as well as other Irish characters, have to be represented in India?'

This book thus seeks to shed a clearer light on Kipling's representation of the Irish in India, by analysing this in the context of the imperial connections between British colonies, especially those between India and Ireland. It argues that Indo-Irish analogies and comparisons became especially important in representing imperial integrity in the late nineteenth century, and as such became the very site where the image of the British Empire was contested. This book compares and contrasts two different ways of representing the connections between India and Ireland: firstly, an 'imperialist' mode of representation, which sought to interpret Irish participation in the Raj as the strongest proof of Irish loyalty to the Empire; and secondly, an Irish and Indian 'nationalist' mode of representation, which strove to form anti-imperial networks between India, Ireland and beyond, characterizing Indo-Irish connections as the cooperation between two colonies suffering from the common fate of being ruled and exploited by England. Therefore, this book, with Kipling as its central and recurrent focus, will look at both imperialist and nationalist modes of representing Indo-Irish connections. Nationalist discourses are shown to have been formed in close interaction with contemporary imperialist networks and discourses, which they often quoted in order to scrutinize and condemn; Indo-Irish nationalist connections not only 'positively' created each other's nationalist identities through interactions, but were 'negatively' constructed against the imperial network of comparisons to destroy them: as one reviewer in *Blackwood's Edinburgh Magazine* rightly predicted in 1880, Irish nationalist 'deeds, speeches and writings' were soon to 'operate as bad examples in other parts of the empire'.[12] Indeed, imperialists and nationalists were fairly familiar with each other's discourses, which makes the sharp discrepancy between the two truly unsettling. The overall supposition of this book is that Kipling was highly sensitive towards the emerging connections between Indian and Irish nationalists and that his text took part in the discursive war of analogies being fought between imperialist and nationalist modes of representing Indo-Irish connections. Kipling's placement of his Irish characters in the Indian setting can be seen as the most illustrative and influential example of the 'imperialist' mode of representing the Irish involvement in the Empire. By superimposing an Irish space on India, Kipling purposefully creates a combination of India and Ireland in his literary world to reproduce the sense of imperial integrity which the Indo-Irish connections traditionally represented, and also to reject the rebellious connections between the two colonies as treacherous and inauthentic.

This book is thus indebted to, and also seeks to make a significant contribution to, recent understandings of the British Empire as comprising networks and connections between colonies, which seek to modify the conventional understanding of the colonial relationship as the dichotomy between the colonizer and the colonized, or between the dominating metropolis and its colonial peripheries. Especially, the imperial connections between India and Ireland have recently received much scholarly attention as a crucial example of intercolonial relationships and exchanges.[13] It is not only the case that many personal and political alliances were made between the two colonies during the long period of being under the same imperial rule, but also that the comparisons and analogies between India and Ireland, two major components of the Empire, greatly influenced the way in which the Empire was viewed and understood. According to Javed Majeed, as early as the late eighteenth century, when the British Empire started expanding, there was already a search for 'an idiom in which cultures could be compared and contrasted', through which 'the cultures of the heterogeneous British empire could be compared, the nature of British rule overseas determined, and the empire unified by the same ethos'.[14] Comparisons between colonies offered the perfect paradigm for this search for a common idiom, and Ireland, as the oldest colony of England, served as a model, a point of reference against which new colonial experiences abroad were assessed, and India, the brightest and biggest jewel in the Empire, inevitably invited frequent comparisons with Ireland. Politicians often had experiences of dealing with both colonies, and experience in one colony played an important role in making policies in the other. This tradition of analogical, administrative and human exchanges between India and Ireland is delineated by Scott B. Cook, in his pioneering work *Imperial Affinities: Nineteenth-Century Analogies and Exchanges Between India and Ireland* (1993). Cook examines the ways in which the Indian administrative policy during the nineteenth century was influenced by comparisons and analogies between India and Ireland. He refutes the recent revisionist view that the British Empire as a consistent and uniform entity did not exist except as a myth, and that in reality imperialism was a motley of diverse and dissimilar areas, 'fractured and mutated at the various junctures of contact'.[15] Instead, he argues that the empire had 'a substantial degree of cohesion', and that 'the frequent use of analogies by officials and other contemporaries of empire'[16] helped create similarities and continuities in 'outlook, motive, method, policy, and even, to a limited extent, practice between such very different and distant components of empire as India and Ireland'.[17] Such associations were also the visible reality for British subjects who, for example, daily read Irish and Indian news side by side in *The Times*, and could make their own analogies and comparisons to form their opinions about the working of the British Empire.

The comparison between India and Ireland took on a new significance when it was adapted by Irish and Indian 'nationalists' as a mutual source of inspiration for their nationalist movements. As Michael S. Silvestri puts it, 'Irish and Indian nationalist leaders shared to varying degrees romanticized notions of a common struggle against the British Empire'[18] and, for some Indian nationalists, 'the Irish experience provided a heroic model of anti-colonial resistance, as well as what seemed to be a blueprint for national liberation'.[19] This is the central focus of Elleke Boehmer's *Empire, the National, and the Postcolonial, 1890–1920: Resistance in Interaction* (2002), in which Boehmer analyses the political cooperation, intertextual connections and mutual inspirations which took place between colonial peripheries, examining the extent to which cross-border and cross-nationalist contact between native intellectuals helped to form anti-colonial resistance and national identities.[20] Irish nationalists' fascination with Indian mysticism has also received attention as a vital aspect of these Indo-Irish nationalist connections: to name only a few examples, Rabindranath Tagore's literary collaboration with W. B. Yeats as the meeting of Orientalism and Celticism; Margaret Noble, alias Sister Nivedita, the most devoted disciple of Swami Vivekananda; and Annie Besant, leader of the Theosophical Society as well as the president of the Indian Home Rule League.[21] The forgotten lives of James Cousins, an Irish poet who went to India, and his wife, Margaret, have recently been uncovered as another example of such connections. According to Gauri Viswanathan, for example, James Cousins reached out for internationalism and went beyond the limits of race, through his identification with Indian spirituality.[22] Irish nationalists worked hard to organize anti-imperial connections with other colonies, and Ireland's long history of resistance against England was something which Indian nationalists could readily appropriate, giving them a strong incentive to cast off the limitations imposed on them as Asians. Irish nationalists also took much inspiration from their cooperation and vicarious identification with Indians, allowing them to portray themselves as the authentic Other of England.

Recent scholarly focus on Indo-Irish connections touches on the sensitive topic of the applicability of postcolonial theories to Irish studies. Stephen Howe, in his controversial *Ireland and Empire: Colonial Legacies in Irish History and Culture* (2002), questions Ireland's status as a colony and Irish critics' claim that Ireland has had experiences analogous to those of other former British colonies. Howe's work interestingly reveals how much Irish studies has relied on comparative models: 'a great deal of contention both academic and political has been framed by questions as to which comparative points of reference are most appropriate and enlightening for Ireland: for instance, whether colonial parallels, or continental European ones, are more useful'.[23] Howe demonstrates the fallacies and pitfalls of these comparative models, and his attack on the postcolonial use of comparative methods is particularly scathing:

> The central trope of 'postcolonial' Irish writing is . . . a claim that there are significant similarities, past and present, between Irish experience and that of African, Asian and other formerly colonised territories. We

> have shown at length how poorly the colonial and postcolonial models fit modern Irish experience itself. Yet in fact much of the invocation of Afro-Asian parallels for contemporary Irish developments is as misleading also about the former as about the latter . . . Analogies between Irish and Afro-Asian cultural nationalism have often been equally misplaced . . . On other levels the postcolonial comparisons immediately collapse.[24]

Irish 'postcolonial' critics, instead of arguing back to Howe that the use of postcolonial theory is not necessarily reducible to comparisons with other former colonies, have set out to prove that comparative methods are indeed relevant, and that historically there have been substantial connections and influences between Ireland and other parts of the world.[25] Joseph Lennon's recent *Irish Orientalism: A Literary and Intellectual History* (2004) is a prime example of this, which seeks to demonstrate the existence and relevance of Irish-Oriental connections from the Middle Ages to the present date: the book presents an impressive catalogue of, as well as profound insights into, various ways in which India and Ireland have had cultural, historical and 'semiotic' links to each other. However, this book problematically perpetuates the gesture of Irish Orientalism which it analyses, namely, the arbitrary appropriation of India and other 'Oriental' countries, in order to give expression to Irish colonial experiences.[26] A similar trend can be witnessed in two recent collections of essays on the relationship between Irish studies and postcolonialism: Glenn Hopper and Colin Graham (eds.), *Irish and Postcolonial Writing: History, Theory, and Practice* (2002) and Clare Carroll and Patricia King (eds.), *Ireland and Postcolonial Theory* (2003). One of the three sections in Hopper and Graham's collection is titled 'Comparisons' and comprises five essays comparing Ireland with other colonies,[27] while Carroll and King's book testifies to the growing popularity of the theme of Indo-Irish connections in Irish studies, including three essays which deal with the comparison between India and Ireland.[28] Carroll and King's collection notably features David Lloyd's essay which argues against 'the revisionist argument that Ireland is different from other colonies',[29] advocating instead the relevance of comparative methods in Irish studies. Lloyd points out that comparison is extremely useful in grasping 'the particularity of Ireland's or of any other country's experience within the larger economies of colonialism',[30] drawing out 'not only the ubiquity and replication of forms of colonial rule but also the remarkably diverse ways its rationalizing drive is deflected by the particularities of each colonized culture'.[31] In order to avoid the simplification and abstraction which comparative methods can easily fall into, Lloyd suggests the use of the word 'differential' instead of 'comparative', since 'there are no identical situations'.[32] Nevertheless, the comparative spirit, which Friedrich Max Müller, a renowned Oriental philologist, in 1874 proudly declared to be 'the truly scientific spirit of our age, nay of all ages',[33] seems to be still present in Irish studies, as if the imperial project of comparing Ireland and other colonies, the most effective means for the British subjects of the day to substantiate the full extent and power of the British Empire, has been faithfully pursued and preserved in Ireland itself.

This book, instead of asking whether comparative methods are relevant or useful, seeks to enquire into the political and historical implications of comparing Ireland with other colonies. To critics like Howe, who question the validity of comparing Ireland with India and Africa, it will answer that the comparison is indeed valid and worth studying, because both imperialist and nationalist discourses did make comparisons, the traces of which are clearly visible in Kipling's text, and it is important to unravel the ways in which this practice of making parallels between Ireland and other colonies affected colonial policies, discourses and realities, as well as Irish identity. On the other hand, this book also questions the uncritical application of comparative methods to Ireland, which has historically been the frequent subject of comparisons with other colonies. It suggests that Ireland's special position as a colonial point of reference might have deprived it of the power of self-representation and of creating its own historical contexts, leaving it haunted by innumerable ghosts of resemblance to other countries. By the same token, however, comparative methods will indeed be useful for Ireland, for they will help us to retrace the ways in which Irish realities, and the discourses surrounding them, were created out of comparisons and interactions with other colonies. Perhaps it might also help us to think a way out of 'the spectre of comparisons' persistently haunting Irish colonial and postcolonial history.[34]

In this sense, the Indo-Irish connection provides a significant case study, for it clearly marks Ireland's unique double position as the colonizer and the colonized within the British Empire: not only was there a shared experience between India and Ireland of being colonized, but there was also a long history of Irish participation in the imperial expansion. These two stories are fundamentally told separately, though side by side, even in many recent studies addressing Indo-Irish connections. They are the two stories which would not mix well together: the Irish Raj testifies to the 'whiteness' and status as colonizer of the Irish in the colonial space, and this 'whiteness' is the greatest obstacle to the Irish claim to have shared a similar experience as colonized with Asians and Africans, and to the applicability of postcolonial theory to the Irish situation.[35] This book aspires to bring these stories together, or at least to identify where the two stories meet to diverge, by exploring the relationships and interactions between them.

Indo-Irish analogies indeed testify to the imperial associations within which Ireland was deeply embedded, as well as to Ireland's close engagement with colonial rule. Cook, in his essay 'The Irish Raj: Social Origins and Careers of Irishmen in the Indian Civil Service, 1855–1914', challenges the portrayal of Irish history 'as a chronology of resistance and reaction to British domination, punctuated by a number of momentous flash-points of conflict: the repeal movement, land wars, aborted rebellions and the like', which is, in his view, a 'distortion' and 'obsessively crisis-oriented'.[36] Cook instead argues that the British Empire was supported not only by Anglo-Irish and Protestant gentry, but also by many middle-class Irishmen. By focusing on the Irish civil servants who acted as colonizing agents, Cook demonstrates the strong involvement of Irishmen in the cause of Empire. Achieving self-government in Ireland and remaining within the imperial context were, Cook argues, compatible for the majority of the Irish in the nineteenth century. In fact, it was only through the connection with England that Ireland could experience the glory of the British Empire as its own.[37] A similar point is made by Peter Karsten in his essay 'Irish Soldiers in the British Army, 1792–1922: Suborned or Subordinate?', in which he argues that Irish soldiers, who were largely Catholic, were 'faithful to [their] oath, despite the efforts of United Irishmen, Fenians, or Sinn Féiners to win [their] loyalties'[38]: 'On balance one *must* conclude that the typical Irish soldier was "willing", and "easily-managed", as one of his regimental commanders had written, that he was "anglicized", as his nationalist compatriots feared, that he served well those who paid him, that he "earned [his] keep".'[39] These arguments are in stark contrast to the more common version of Irish history in which the Irish, throughout the nineteenth century, struggled to break away from the Union. Assuming that Cook's picture of the Irish Raj, supported both by Catholics and Protestants, is historically correct, how should we interpret the presence of the Irish in India, who fully enjoyed the privileges of the colonizer? Was it the ideologies of the day which forced them to act as colonizers, and therefore is this also further evidence of the colonization of Ireland? Irish people might not have liked English rule in Ireland but they could act like the English with respect to other colonial Others. As Gandhi puts it:

> Some Irish leaders are convinced that the people of Ireland suffer because they live in a particular country, just as Indians suffer because of the colour of their skin. In other words, the Indian people suffer many hardships both in India and outside and are treated as inferior to Englishmen. The Irish people count for nothing in their own land and are oppressed by their English rulers. But no sooner do they go out of Ireland than they enjoy rights quite similar to those of Englishmen.[40]

To be more precise, Irish people counted for nothing in some other places outside Ireland, for example America, where they often had to content themselves with the status of lowest-paid workers. Irishmen enjoyed a similar status to Englishmen only in the British colonies. What Gandhi here points out as an undeniable dissimilarity in the 'colonized' status of the Irish and Indians cannot easily be dismissed. Both, no doubt, suffered under the same imperial rule, but the manner of, and reasons for, their suffering were different, and equating the two might obscure many crucial differences.

The Irish participation in imperial affairs illuminates the fact that large numbers of the Irish to whom the present Irish people are 'biologically' related are not, one may say 'autobiographically', chosen as the precursors of modern Ireland. Irish history has severed kinship ties among the Irish people, choosing, for example, Theobald Wolfe Tone as an ancestor and rejecting his brother William Henry Tone, who successfully served in the East India Company, even though Wolfe Tone himself was elated with his brother's success in India.[41] These contexts, however, by no means testify to the fallacy of the Indo-Irish connections which Irish and Indian nationalists strove to forge. On the contrary, they provide an important background to understanding the full extent of their desperate struggle to carve out any effective counter-discourses to claim their own national space. And the meeting and collaborating of Irish and Indian nationalists is truly amazing, specifically because they combined two different contexts in one single force of resistance.

* * *

'Why is Kim Irish?' – this is one of the questions which have puzzled Kipling's critics. A definitive answer is yet to come, but a great deal of attention has already been paid to Kim's Irishness. For example, J. Mukherjee considers this 'relevant', for the spiritual and supernatural side of the Irish makes Kim a perfect companion for the lama in his search.[42] T. G. Fraser, in his essay tracing the Irish involvement in the Raj, refers to the large Irish population, principally soldiers and missionaries, in India in the nineteenth century, and comments that '[i]t was no accident that Kipling chose the surname O'Hara for his hero Kim'.[43] Rukmini Bhaya Nair points out that *Kim* and Rabindranath Tagore's *Gora* (1910) are both about 'Irish foundlings' brought up as 'Indians', and refers to the Bengali intelligentsia's interest in 'the Irish Question' throughout the nineteenth century, which dated back to as early as the 1820s.[44]

Recent attempts to answer this question have sought to place *Kim* within the context of contemporary Irish politics: the advance of the Irish Home Rule movement supported by the Liberal Government, with two failed attempts to pass a Home Rule Bill in 1886 and 1893, both of which were rejected by the House of Lords; constant terrorist threats from the Fenian organizations, which established secret networks encompassing Ireland, England and America; the foundation of Sinn Fein in 1905, and so on – a whole range of Irish nationalist movements which Kipling found threatening to the integrity of the Empire. According to Phillip E. Wegner, for example, Kim's being Irish reflects Kipling's intolerance of the unloyal Irish: 'With this complication set into place, "India" seems to disappear from the narrative altogether, and *Kim* comes to be "about" the utopian reconstruction of increasingly restive *Irish* populace: a neutralization of the Sinn Fein movement that had been founded, only two years before the publication of *Kim*, to promote what Kipling saw as an intolerable and treasonous opposition to English rule.'[45] Tim Watson similarly argues that Kim's Irishness testifies to Kipling's recognition of, as well as attempt to contain, the Irish nationalist movement at the turn of the nineteenth century.[46] His essay reflects the recent scholarly attention paid to the parallels between Indian and Irish nationalism: according to Watson, in this period 'Irish unrest paralleled Indian unrest', which, 'taken together . . . formed a powerful threat to the Empire'; Kim's Irishness is thus 'a way of containing these problems by joining Irish and Indian dissents'.[47] For both critics, Kim's Irishness marks Ireland's double position as the colonizer and the colonized, 'both rebel and governor at the same time'.[48] Kipling, by representing his imperial hero as Irish, at once contains Irish rebellion and reclaims the Irish as loyal subjects.

Interestingly, both Wegner and Watson, in their discussions of Kim's Irishness, seem to discount the importance of India as the setting of *Kim*: for Wegner, '"India" seems to disappear from the narrative altogether', and Watson refrains from 'suggesting that the India of Kim is a displaced version of Ireland'.[49] Though Kim's Irishness can be easily explained by referring to the contemporary historical contexts, the curious fact that in *Kim* the Irish contexts are relocated to no other place than India is not fully explained. I propose to see Kim as the personification of the imperial connection between India and Ireland. Kim, as a 'hybrid' boy, represents a combination of diverse racial types and cultures: Kim, in whom 'every unknown Irish devil'[50] and 'the Asiatic side of the boy's character'[51] coexist unmixed, can disguise himself as any identity, and he is also 'English'.[52] Kim's hybridity has the same function as the 'Wonder House' (the Lahore Museum) to which he takes the lama, where one can see different cultures amassed in one place (thus it is very symbolic that at the opening of the book Kim is shown as part of the museum, sitting astride the gun Zam–Zammah[53]). In Chapter 4, I will argue that the imperialist discourses had the same effect as the Great Exhibition, where all the colonies of the Empire were displayed side by side without being separated by geographical distance, thus strengthening the sense of imperial unity. As Peter H. Hoffenberg argues, the grand exhibitions reinforced, rather than blurred, national and cultural differences: they were a space where 'the official and unofficial ideas of "Englishness" and colonial identities converged, were actively created, interpreted, consumed, and mediated'.[54] *Kim* is such an international space, and its hero reinforces the boundaries of many cultures and nationalities as he traverses them, in the course of which his Englishness as well as colonial identity are in many ways negotiated.

Although I agree with Wegner when he suggests that Kim's Irishness in India is a way of containing contemporary Irish and Indian dissents by joining them together, I suggest that such joint resistance is more overtly tackled in the figure of Kim's predecessor, Terence Mulvaney, Kipling's favourite Irish soldier, who appears exclusively in India. Mulvaney was created in the mid 1880s, when both Irish and Indian intrigues were starting to be keenly felt, this being the period of the Irish Home Rule Bill and of the formation of the Indian National Congress. Unlike Kim, who is Indian by birth, English by education and only biologically Irish, Mulvaney more directly embodies the impossible position of the Irish within the Empire, being a loyal British soldier defending the Raj, with some curious Fenian past. Through Mulvaney, Kipling's literary world of the Irish in India converges with the reality of the Empire. While in India, Kipling became a personal acquaintance of Lord Roberts (1832–1914), an Irishman and Commander-in-Chief of the British Army in India, who had already been hailed by Mulvaney as a great leader in his first story: 'we three . . . have dhrawn the par-ti-cu-lar attinshin av Bobs Bahadur [Lord Roberts] more than wanst. But he's a rale good little man is Bobs.'[55] In his autobiography, Kipling remembers the day when he 'rode up Simla Mall' beside Roberts, discussing the condition of soldiers, as 'the proudest moment of my young life'.[56] Lord Roberts was Kipling's personal hero and also embodied his dream of India and Ireland joining together to defend the Empire.

Kipling 'put India behind him'[57] with the publication of *Kim*, and also his representation of the Irish in India. This can be seen as due not only to Kipling's increasing disillusionment with the Indo-Irish combination as an effective way to sustain the image of the Empire, but also to his growing fascination with a new model of Empire as a federation of the settler colonies, also known as 'the Five Nations' or the 'White Man's World'. In *Kim*, we see this new imperial vision being palimpsested with the Indian landscape, allowing Kipling to represent the Irish, in the form of Kim, simply as 'a White Man' – or a 'Sahib', to use the novel's terminology – a new child of Empire emerging as a settler. This vision was closely related to Indo-Irish analogies, pointing to an alternative way in which the Irish could, without any problems, turn into loyal imperial subjects. Kipling's changing representation of Empire, from that centring on India to the settler's Empire, is therefore another thread which this book pursues. Kipling's Empire was by no means static: it kept shifting, just as newspapers constantly renewed their narratives to keep pace with the changing situations of Empire. By tracing his representation of Indo-Irish analogies, this book seeks to uncover different visions of Empire which Kipling created in response to the fast changing imperial affairs.

* * *

Chapter 1, 'The Taming of the Irish Afreets', looks at the ways in which Kipling represented his Irish characters in India. Kipling's Irish characters do not miss home, in marked contrast to his English characters, who periodically suffer from intense homesickness. The characterization of the Irish as gregarious immigrants can be seen as reflecting the imperial policy of the day, which solved domestic and social problems by sending them to the colonial space. Within this context, this chapter considers the political implications of Kipling making India the chosen destination of his Irish characters. The Irish rebel, represented as a riddle to be solved by Kipling, is also discussed in this chapter. Chapter 2, 'When East Meets West: Kipling's India of Anti-Gravity', contrasts Kipling's early Indian stories, written in India, with the later stories, especially *Kim*, which were written after he had left India. Unlike the former, in which the colonizers are shown to struggle against the corrupting force of the native ground in order to retain their character as English, the latter are strikingly *ground*less: Kipling successfully turns India into an ideal imperial space where all the different elements of the Empire are seen together and freely traverse without being constricted by the subversive colonial ground. Chapter 3, 'Exiled Home: The Voice of the Irish Soldiers', concentrates on Kipling's representation of the voice of the Irish soldier, Terence Mulvaney. Mulvaney's voice serves as a powerful counter-representation to the Irish nationalist voices which were raised against the Empire, and yet also figures as a subversive voice, which needs to be constantly controlled by the narrator. In Chapter 4, 'Shamrocks in the Veldt: Two Types of Aphasic Empire', by applying Roman Jakobson's distinction between metonymy and metaphor, I characterize the imperialist discourse as 'metonymic' and the nationalist as 'metaphoric': the former *combines* originally different elements into one imperial context according to spatial or temporal *contiguity*, while the latter forms the anti-imperial associations by means of identifications and substitutions based on varing degrees of *similarity*. Within this framework, I examine the contest between these two types of analogies during the Boer War. Chapter 5, 'Kim in South Africa', discusses *Kim* as a 'Boer War' novel, in which Kipling's new vision of the white Empire meets his old India. His South African stories, in contrast, loom as uncanny and unsuccessful doubles of *Kim*, testifying to the fall of Indo-Irish imperialist analogies as an effective means of representing the imperial unity. The final chapter, 'The Dynamite War of Analogies', characterizes the battle between imperialist and nationalist analogies as a 'newspaper' war, with which Kipling as a journalist was deeply involved. This chapter also explores ways in which Indo-Irish connections served Irish nationalists as a means of recovering their own national voice, through their identification with India, and takes Maud Gonne's characterization of Queen Victoria as the 'Famine Queen' as an example.

Chapter One

The Taming of the Irish Afreets

1

> The great Slave has been born in our household, like Abraham's steward: his feats are too familiar to cause us any surprise: we confide our best to him without a fear of his fidelity. No Frankenstein, though fancy may still play with that thought and laugh at itself for the whim.[1]

P. J. Keating, in his *The Working Classes in Victorian Fiction* (1971), points out that Kipling's Indian poems and stories opened the way to represent the lowest stratum of the British working classes in the nineties; many unemployed working-class people became soldiers simply because they had no other choice. As Kipling's biographer Charles Carrington puts it, 'Socially, the private soldiers were in fact drawn from the unemployed or unemployable, so that "going for a soldier" was, in the respectable working class, regarded as the last degradation, analogous with "going to the bad".'[2] Kipling had plenty of opportunity to observe these soldiers in India instead of in the East End of London to which they originally belonged, which, Keating argues, made it possible for him to create a more realistic, humane and vivid stereotype of the working class.[3]

By identifying the soldier in India as a former working-class outcast from East London, Keating has presented us with a direct link between Great Britain and India as well as a link between the issues of class and imperialism. However, Keating is mainly preoccupied with finding out how Kipling's literary representation reflects the reality of the working class in the late nineteenth century, and does not really question the ideological side of this representation: why do the working class have to be represented in India as soldiers? What is more, he defines Kipling's soldiers only in terms of class, and dismisses all other aspects: for example, Mulvaney is for Keating nothing but a working-class character from one part of Britain, namely, Ireland, just as Learoyd is from Yorkshire and Ortheris from London: 'Although they come from different parts of Britain and speak different dialects, they share working-class attitudes, amusements and emotions . . . Their memories of civilian life serve rather to reinforce than alleviate their outcast state, for in the social structure of Anglo-India they occupy very much the same position as they did at home in England.'[4]

Nevertheless, Keating does notice some differences between Mulvaney and the other two: whereas Ortheris and Learoyd are 'more conscious of the ineradicable ties they have with their pre-army lives', Mulvaney, 'the central and more fully rounded character' is

> someone who belongs so completely to barrack life that it is impossible to believe he has ever experienced any other kind of existence. He attains, as Andrew Lang was first to point out, 'mythical' status. His social background is never exactly pinpointed; it is a cornucopia of memories and adventures from which he can draw fabulous tales as and when the occasion demands.[5]

We may here try to elucidate Mulvaney's pre-war background mystified by the author. According to *The Readers' Guide to Rudyard Kipling's Work* (1961), it is presumed that Terence Mulvaney was born in Portarlington, Queen's County, Ireland, sometime between 1844 and 1850, and enlisted as a soldier between 1863 and 1868.[6] That is to say, he was born during the Great Famine and was brought up when Ireland was struggling to recover from its devastating aftermath. If Mulvaney had to be a soldier, it is not because he was literally born in the slums, but rather because at that time for much of its population Ireland was no better than the slums, so that, besides encouraging emigration, to send its young men off as soldiers to the front line was the surest way of relieving the distress of Ireland. We may say that Kipling's mystification of Mulvaney's pre-army life operates to cover up the hard reality of Ireland, as well as indicating his difficulty in representing it as it was.

Kipling, instead of giving the slightest hint about the condition of Ireland from which his Irish characters had to escape, describes how they adjust themselves pretty well in India. In 'The Daughter of the Regiment' (1887), the McKennas, a prolific Irish couple, tired of thinking of new names for their coming children, decide, instead of numbering them off as the husband proposes, to 'christen them afther the names av the stations they was borrun in': 'So there was Colaba McKenna, an' Muttra McKenna, an' a whole Prisidincy av other McKennas, an' little Jhansi.'[7] This peculiar combination of Indian place names and the typically Irish surname not only allows us to follow the itinerary of the Irish regiment and see how the Irish spread and took root in the Indian soil, but also indicates how they truly transformed themselves into imperial subjects by incorporating India into themselves and literally becoming a part of it.[8] Mulvaney acts as a matchmaker between Jhansi McKenna and an Irishman in the regiment; thus Irish fertility is safely relocated to India, where epidemics and the hot weather will take care of any excess of population; in fact, none of the children except Jhansi survive the harsh living conditions in India.

While the Irish characters marry and make India their home in Kipling's fiction, India can by no means be called 'home' for the English Ortheris and

Learoyd. Mulvaney is the only one of the 'Soldiers Three' who marries; the other two stay single during their service in India. If the notion of 'home' in the Victorian period required the presence of a woman as the angel in the house tending its sacred hearth, there is no 'home' for Ortheris and Learoyd in India, for both of them left a woman whom they wished to marry in England: the domestic home and England as Home are inseparably intertwined.[9] 'If I'ad a stayed at 'Ome, I might a married that gal and a kep' a little shorp in the 'Ammersmith 'Igh',[10] laments Ortheris, when he is suffering from the homesickness which seems to assault him from time to time. For him, 'home' is London, where he might have married and settled down. Learoyd, in 'On Greenhow Hill' (1890), also talks of his first love, 'Liza Roantree, a girl whom he fell in love with in England. The story tells us how Learoyd found, through 'Liza, a true home space, and then lost it for ever. Learoyd, who came to Greenhow Hill 'because of a little difference at home',[11] found himself lying in bed in 'Liza's house with his arm broken; he had been carried into her house after falling off a wall and being knocked unconscious. 'Liza nurses Learoyd back to health, which gives us another example of what Miriam Bailin calls the sickroom scene in Victorian fiction, in which the characters, through the act of being nursed and nursing, leave the 'social roles and norms by which they previously defined themselves'[12] and accept new ones in order to create a better family and community. Learoyd, who had been a lawless young lad, becomes a member of the Primitive Methodist church, under 'Liza's influence. 'Liza figures as an ideal angel in the house, a dutiful daughter with all the domestic skills such as sewing and making tea. Since she rarely leaves home, except to go to the chapel, Learoyd's longing for her is almost equated with his visiting her house or seeing it from a distance; it was the only place where he found himself at home. His love for her was so strong that he was even tempted to murder a man who was his competitor in love. However, it turned out that 'Liza's health declined and she would soon die; this made Learoyd decide to be a soldier. He said goodbye to a dying 'Liza at her home and joined the army; his loss of the girl and the domestic hearth therefore coincides with his self-banishment from England as Home.

Moreover, as many critics have already suggested, any love affair between an Englishman and a native girl never fails to end in tragedy in Kipling's world (Lispeth is jilted, both of Bisesa's hands are cut off and 'Georgie Porgie' deserts his Burmese wife to marry an Englishwoman[13]). It seems to me that this is not only due to Kipling's fear of, as is often argued, the possible racial mixture, but also because he has to guard the idea of the English 'home' itself against contamination. For example, in 'Without Benefit of Clergy' (1890), John Holden, an English official, provides a tiny home for his native wife, Ameera. Holden sincerely loves her, but the harsh climate in India and a cholera epidemic take his son and then his wife away from him.

The landlord, who first plans to let the house to somebody else, changes his mind after hearing Holden's wish to keep the home as his, and declares that he will have it pulled down so that 'no man may say where this house stood'.[14] Englishmen are not allowed to have a 'home' outside and other than England.

The contrast between the adaptability to India which the Irish characters show and the incapability of the English characters to make a home in India may become clearer if we note that it is mostly the English characters who experience difficulty with life in India. As we have already seen, of the Soldiers Three, it is not the Irish Mulvaney but the other two who suffer from homesickness (Ortheris) and homelessness (Learoyd). Also, in 'Thrown Away' (1888), a young English officer, whom the narrator refers to as Boy, commits suicide, for he takes all things too seriously in India, 'a place beyond all others where one must not take things too seriously'.[15] Just before he kills himself he spends 'half the night' in writing to 'his people, to his Colonel, and to a girl at Home',[16] looking at their photographs. This distinction in representation between the English characters and the Irish ones seems to correspond neatly to the contrast which Abdul R. JanMohamed makes between the exile and the immigrant in his essay on Edward Said. According to JanMohamed, although both of them 'cross the border between one social or national group and another', the immigrant can show a far more positive attitude towards the host culture, because the immigrant, unlike the exile, does not suffer from the nostalgia caused by 'the absence of home', that is, 'an involuntary or enforced rupture between the collective subject of the original culture and the individual subject', which 'often makes the individual indifferent to the values and characteristics of the host culture'.[17] The Boy in 'Thrown Away' dies from this rupture. If letter-writing stands for the long distance which separates him from Home, the photograph, showing both the absence and the partial presence of the object, indicates that, though his home is absent, he has nevertheless brought part of his home, his life at home, with him, which makes his separation from Home even more painful. The immigrant, on the other hand,

> is not troubled by structural nostalgia because his or her status implies a purposive directness toward the host culture, which has been deliberately chosen as the new home. Most importantly, his or her status implies a voluntary desire to become a full-fledged subject of the new society . . . indeed, his or her success as an immigrant depends on what Said calls 'uncritical gregariousness', that is, on an ability to identify rapidly and to merge with the structure of the new culture's collective subjectivity.[18]

Thus we may say that, following JanMohamed's distinction between the immigrant and the exile, Kipling's Irish characters are represented not as exiles but as immigrants, who do not miss Ireland and are willing to accept their new life in India. Just as the McKennas in 'The Daughter of the Regiment' 'uncritically' merge their Irish surname with Indian place names, the Irish in Kipling's world have no problem accepting the place and its culture as part of themselves. Their children are born not as Irish but rather as Anglo-Indian, into a new identity, with India already incorporated as part of them. Indeed, JanMohamed's dichotomy between the exile and the immigrant corresponds all too well with the differences in Kipling's treatment of the English characters and the Irish ones. In other words, he denies any aspect of the 'exile' to his Irish characters, and only presents them as immigrants who uncritically accept the place to which they have moved.

Whereas Kipling locates his Irish characters in India as immigrants, his English characters, if they are 'English' enough, eventually escape from India and go back Home. Even Strickland, the English police officer versed in the native culture and languages and the art of disguise, who figures as the guardian of the Raj in some of Kipling's stories and *Kim*, returns to England where he regularly accompanies his wife to church after his retirement.[19] 'Englishness' even splits the strong ties uniting the Soldiers Three. Both Ortheris and Learoyd go back to England after time-expired; Ortheris's long-standing dream to open a '"little stuff" birdshop' in London will come true and Learoyd will be 'back again in the smoky, stone-ribbed North, amid the clang of the Bradford looms',[20] while Mulvaney chooses to live in India as a civilian. Mulvaney does go home as well, 'in the *Serapis*, time-expired', but he soon comes back to India with his wife, Dinah, in order to work for a new Central India line:

> It was all Dinah Shadd's fault. She could not stand the poky little lodgings, and she missed her servant Abdullah more than words could tell. The fact was that the Mulvaneys had been out here too long, and had lost touch with England.[21]

It is interesting here that Mulvaney has lost touch with 'England', not 'Ireland'. Mulvaney might have geographically gone back to Ireland, but ideologically he has gone back to England, to which Ireland belongs within the imperial context. Among the many aspects of England with which the Mulvaneys have lost touch are the poor conditions of life which the Irish had to endure as colonized subjects, and which contrast strikingly with the privileges that any 'British' colonizer could enjoy in India. The British colonies were an exceptional space within which the differences in class and ethnicity inside 'England' easily disappeared and everybody could equally assume an English identity, regardless of their status at home. As Francis G. Hutchins puts it, 'Englishmen in India, high and low, *were* of a class, sharing a common lot and forced to bury the differences which would have separated them in England';[22] this was at least the British portrayal of the Raj, which made India appear free from any social problems at home.[23] Even the Irish Mulvaneys, who have to live in one of 'the poky little lodgings' in Ireland, can be treated like sahibs by native servants in India. (It is interesting that Dinah Shadd, in the quotation above, objects to going back to England more than Mulvaney. As an Irishwoman, she would be placed not only under the English but under the Irishmen in the social hierarchy. In India, on the contrary, she secures a status which enables her to command, as a memsahib, her Indian servant Abdullah).[24] Kipling, instead of putting Mulvaney back into a miserable life in Ireland, chooses to let him live comfortably in India. A curse was cast on him in 'The Courting of Dinah Shadd' (1891) that he should die 'in a strange land',[25] and he is indeed destined never to return home, never to go back to Ireland. The narrator in 'Private Learoyd's Story' (1888) describes Mulvaney as a 'grizzled, tender, and very wise Ulysses, sweltering on the earthworks of a Central India line'.[26] Indeed, Mulvaney can be said to be a 'Ulysses', for he wanders away from his home, but in what way is he 'wise'? Wise enough to bring his Penelope with him, so that he does not have to suffer the longing for home? Or wise in the sense that he stays away from Ireland and lives in India, knowing that this is the only way to make being at once Irish and British possible?

For whatever reason, Kipling chooses not to represent his favourite Irish character Mulvaney in Ireland, except in his reminiscences, as if his return to a troubled Ireland under British rule might disrupt the integrity of England as Home and Mulvaney's identity as the loyal 'English' soldier. In fact, Kipling's sympathetic treatment of Mulvaney the Irishman as a 'Tommy Atkins' is in sharp contrast to the 'ape-like' representation of the Irish formed under the influence of Darwinism during the nineteenth century. According to L. P. Curtis, the assumption that Anglo-Saxons and Irish Celts were completely different races or breeds, along with the increasing fear of Fenianism, accelerated the degeneration of the Irishman's image from 'the peasant Paddy' to 'the white negro' and the simian orang-utan and gorilla.[27] The Irish as well as the working class, abhorred and distorted into hideous stereotypes at home, had to be placed far away from this home before they could be more 'humanely' treated. Cecil Rhodes's view of the relationship between imperialism and social problems at home, well known since it is cited by Lenin, may be worth citing again here:

> I was in the East End of London (working-class quarter) yesterday and attended a meeting of the unemployed. I listened to the wild speeches, which were just a cry for 'bread! bread!' and on my way home I pondered over the scene and I became more than ever convinced of the importance of imperialism . . . My cherished idea is a solution for the social problem, i.e., in order to save the 40,000,000 inhabitants of the United Kingdom from a bloody civil war, we colonial statesmen must

> acquire new lands to settle the surplus population, to provide new markets for the goods produced in the factories and mines . . .[28]

Kipling's soldiers in India were those safely removed from the East End of London, where they had been clamouring for bread. If Kipling's representations of the working class are more or less 'objective' and 'humane', it is not because Kipling was, as Keating argues, 'the first important Victorian writer who was not scared of the working classes'.[29] It is rather because his stories are themselves the literary practice of the imperial policy expressed by Rhodes as well as the faithful description of its outcome: imperialism was to relocate home problems to make them safer.

It is worth noting that Kipling chooses to relocate the Irish Question only in India and not in any other place; India was one of the few places where the Irish could be represented safely. America, a major destination for Irish emigration together with Canada and Australia, was particularly notorious as a breeding ground of Fenianism; as one contributor to the *Nineteenth Century*, commenting on the result of 'deporting troublesome Irish subjects to America', remarks, 'it might have been safer to have such men, if they conspired at all, conspiring within reach of British law rather than beyond it'.[30] The Irish should be contained within the Empire to be supervised, and this may explain why Kipling strongly objects to the suggestion that William McMann, a former Irish soldier in India but now a resident of San Francisco, was a model for Terence Mulvaney: 'There is but one Terence, and he never set foot in America and never will.'[31] Mulvaney, in order to remain a loyal 'Irish' soldier, should stay clear of any association with his fellow-Irishmen in America. India was, along with other major colonies such as Canada and Australia, a territory in which the law of Great Britain could punish conspiracies. What is more, India had one advantage which Canada and Australia did not have: it was under direct military control. In fact, many Irish people went to India to be soldiers – the percentage of Irishmen in the Indian army was always high[32] – which is to say that they came all the way to India to place themselves under direct military discipline as well as to be the very force which checked any mutinous uprising against the Empire. Only in India would the Irish degeneration into and reappearance as Fenians be checked.

The Irish who escaped British control became an even more formidable enemy, for they gathered strength in foreign capitals and sought aid from other anti-imperial forces. Indeed, in Kipling's work, the subversive power which attempts to overthrow the British Empire is often represented as an international conspiracy, which the Irish are either working at the very centre of or are ready to assist. Kipling's suspicion of foreign conspiracies was confirmed by the 'news' that Maharaja Dhulip Singh (1837–93), the last Sikh ruler of the Punjab, who was deposed by the British government at the age of twelve, conspired to overthrow the British in India with Russian support in 1889. Kipling composed a poem on this issue, titled 'The Irish Conspiracy'; it is significant that he calls the conspiracy by an Indian Prince with Russian support *Irish*, and not Indian or Russian. That is to say, the most shocking part of the conspiracy was that Dhulip Singh took it for granted that he could also procure support from the Irish regiments in India. The poem was written in response to an article in the *Pioneer* (15 February, 1889), which reported the news that another Indian Mutiny is planned by Dhulip Singh:

> The Maharaja Dhulip Singh has issued a manifesto addressed to the Princes and People of India. In it he declares that there are supporters in Europe and America, who are ready to form an army for the overthrow of British rule in India, but a fund of four million pounds is necessary for the purchase of munitions in order to carry out that object. Besides the Punjabis the Irish soldiers serving in British regiments in India would assist in the movement.[33]

In the poem, Mulvaney is asked to have a look at the article by the narrator, who is indignant at the rumour of an Irish conspiracy. Mulvaney, after reading the article, at first eloquently decribes how the Mutiny might succeed with the help of 'six Oirish Regiments' and then, in the very last stanza, sternly denies the rumour that the Irish regiments would assist in any such attempt. This last stanza is separated from the rest by three asterisks, as if to protect Mulvaney's loyalist last word from his prior open approval of another Indian Mutiny, given, though, as in jest.[34]

Another Irish conspiracy was planned in 'The Mutiny of the Mavericks' (1891), a story in which a Fenian organization in the United States sends an Irish-American boy to the Mavericks, an Irish regiment in India, with a view to inciting a mutiny to produce 'vague, unhappy mistrust about the English rule in Ireland:

> The English people, when they trouble to think about the army at all, are, and with justice, absolutely assured that it is absolutely trustworthy. Imagine for a moment their emotions on realizing that such and such a regiment was in open revolt from causes directly due to England's management of Ireland.[35]

The recent 'Irish Conspiracy' plot lingers in this story, for the Fenian organization acts on its supposition that the Irish regiments in India are 'already half-mutinous, quartered among Sikh peasantry, all wearing miniatures of His Highness Dhulip Singh, Maharaja of the Punjab, next their hearts, and all eagerly expecting his arrival'.[36] The Mavericks are chosen as the target of incitement because the fenian organization considers them to be 'masterless and unbranded cattle – sons of small farmers in County Clare, shoeless vagabonds of Kerry, herders of Ballyvegan, much wanted "moonlighters" from the bare rainy headlands of the south coast, officered by O'Mores, Bradys, Hills, Kilreas, and the like'.[37] The despicable degeneration of the Irish outside the Empire and their cooperation with other foreign forces is symbolized by the hybridity of Mulcahy, 'Irish American-Jew boy'[38] sent to the Mavericks, who sucked 'that blind rancorous hatred of England that reaches its full growth across the Atlantic . . . from his mother's breast in the little cabin at the back of the northern avenues of New York' and 'had been taught his rights and wrongs, in German and Irish'.[39]

Mulcahy tries to talk the Irish soldiers into a mutiny by generously buying them drinks and circulating copies of Irish papers. The Mavericks, however, prove to be totally immune to such persuasion. The soldiers congenially listen to Mulcahy in order to let him pay for more drinks (in this way, they absorb the Irish-American capital invested for the purpose of overthrowing the Empire), though they deeply detest his urging them to 'join with the niggers, and look for help from Dhulip Singh and the Russians'.[40] Whereas, from the Fenian point of view, Irish men owe a duty to Erin to mutiny against England, Kipling's Irish soldiers seem to embody the purity of the loyal Irish preserved in India. At the end of the story, it turns out that even an Irishness corrupted by Irish nationalism and its foreign associations can be purified through service in India, for Mulcahy dies in the front line, ironically, as a hero who 'would have been recommended for the Victoria Cross had he survived'.[41]

In both 'The Irish Conspiracy' and 'The Mutiny of the Mavericks', the Irish are represented as willing participants in international conspiracies against the Empire, and Kipling represents the loyal Irish soldiers in India as thwarting these 'Irish' conspiracies. I suggest that *Kim*, a story about an Irish boy in India, should be understood in the same context. In the novel, the Great Game is played to secure India's north-western border, endangered by what Kipling describes as some conspiracies against the Empire: the spies appearing in the novel are Russian and French, and a plot uncovered by the Indian Secret Service involves 'the five confederated Kings, the sympathetic Northern Power, a Hindu banker in Peshawur, a firm of gun-makers in Belgium, and an important, semi-independent Mohammedan ruler to the south'.[42] When the Russian spy refers to Hurree as 'the monstrous hybridism of East and West', he is in fact referring to the anti-imperial network of which he is part, calling for the 'hybrid' Hurree, as 'little India in transition', to join the camp.[43] Moreover, this entire plot will be, at least in Kipling's imagination, readily supported by the Fenian Irish. In this sense, Kim's Irishness functions similarly to that of Mulvaney's and the Mavericks' (his father's regiment), representing the loyal Irish in India who fight on behalf of the Empire against foreign conspiracies. Far from being accidental, Kim's Irishness is meant to function as a powerful antidote to Irish conspiracy.

2

> The Victorian age is like one of those Magicians of eastern story who caught and bound to the accomplishment of their will some of the great Genii, Afreets, Jins, whatever the name Oriental fancy may have given them, whose force infinitely transcended every human force, yet who were at the mercy of the wise man who knew how to secure and train them.[44]

The expansion of the Empire was often seen as an oriental tale of taming the untameable, as can typically be seen in Margaret Oliphant's 1897 essay celebrating the year of the Diamond Jubilee, which looks back on the Victorian era as an eastern story of 'the great Genii, Afreets, Jins'. Such 'Oriental' genii, according to Oliphant, ranged from the telegraph and the steam engine to the Colonies, 'the loving Servants of the Queen'[45] themselves, which the marked innovations in methods of communication allowed Britain to grip more firmly. For this imperial fantasy of taming the Afreets, the fear of the Slave's fidelity should be just a 'whim', the imperialist representation of Empire operating like a spell which daily renewed its control over the Slave. Kipling also shared this fantasy, Irishness being an Oriental creature whose protean quality can be pinned down only by great magicians who know 'how to secure and train them'.

The genie-like side of Kim is closely examined by J. Mukherjee in his essay 'The Relevance of the Irish Aspect in Rudyard Kipling's *Kim*'. According to Mukherjee, a 'Druidic, Celtic heritage' enables Kim to 'absorb, understand and appreciate the occult' in India; Kim's adventure is that of an Irish boy made to seem natural in India due to the shared supernatural heritage of the two countries, allowing him to 'disappear into the landscape at will, like the Siddhi or Celtic Fairy folk'.[46] Kipling depicts his Irish characters as having a certain affinity with the most mysterious side of India, and Mukherjee thereby deems Kim's Irishness relevant to Kipling's Indian story. It seems to me, however, that in seeking to understand the 'relevance' of Kim's Irishness and his Celtic legacy, the 'politics' of this identity should be examined first. The Irish and the Indian, the two most supernatural elements found in the British Empire, geographically far apart, are, in Kipling's work, summoned, deliberately overlapped and almost identified in order to naturalize the Irish presence in India, which became possible only as a result of British rule in both countries.

According to Murray G. H. Pittock in his book *Celtic Identity and the British Image* (1999), 'characterizations of the Celt from *outside* have been primarily ethno-cultural, while internal self-definition has dominantly emphasized the civic and territorial, even while appearing to stress the ethnic'.[47] To characterize the Irish as supernatural is to define them solely in ethno-cultural terms, at once essentializing them as the 'mystical' others of the English and refusing to let them have any political identity which would threaten the British 'self-definition'.[48] During the expansion of the British Empire, the entire colonial space was similarly studied and understood in ethno-cultural terms, allowing the British to export and extend their civic and territorial identity to the colonies – the prior experience with Ireland no doubt informed this process. Kipling freely uses the slippage between Ireland and India, via the shared stereotype as an ancient and mythical land, to naturalize British rule in both countries. By using the Indian setting, Kipling could more easily catalogue the Irish as another oriental race, knowable and therefore governable, while on the other hand India is treated as another Ireland, the safe playing-ground of his favourite Irish characters. Furthermore, the association thus made between the two colonies serves to represent the strength of the imperial bond, best illustrated in the friendship betweem Kim and the lama.[49]

As far as the 'Druidic, Celtic heritage' of the Irish characters is concerned, Kipling seems to make full use of the supernatural legacy of both India and Ireland in order to forge a natural connection between the two colonies. It is interesting that the violation of imperial hierarchies by the supernatural, which Peter Morey sees as characteristic of Kipling's supernatural Indian stories, does not apply to the ones in which his Irish characters figure.[50] Many of the English characters are defeated by supernatural and inexplicable incidents, which the Irish characters seem to be better able to cope with. The supernatural is not necessarily represented as in opposition to reality, nor does it disturb the everyday life of the Irish characters. It is depicted more or less as natural, as if part of the Irish reality. For example, in 'The Courting of Dinah Shadd', both Mulvaney and Dinah readily accept 'the Black Curse of Shielygh', cast on them by 'ould Mother Sheehy', without asking whether it is valid or not.[51] In 'The Solid Muldoon' (1888), clearly a ghost story, in which Mulvaney tells how he had to fight with the ghost of a man while courting a married woman, the moral of the story is 'kape out av the Married Quarters',[52] and meeting a ghost itself, though Mulvaney admits that it is '*not* an ivry-day expayrience',[53] is nevertheless not treated as an impossible event. In fact, in this story the supernatural seems to draw India and Ireland closer together, suddenly ending with Mulvaney's looking back on his days in Ireland, which comes rather out of the blue for the reader: 'An' that's fourteen years gone! Eyah! Cork's own city an' the blue sky above ut – an' the times that was – the times that was!'[54] This almost gives us the impression that the whole story in fact took place in Ireland, though the story's setting is India. The supernatural elements merge the two places into one, as safe places nostalgically associated with the good old days.

Kipling's view of the Irish as a race is well summarized in 'The Mutiny of the Mavericks', which describes the Irish as 'that quaint, crooked, sweet, profoundly irresponsible and profoundly loveable race that fight like fiends, argue like children, reason like women, obey like men, and jest like their own goblins of the rath through rebellion, loyalty, want, woe, or war'.[55] It is interesting to note that this remark curiously echoes his own earlier description of *Indians* in a letter to his cousin Margaret Burne-Jones: 'A queer people indeed. Touchy as children; obstinate as men, patient as the High God's themselves; vicious as Devils but always lovable if you know how to take 'em.'[56] In using the same stock expressions to describe Indians and the Irish, Kipling implies that to know one race is to know the other. Furthermore, the Irish and Indians merge together in these two accounts, forming, as it were, a colonial riddle of the Sphinx – what is this creature that appears alternately as men, women, children, goblins, Indians *and the Irish*? (Kipling refers to India, in terms of colonial administration, as the 'great Sphinx of the Plains'.[57]) With this riddle in mind, it is important that in *Kim*, the boy's identity is also described as 'the tremendous puzzle'.[58] Kipling the imperial ethnographer thus takes up Oedipus' task of solving this riddle – otherwise known as 'the Irish Question' – which, if not solved, would condemn British rule to be devoured by the monstrous hybrid; the successful naming of the creature would immediately tame him into the fighting force of the Empire.

In 'Namgay Doola' (1891), a little Indian kingdom is threatened by a red-haired rebel, Namgay Doola, who not only refuses to pay taxes but also stirs the people 'up to the like treason'.[59] The narrator is 'puzzled' by the identity of this rebel, who cuts off the tail of the king's cow and steals the narrator's camera-cloth, yet always seems to get away with mischief, being a merry-faced man with a 'soul-compelling grin'.[60] The narrator eventually identifies him as being of Irish descent: he is a Eurasian whose father is an Irish soldier in the East India Company and whose mother is a woman of the hills. The most crucial evidence of the rebel's Irishness is his father's name, 'Timlay Doola', which the narrator, by making the rebel pronounce it thrice or four times, successfully identifies as the Irish name 'Thimla Dhula'.[61] Likewise, the strangely familiar song which Namgay Doola repeatedly sings turns out to be a corrupt version of 'The Wearing of the Green',[62] a popular Irish nationalist song. The narrator then advises the king to make this man the chief of his army: 'Feed him with words and favour, and also liquor from certain bottles that thou knowest of, and he will be a bulwark of defence'.[63] The Irish, though rebellious in nature, become the most reliable subjects when they are well treated and their pride is flattered, and if, as the narrator boasts, you 'know that breed',[64] that is, how to deal with the Irish.

'My Lord the Elephant' (1892) makes a similar point: the rebellious quality of the Irish is subdued by the one who knows the race best. In fact, here it is the Irish Mulvaney who figures as an orientalist with specialist knowledge of the Irish. In this story, Mulvaney tells how he once tamed an elephant which had suddenly become so unruly that even his mahout could not control him. Mulvaney the narrator tries many different names to speak to the elephant: he is interchangeably 'a Kumeria of the Doon',[65] 'ould rapparee',[66] 'Ould Grambags',[67] 'Ould Barrel-belly',[68] 'Ould Thrajectory',[69] 'ould Potiphar',[70] 'Ould Double Ends',[71] 'Ould Typhoon'[72] and so on. This act of naming is noteworthy because it presents a story of taming as that of naming: just as Adam named his animals as he tamed them, this animal has to have a 'proper' name to be tamed. Mulvaney's narrative device of inventing new names for the elephant retraces his desperate efforts to calm down the 'murderin' volcano',[73] and Mulvaney even tries the names associated with domesticated animals, such as 'Good dog', 'Pretty puss', 'Whoa mare',[74] as if to downsize the elephant. Importantly, the variety of names represents the elephant as a kind of protean being which eludes any definition lest it should be caught. Informed by a sergeant that the elephant became rebellious because he resented being put to the gun-team instead of carrying tents, the job which he took most pride in doing, Mulvaney sympathizes with him and comes to the conclusion that the elephant is an Irishman: 'He's an Irishman . . . for all his long Jew's nose, an' he shall be threated like an Irishman',[75] and the 'proper name' which Mulvaney finally comes up with is 'Smith O'Brine'.[76] He starts treating him as an Irishman, that is, talking to him, cleaning him and having a drink with him to 'let bygones be',[77] and by these means successfully tames the elephant. At the end of the story, Mulvaney's insight that the elephant is an Irishman proves to be true: the elephant's real name is Malachi, the name of an Irish saint and also that of a brave Irish king who fought against the invasion of the Danes.[78]

Interestingly, Mulvaney does not reveal the elephant's name to be Malachi from the beginning of his story, despite the fact that he already knows this name when he retrospectively tells the story to the narrator. The initially resentful and mutinous nature of the elephant is encapsulated in the other Irish name 'Smith O'Brine' – here the reference to William Smith O'Brien (1803–64), an Irish revolutionary whose rising in 1848 ingloriously failed, is quite obvious. It is not until the elephant 'let[s] bygones be' and is transformed into a loyal and obedient servant of the Empire that Mulvaney can address him as Malachi, his *true* name, thereby rendering 'Smith O'Brine', the elephant's name as a mutineer, temporary. Irish rebelliousness is also represented in the form of Mulvaney's extravagant and unmanageable imagination, which causes his narrative course to correspond to that of the rampant elephant: the story can be read as the taming of the Irish by the Irish through storytelling, with the help of Kipling the narrator. Throughout this story, then, Kipling draws a clear parallel between the Irish and the elephant. The Irish are not the tiger, that animal which stands for the most ferocious and untameable side of nature, which has to be killed and excluded in order to make exploitation of the land easier for the colonizer, and to which the Indian natives were often likened;[79] rather, the Irish are the elephant, ferocious yet manageable, who, once tamed, will be the most reliable and efficient vanguard of imperialism.[80]

Kipling presents the plot of taming the Irish Afreets as the solving of a puzzle, which takes the form of identifying a baffling and rebellious creature found in the Empire, whose true name always turns out to be 'Irish'. A large part of the narrative is thus devoted to the guessing process, enticing the reader with the intricate art of imperial ethnography. Kim is another protean creature who freely turns into an Oriental, a sahib, Irish, English, a *chela* and whatever he chooses to be, and thus presents himself as a puzzle to be solved. However, while in 'Namgay Doola' and 'My Lord the Elephant' the puzzle is satisfactorily solved by finally identifying the rebel as Irish, Kim's identity as Irish is established quite early in the novel, and the question 'Who is Kim?' naturally requires different answers. Nevertheless, *Kim*, like 'Namgay Doola' and 'My Lord the Elephant', does also make a riddle out of the Irishman's identity. Indeed, Namgay Doola, identified as Irish from his father's name and thereby reclaimed by the Raj, is undoubtedly Kim's predecessor, except that Kipling takes great care to show that Kim is purely Irish, not a half-caste. Kipling therefore repeats 'Namgay Doola' in *Kim*, but with a difference; accordingly, the nature of the Indo-Irish hybrid as a riddle is also given a different twist.

Before concluding this section, I would like to note one other aspect of Kipling's stereotype of the Irish: theatricality. In Kipling's world, the Irish are actors who can play any role. Just like Kim who turns into anything, Mulvaney impersonates Krishna extempore and can even act as an efficient British soldier. It is interesting that what information we have about Mulvaney's life in Ireland is mostly associated with a place called 'Silver's Theatre' in Dublin. This theatre, always short of money, gave anybody a chance to play who would pay for the role. Mulvaney, who was, according to himself, 'a patron av the drama'[81] when he was young, was once supposed to play the role of Hamlet, but it was taken over by somebody else in his regiment, named Hogin. Mulvaney went to see the play and disturbed the performance by inciting the audience to ridicule the costume. The whole theatre then became a stage in which not only actors but also the audience played. In this way, Kipling successfully locks Ireland in a theatre, inside a representation, where 'reality' is, if only for a short time, suspended. '[A]fther this performince is over me an' the Ghost'll trample the tripes out av you, Terence, wid your ass's bray!'[82] retorts Hogin, still on stage, knowing the ringleader was Mulvaney. However, he is not likely to be able to take his revenge on Mulvaney, because in Kipling's world, the Irish characters are transfixed in Silver's Theatre and the performance will never be over. Furthermore, the Irish talent for theatrical representation should never be used to represent themselves in the political arena; the Irish have to keep on playing their stereotype, the stage Irishman.[83]

Chapter Two

When East Meets West

Kipling's India of Anti-Gravity

> *Hospitalität* [hospitality], a word of Latin origin, of a troubled and troubling origin, a word which carries its own contradiction incorporated into it, a Latin word which allows itself to be parasitized by its opposite, 'hostility,' the undesirable guest which it harbors as the self-contradiction in its own body.[1]

Hospitality is, according to Derrida reading Kant, 'the right of the stranger' to be cordially welcomed on his arrival, 'which is reciprocally the duty or obligation of the host who is master in his house, who is *what he is* in his house'.[2] Hospitality, however, could in a split second slip into its opposite, hostility, rendering a welcomed guest into an undesirable intruder, into an enemy within the host's territory. Colonization is an infringement of the law of hospitality, for the guest, once invited in, takes over the territory and assumes the role of master, which Kant describes as conquest, 'the *inhospitable* conduct of the civilized states of our continent', responsible for 'the whole litany of evils which afflict the human race'.[3] In the nineteenth century, the colonizing British were determined to make themselves *at home* and to become masters of the foreign lands in which they were initially received as guests. This inhospitable intrusion was carried to the extreme in the settler colonies, where the native population was decimated to near extinction. English, the mother tongue through which they could easily act as hosts at home, was imposed wherever the British migrated – as Derrida puts it, 'when I begin to speak in my language, which seems to suppose that I am here <at home> master in my own home, that I am receiving, inviting, accepting or welcoming you, allowing you to come across the threshold, by saying "*bienvenu*," "welcome", to you'[4] – keeping the natives and their languages servilely waiting outside the threshold as translation.

Even in India, where they did not and could not purge the land of its native inhabitants, they successfully established themselves as 'Sahib', the master. However, one interesting aspect of British India was that the Englishman, the master, nevertheless remained as a *guest* of the place, for India shattered the colonizer's dream of making it his home, for it was too hot, too unsanitary and almost uninhabitable for the white population. India proved to be, to quote Rudyard Kipling and Wolcott Balestier, 'a great big Bad Lands – morally, physically and agriculturally, Bad Lands . . . no place for white men, let alone white women'.[5] Not only was there the physical impossibility of the colonizer settling, but there was also a great deal of aversion to being assimilated by India. Englishness and settling down in India were thought to be almost mutually exclusive. The English were constantly threatened with erosion and hybridization in their contact with the Indian climate and in their close proximity to native bodies. Accordingly, the experience of British India was presented as a constant contest between the English *character* and the corruptive Indian *ground*, and was characterized as the search for a space similar to the home country where their standards and identity could be easily maintained. As Francis G. Hutchins puts it, 'the British never became Indianized, as had earlier conquerors. Earlier conquerors had not possessed a foreign home from which they continuously drew their standards and which induced them to look upon India only as a place of permanent exile.'[6] Thus the English, the masters of India, were never quite a host, and India responded to the half-hearted hospitality of the master with plenty of hostility *and* the relentless force of assimilation.

In this chapter, I will discuss Kipling's representation of India, in which the imperial mission is represented as the Englishman's heroic struggle to retain his Englishness against the corrupting Indian influences. I illustrate this as the battle for survival of the English *figure* (character) against the Indian *ground*. I will then trace the change in Kipling's representation of India in the 1890s, which reflects the fact that Kipling left the physical force of the Indian ground (he left India in 1889), and also his changing views of the Empire. For example, *Kim* underplays the conflict between the English and the hostile India, which was the principal theme of Kipling's earlier representation of British India. Instead, India is presented as a rather habitable place – almost like an ideal settler colony – in which the colonizer's difficulty and his physical limitations are miraculously and technologically removed.

The distinction between the settler colonies and the non-settler colonies is crucial when considering Kipling's Empire. His earlier representation of the British Empire, in the 1880s and 1890s, was predominantly made through India, a non-settler colony, while his later representation of the Empire, during the time of the Boer War, is constructed around an ideal federation of English-speaking white settler colonies. The latter was a dream of world domination by Anglo-Saxons which Kipling shared with his friend and hero Cecil Rhodes, a dream well typified in the title of his book of poems *The Five Nations* (1903) – Canada, Australia, New Zealand, South Africa and 'England' – in which collection his famous poem 'The White Man's Burden' appears. If the Irish were always represented as immigrants in his earlier stories, Kipling perhaps foresaw his future vision of the Empire in this representation of the Irish in India, for the mass emigration from Ireland was a propelling force of the English-speaking white settlers' dominion. At least, as Kipling becomes more preoccupied with the issues of Empire as the settler colonies' federation in the late nineteenth century, his India seems to have become increasingly a more habitable place, as if Kipling, as an unofficial bard of the Empire, altered his tactics to best represent imperial prosperity and solidarity. It is within these contexts that I wish to discuss Kim the Irish boy, made to inhabit the subtle but intriguing differences between hospitable and uninhabitable India, the 1880s and the 1900s, Englishness and Britishness, India and the British Empire.

1

In the spirit of 'the exception proves the rule', I will start this chapter with a story by Kipling which is in many ways 'exceptional' as an Anglo-Indian story, '"Yoked with an Unbeliever"' (1886). It is exceptional, firstly, because the story does not *at all* register any of the difficulties or struggles characteristic of English life in India. The story is set 'somewhere between Darjeeling and Kangra',[7] where the climate is rather good and there is little chance of suffering from sunstroke and hallucinations. Secondly, even though it is set in a habitable hill region, the story does not particularly focus on the Anglo-Indian community, nor does it dwell on the unbridgeable racial divide between the English and Indians. On the contrary, an Englishman marries a native girl, and, unlike others of Kipling's stories dealing with inter-racial unions, this story ends with a happy-ever-after, with Phil and his native wife blessedly united in their married life. And lastly, the aforementioned Englishman, Phil Garron, completely loses touch with England and decides to *settle down* in India, which no Englishman should consider as his home.

This story, which demonstrates the peculiar power of assimilation which the colonial space exercised over the colonizer, ironically starts with a 'stereotypical' view of India, which fails to register the true nature of the dangers encountered by Englishmen out in the colonies:

> [Miss Agnes Laiter] had reason to cry, because the only man she ever loved – or ever could love, so she said – was going out to India; and India, as every one knows, is divided equally between jungle, tigers, cobras, cholera, and sepoys.[8]

The rest of the story reveals that it is not jungle, tigers, cobras, cholera, sepoys or even the famous Indian heat which causes Agnes to lose her true love Phil Garron. It is what lies in the background of these fixed figures that is actually responsible for their break-up, namely, the powerful force of the ground which firmly grips Phil and transforms him over time. This transformation is underlined by Phil's gradual deviation from his initial plan of '[saving] a large proportion of his magnificent salary yearly' and 'triumphantly' returning to marry Agnes Laiter.[9] Phil soon forgets about Agnes, his ambition and England altogether, marries a hill-girl, Dunmaya, and happily settles down in India, whereas Agnes, though the circumstances also force her to marry another man in England, remains faithful to Phil at heart, believing in a letter which he wrote to her in a fit of sentimentality. Phil's process of acclimatization is virtually described as his gradual loss of Englishness :

> It is to be remembered that Phil was living very comfortably, denying himself no small luxury, never putting by a penny, very satisfied with himself and his good intentions, was dropping all his English correspondents one by one, and beginning more and more to look upon India as his home. Some men fall this way, and they are of no use afterwards. The climate where he was stationed was good, and it really did not seem to him that there was any reason to return to England.[10]

There is no satisfactory explanation nor reason given for Phil's transformation, except that we are told that Phil is 'the least little bit in the world weak'.[11] This weakness in his character turns out to be fatal, for it means that he is neither self-disciplined nor strong enough to sustain himself as an English figure; he lets his new circumstances recreate him. By the time Agnes, after her husband dies, goes over to India to join him, he has become totally inseparable from native life, being presented in the text only with his new background: 'She found him. She spent a month over it, for his plantation was not in the Darjeeling district at all, but nearer Kangra. Phil was very little altered, and Dunmaya was very nice to her'.[12] The Phil whom Agnes retrieves is not so much Phil per se as Phil inseparable from the Indian landscape and his wife, who has 'a reasonable estimate of her husband's weaknesses'.[13] This story, in which an Englishman who is 'the least little bit in the world weak' becomes very easily naturalized in India, eloquently proves the general rule that the colonizer was required to have a strong character in order to sustain his original identity as English against the assimilating force of the colonial ground. Somerset Maugham, a later colonial writer, names this effect of the ground as 'The Force of Circumstance', the title of a story in which an Englishwoman finds that her newly married husband, with whom she came to Malaya to live, had a native wife and three children by her before their marriage. The 'force of circumstance', or the physical and affective ties which the colonizer forms with the place during his long residence, proves to be stronger than the couple's racial affinity: 'You belong to them, you don't belong to me . . . It's a physical thing, I can't help it, it's stronger than I am.'[14] As soon as the bond breaks, each of the two is pulled back to the ground to which each most naturally belongs: the wife goes back to England and, once she has left, the husband calls his deserted native wife and children back to him. The man in the story is English by blood, but is described as having less powerful ties with England, having been born and brought up in Sembulu: 'After all, England's a foreign land to me.'[15] Although England is supposedly the home ground of Englishness, and he desires to have an Englishwoman as his wife, he does not feel any urge to go back to England in order to form a true tie with the land of his racial identity. Thus he lets himself become less and less English, becoming more and more rooted in a foreign land. This was the risk which the English had to take by extending their territory: the Englishness of the English, deprived of its own ground, was to be attenuated, exposed and subject to change in the colonies.

The nineteenth century was a period in which the transforming power of foreign places was strongly felt, because of the unprecedented scale of imperialist expansion. The colonizers spreading themselves all over the world provided the best examples of Darwin's theory of natural selection and geographical distribution.[16] While their adaptability to a foreign ground ensured the possibility of colonization and settlement, the same trait proved to be double-edged, for it inevitably suggested that the 'Englishness' of the colonizer was fundamentally corruptible. Dane Kennedy, in his *The Magic Mountains: Hill Stations and the British Raj* (1996), argues that the racial identity of the British was seriously threatened both by the effect of the harsh foreign climate and by 'miscegenation' with local women. While the view that Europeans physically degenerated over time owing to exposure to high temperatures and tropical diseases was accepted by medical and administrative authorities as true, this 'threat of physical extinction' was aggravated by 'the prospect of miscegenation', which would threaten 'the possibility of a European settler population's surviving over several generations *as* Europeans'.[17] The English had spread their territory at the cost of being 'corrupted' and assimilated into the soil which they had colonized. So, the 'colonial desire' of those who stayed long in the colonial space was by no means simply the desire to transgress a forbidden sexual border. It was rather the desire to clearly demarcate and retain a firm boundary between themselves and their racial 'others', so that their identity as the colonizer, threatened and hybridized through their contact with the place and their personal and sexual involvement with natives, would be safely maintained.[18]

Kipling, who spent a substantial time away from England, was fully aware of the force of the foreign ground, and it seems to me that his writing markedly shows this awareness. Alan Sandison argues that Kipling's Indian stories are *not* the presentation of imperial heroes, tough and resourceful English administrators and subalterns who are dedicated to their duties; his stories are rather the presentation of the colonizer's desperate effort to maintain 'self-consciousness, identity and moral integrity'[19] in the face of 'great, grey, formless India', which is the true main character in Kipling's Indian stories, with its 'inexorable powers of assimilation'.[20] India represents 'the forces of persecution raged against the individual in his struggle to sustain his identity. Physically and morally it overwhelms and crushes. One's own truths and moral definitions blur and diffuse themselves into meaninglessness.'[21] Kipling's characters identify themselves with the values of the Empire in the hope that sticking to their own cultural ethos might help them sustain their identity, even though they run the risk of failing to understand the people they govern and imposing blindly their own cultural values on them.[22] To put this differently, India is more likely to be represented as a harsh and hostile place in order to accentuate true 'Englishness' as the strength to fight against it. Englishmen wholeheartedly embraced by India, like Phil Garron, can only be denounced as 'weak' characters.

Phil Garron is indeed an exceptional character in Kipling, figuring one of the few instances in which Kipling lets the power of the ground win over the Englishman. In Kipling's world, it is usually 'English' characters with characteristically Celtic names (but not specified as Irish) who suffer the most dishonourable defeats at the hands of the Indian conditions, often in spite of, or perhaps because of, their top academic education. For instance, Aurelian McGoggin, a 'brilliantly clever' disciple of Comte and Spencer with many 'isms' in his head, suddenly falls into a temporal aphasia because of the Indian heat.[23] McIntosh Jellaludin, 'an Oxford Man' and a first-rate scholar, ends up in the lowest stratum in India – in an opium den among half-castes – taking a native woman as his wife and being converted into a Muslim: 'When a man begins to sink in India, and is not sent Home by his friends as may be, he falls very low from a respectable point of view.'[24] McIntosh Jellaludin, however, is an important character in *Plain Tales*, who is no doubt an alter ego of the author. He likens himself to Dante descending into an Inferno and is the author of 'the Book of Mother Maturin', a big bundle of manuscripts which he entrusts to the narrator shortly before he dies;[25] Kipling's own unfinished manuscript, which it seems that he later destroyed, was also called 'Mother Maturin', and was a story about an old Irish woman who kept an opium den in Lahore, which allegedly dealt with 'the unutterable horrors of lower class Eurasian and native life as they exist outside reports and reports and reports'.[26]

McIntosh Jellaludin is the side of Kipling which was wholeheartedly seduced and embraced by the force of the native ground, and Kipling significantly represents this 'weaker' side of himself as Celtic. We may even say that he splits himself between the *Celtic* loafer McIntosh Jellaludin and the *English* policeman Strickland in his fascination with native life. McIntosh Jellaludin and Strickland both know native life inside and out, but how they come to know the natives is fundamentally different. While McIntosh Jellaludin has 'his hand on the pulse of native life'[27] by hybridizing himself with India, as his name – half Celtic, half Indian – symbolizes, Strickland comes to know 'as much about the natives as the natives themselves' by perpetually 'going Fantee' among them, *without* losing either his character or his power over the natives as English. Strickland disguises himself as a native but never becomes one, and his marrying a white woman further safeguards his stability as English while living in India.[28] In 'To Be Filed for Reference' (1888), Strickland helps the narrator sort out McIntosh Jellaludin's manuscript and judges it of no use, whereas Jellaludin derides Strickland as 'ignorant West and East',[29] an unauthentic amalgamation of the two. If, as is commonly thought, *Mother Maturin* over time matured into *Kim*, in which Strickland figures as the Superintendent of the Game, this may mean that Kipling over time comes to choose Strickland's India over McIntosh Jellaludin's India. At any rate, this overall framework makes it even more interesting that the Irish settlement in India is, as I have shown in the previous chapter, treated as more or less natural immigration. The Irish are not required to miss Home, and their failing to return is in no way treated as weakness. Kim, unlike Phil the Englishman or McIntosh Jellaludin, manages to escape being permanently caught by one native location (or woman) and retains his mobility and his adaptability to any new ground which he crosses. The Irish are given a role which their English counterparts cannot possibly achieve: they live in India without losing their outline as 'English'.

2

The colonizers did not passively wait to be endangered by the new environment to which they relocated themselves, but on the contrary attempted to dominate and transform it so as to meet their demands. We have to recall that in the nineteenth century to colonize was to conquer the natural resources of a new land for the colonizer's use – rivers, jungles, mountains, animals, climate and so on – as well as the natives who were part of the landscape. From the colonizer's point of view, it was not so much a psychological, face-to-face confrontation between the colonizer and the native inhabitants as a challenging process of overcoming the physical obstacles and resistances which he found in his way. In this context, the biggest crisis in British India, I suggest, has to be seen neither as 'the Indian Mutiny' nor as 'the First War of Independence', but rather as the spontaneous restoration of the original shape and equilibrium of the Indian grounds which had been greatly disturbed by its exploiter.

Lord Roberts (both Anglo-Irish and Anglo-Indian), looking back on the 1857 Uprising, which he himself had helped to suppress about forty years before, recollected that any delay in retrieving Delhi was felt to be fatal for the efficient officers: 'If Delhi were not taken, and that speedily, there would be a struggle not only for European dominion, but even for European existence within the Punjab itself.'[30] The 'Indian Mutiny' was not merely the battle fought to preserve British rule in India and to prove British superiority over the natives; in reality, it was rather the desperate struggle for survival of the British figures – so as not to be erased from the Indian ground. The success of the Mutiny meant for the English in India not only the dissolution of English ideologies and values – which protected and 'vaccinated' them against the Indian ground, allowing them to safely prefigure as English – but also the loss of the ground in which they could exist at all. With the outbreak of the Mutiny, the English suddenly found themselves fully exposed to the natural forces of the foreign ground. The early battles were fought in the most oppressive climate of the year (the Mutiny broke out on 10 May at Meerut, and Delhi was recaptured on 21 September; the European troops had to fight through both the hottest and rainiest seasons). Soldiers were struck down by heat and exhaustion, and epidemics reduced the limited human resources at an alarming rate even before the actual fighting began. Quite a few officers had to give up their commands owing to ill-health or died.[31] Not only the climate but also the configuration of the land hindered the swift progress of the British troops and caused further delay, while giving the natives a great advantage, allowing them time to attack weaker places and reduce the number of Europeans. As Roberts recalls, the bad weather and ground conditions were the more formidable enemies which relentlessly robbed the English troops of their time:

> It proved a most difficult march. The rain fell in torrents, and the roads were mere quagmires. In the first nine miles two swamps had to be got through . . . while running round the enemy's right and rear was a huge drainage cut, swollen by the heavy rain. The cut, or nulla, was crossed by a bridge immediately behind the rebels' position. Nicholson advanced from a side-road, which brought him on their right with the nulla flowing between him and them. Even at the ford the water was breast-high, and it was with much difficulty and not without a good deal of delay that our troops crossed under a heavy fire from the serai. It was getting late, and Nicholson had only time to make a hasty reconnaissance.[32]

According to Paul Virilio, 'Speed is Time saved in the most absolute sense of the word, since it becomes human Time directly torn from Death – whence those macabre emblems of decimation worn down through history by the Assault troops, in other words, the *rapid troops*.'[33] Indeed, the success of the Assault of Delhi depended absolutely on how rapid the British troops could be. As Richard Baird Smith, the Chief Engineer of the Delhi Troops, puts it in reply to Commander Archdale Wilson, 'waiting for reinforcements involved inaction – an inaction which might last for weeks. Such inaction

. . . involved a risk greater even than the risk of a repulse before the walls of the city.'[34] It was a case in history in which inaction – the lack of speed – literally meant perdition. The problem was, however, that the British troops combating the Indian Mutiny were deprived of the speed necessary, because they were fighting in and against the very plane on which they moved. Roberts, in his accounts of the initial stage of the Mutiny, repeatedly draws a contrast between the natives, who, having a geographical advantage, proceeded speedily and 'lost no time',[35] and the British, who failed to take action 'with sufficient promptitude'[36] and therefore suffered from 'unaccountable delay':[37] 'every hour that passed without assaulting was a loss to us and a gain to the enemy'.[38] At night, when the battles were not fought, further delay occurred, because the mutineers secretly succeeded in effecting the breaches, 'notwithstanding the steady fire we had kept up'.[39] Moreover, as we will see later in this chapter, these summer nights were exhaustingly hot.

The feeling that any more delay would be fatal was further intensified by the fact that Wilson, who had assumed the command of the Delhi field force, was reluctant to attack the city, preferring to wait for the reinforcements of European troops which he believed were available. Roberts quotes a letter sent from John Lawrence (an Anglo-Irish commander) to Wilson, in which Lawrence urges Wilson to take immediate action: 'There seem to be very strong reasons for assaulting as soon as practicable. Every day's delay is fraught with danger. Every day disaffection and mutiny spread. Every day adds to the danger of the Native Princes taking part against us'.[40]

The Siege of Delhi typically illustrates the dilemma which the colonizer had to face: he could maintain his rule over a ground only if he did not touch the ground. Too close a physical contact with the ground might undermine his existence and identity as the colonizer. To solve this dilemma, the colonizer of the nineteenth century set himself the unusual task of erasing the ground as he owned it, with the help of 'speed', moving so rapidly that he barely touched the ground. Modern transportation, be it the train, automobile or aeroplane, all of which saw dramatic improvements during the nineteenth century, was the realization of the colonizer's deepest wish to 'go over every kind of terrain' and erase obstacles; as Virilio puts it, 'With it, earth no longer exists. Rather than calling it an "all-terrain" vehicle, they should call it "*sans-terrain*" – it climbs embankments, runs over trees, paddles through the mud, rips out shrubs and pieces of wall on its way, breaks down doors . . . It offers a whole new geometry to speed, to violence.'[41] With the speed acquired thanks to modern technologies, mankind can now disregard the force of the ground. (Virilio's quote from Marinetti's 1905 text to illustrate the power of speed as 'sans-terrain' is worth quoting again: 'Hoorah! No more contact with the vile earth!'[42])

The view that modern technology was the sole means of overcoming the destructive effect of the Indian ground was clearly articulated at that time; for example, evidence was given to the Select Committee on Colonization and Settlement in India 1857–8 – a British attempt to re-examine the possibility of a European colonization of India in response to the outbreak of the Mutiny – stating that Europeans could not possibly 'thrive or exist on the plains in India' but for 'means of communication', such as 'connecting the trunk lines of railway by branches to the hill stations'.[43] Improvements were made accordingly, and Lord Roberts concludes, in the preface to his memoirs, that the Indian Mutiny eventually contributed to consolidating British power in India, as it 'hastened on the construction of the roads, railways, and telegraphs', which 'have done more than anything to increase the prosperity of the people and preserve order throughout the country'.[44] The new technologies, such as 'roads, railways, and telegraphs', radically diminished the danger of delay which had proved fatal during the Indian Mutiny, made the ground spatially shrink and minimized the duration of time necessary to cover the vast spatial distances inside India.

Among British technological achievements, the electric telegraph most radically annihilated space and time. As James W. Carey argues, it decisively separated 'transportation' and 'communication', which had been identical till the advent of the telegraph: the telegraph 'not only allowed messages to be separated from the physical movement of objects; it also allowed communication to control physical processes actively'.[45] It made it possible for information to be sent independently of geography, and, what is more, gave the user the power and time to intervene in the course of events. The telegraph was first introduced during Lord Dalhousie's era by an Irishman, William Brooke O'Shaughnessy (1808–89), Assistant Surgeon and Professor of Chemistry in the Medical College at Calcutta, and another example of the close involvement of the Irish in the Raj. The telegraph, in fact, turned out to be 'the most powerful weapon with which Lord Canning confronted the mutiny'.[46]

Of course, in the nineteenth century the materiality of time and space was yet to be overcome. Transportation (or the movement along the physical plane) was, and still is, to a certain extent inevitably caught up with the force of ground. As Hurree Chunder in *Kim* puts it, 'you cannot occupy two places in space simultaneously. Thatt is axiomatic'.[47] However, it is this axiomatical impossibility that modernization has nevertheless been trying to disprove: to speed up against the ground effect, in order to obliterate space and time, and occupy more than one place at the same time, which will make the force of the ground almost unnoticeable, and in the end eliminate the need to touch the ground altogether. After the Mutiny, transportation was asked to catch up with the speed of communication enabled by the new technology as the colonies of the British Empire were quickly networked by the telegraph, which unified the Empire not so much by a sense of shared geographical territory as by what Benedict Anderson calls an 'imagined community' sustained by shared time and information.[48]

3

Kipling's earlier Indian stories were written with the pull of the ground's gravity, the same force which could have annihilated the Delhi troops in the Indian Mutiny. The sudden removal of this ground-effect affected his later stories, written outside India, as much as its presence left a deep mark in his earlier writing.

A few critics have already noted that there was a change of tone in Kipling's writing after he left India. For example, as early as 1896, E. Kay Robinson notes that 'On leaving India Kipling was plunged into a new world, and to some extent seems to have lost his bearings, while his Indian writings – of jungle life, etc. – are losing the exactitude of local colour which marked his earlier work.'[49] Also, J. H. Fenwick writes, concerning the stories of *Soldiers Three*, 'After Kipling leaves India the soldiers continue to appear, but one can mark the way in which the old frame formula is becoming anachronistic, often effective in itself, but seldom serving an exploratory or analytic purpose.'[50] According to Fenwick, Kipling's later soldier stories no longer show 'a real and successful balance between the problems of the individual and that of military society as a whole',[51] which he values in the earlier stories. Instead, the stories become more tactless and overtly ideological, and Fenwick finds that the narrator of the later stories is 'as a civilian . . . unbearably presumptuous in his outspokenness', and notes 'an increasing tendency to rhetorical persuasion': 'The rhetoric is sometimes crude, sometimes effective, but its very existence shows that Kipling's aim is no longer strictly fictional – that it verges at times on the propagandist.'[52] I will go on to argue here that Kipling's earlier Indian stories written in India are a little different from the later ones written after 1889, when he left India. This may trouble some readers, because what I am suggesting could lead one to read differences between *Plain Tales from the Hills* (1889) and *Life's Handicap* (1891), both of which are often discussed in the same context.

Kipling's later Indian stories are not only seen to be more imperialistic, but are also often criticized for failing to register 'time' and 'reality'. His India is likened to the Garden of Eden, where the colonizer can still enjoy a full sense of power and from which the changing colonial realities are all left out.[53] For instance, Edward W. Said criticizes 'a radical misreading' by Kipling's admirers who understand his Indian writing as a truthful representation of India as 'a timeless, unchanging, and "essential" locale, a place almost as much poetic as it is actual in geographic correctness'. He nonetheless agrees that Kipling's India *is* indeed timeless and placeless – 'it was because [Kipling] deliberately saw it that way' – that is, to mask the changing realities of British India at the turn of the century and to perpetuate the hegemony of the Empire.[54] Similarly, Kipling's world, in stories like *The Jungle Books* and *Kim*, is often referred to as 'adolescent; caught between childhood and adulthood',[55] as if, unlike in England where maturity was associated with the idea of tradition and progress, any transformation in time which India might experience immediately meant hybridization with, therefore degradation into, Indian nationalism. This sense of timelessness or groundlessness indeed makes a striking contrast with Kipling's earlier version of India, characteristically marked by various pernicious effects of the Indian ground. Especially, the hot Indian weather can be seen everywhere in his early stories and letters, which makes its absence in his later work far more interesting.

Kipling's departure from India – his freeing of himself from the Indian ground – interestingly coincides with both the beginning of his literary fame and his becoming more obviously imperialistic. We can assume that these two phenomena are probably interconnected. By the time he went back to England his name was well known among the English public. Edmonia Hill, one of Kipling's close friends during his days in India, writes in her diary in April 1888:

> I shall never forget the glee in which RK came in one afternoon saying, 'What do you suppose I just came across in reading the proof of this week's English letter? Andrew Lang says, "Who is Mr Rudyard Kipling?"' He was so pleased that they really had heard of him in England, for in all modesty he intends to make his mark in the world.[56]

This is a significant moment, in which Kipling realized that his name had not only become known in England, but also become a byword for the representation of India and Anglo-Indian society. The period in which Kipling wrote anonymously or under various pen names in the Indian newspapers was over. When Kipling reached England in person, his name had already become an author's name, and shortly became identified with certain discourses which were very powerful at the turn of the century, namely, discourses of empire and race. Within the text which bore the name 'Kipling', the reader could vividly visualize British India, the solidarity of the British Empire and even racial differences between black and white, all of which were supposed to exist. Kipling quickly responded to the expectations of the British public. In order to make the Indian background more accessible to a British audience, he made changes to the first English edition of *Plain Tales from the Hills* (1890), in which 'anna' becomes 'penny', 'this country' becomes 'India', 'you know' becomes 'every household in India knows'.[57] Kipling's stories became the Anglo-Indian gift to the imperial centre, whose local and partial view of the colonial margin was translated into the representative text of the Empire by the repositioning of the narrator and the author. Kipling adopted the same strategy as the Anglo-Indian force combating the Mutiny, that is, the erasure of the Indian ground through the creation of a timeless and groundless India, as if to protect the representation of the Raj from hostile forces. We may also say that this strategy was to disavow the white men's panic and their inability to retain their Englishness in the face of the corruptive native ground-effects.

The colonizer's new India, woven through networks of simultaneous communication and speedy transportation, has much in common with what Benedict Anderson calls 'empty, homogeneous time',[58] a new temporal consciousness emerging in the eighteenth century, and providing the basis for re-presenting 'the *kind* of imagined community that is the nation'.[59] This new temporality is, according to Anderson, exemplified by daily newspapers and multi-plot novels: events simultaneously happening somewhere in the world become an important part of the readers' reality, giving a sense of connectedness and communal solidarity with people whom they have never met. Irene Tucker, in her summary of Anderson's *Imagined Communities* 1991, aptly calls this new temporality 'the placelessness implicit within modern notions of culture – a placelessness that will turn out, however paradoxically, to be essential to a sense both of culture's nationalness and of its spatiality'. Tucker argues that not only national, but also *international* consciousness took place in this placelessness, for the connectedness conveyed through newspapers was 'among *different* nations'.[60] Kipling's new, timeless India, achieved through the partial erasure of his earlier version of India, aims to capture this 'placelessness', the Empire as a non-place, imagined as the networks and connections of different colonies and nations internationally united. The Anglo-Indians achieved their fondest wish of creating a space free of the Indian ground, in which they could survive as English, through the communication networks of the hill stations and in the columns of international and colonial news (in contrast to local news) assuring them of the existence of the Empire, which Kipling, as a journalist, was in touch with.

While Kipling's earlier narrator is restricted by his body and the oppressive Indian climate in his storytelling, his later stories characteristically feature an omniscient and omnipresent narrator, whose all-knowing perspective, according to Anderson, is indispensable in creating the imaginary world of interconnection.[61] Kipling, in his transformation from the Anglo-Indian writer into the bard of the Empire, adopted such a viewpoint, which could redefine and disavow his rather gloomy and demoralizing earlier Indian experience.

4

The fact is, we must get this work over, or the sun will become very deadly.[62]

By the time William Howard Russell, a special war correspondent for *The Times*, arrived in India in January 1858, the Mutiny had been virtually suppressed. However, Russell, who stayed in India until the retaking of Lucknow, went through a war as formidable as that against the Indian rebels, that is to say, the experience of living through one whole Indian summer. During the march under the burning sun he witnessed European soldiers being carried past him 'fainting, or dead'[63]. He himself fell ill on the way and was unfit for duty for quite a long time. Russell found that work and the climate were not compatible in India, especially during the summer, and later wrote an essay titled 'The Climate and the Work', in which he identifies the Indian climate as the most formidable enemy of the Raj, simply because '[t]he climate kills as many as the sword':[64]

> There would be less envy of Great Britain, on account of her Indian possessions, if the world could be made aware of the price of their retention . . . See, mail after mail, how the list of the dead lengthens out! What household is there which does not own its losses? What family is there which has not to say of some loved one – 'He died in India'? . . . It may be true that few of the great statesmen of India died in office, though some there have been who did; but the number of those who have fallen victims to the effects of climate, incessant mental exertion, and physical suffering, and exposure, cannot be easily estimated.[65]

Kipling's 'Seven Years Hard', the period during which he stayed in India as a journalist, was also the period of his painful effort to work in the tremendous summer heat. Kipling found the climate in summer totally unbearable. Indeed, just a brief look at Kipling's correspondence during his Indian days makes us realize that his own experience in India was far from Edenic, and very different from the way he would later present India in *Kim*. His letters most frequently mention the temperature of the day: 'Would 94° in the office interest you? It has no charms for me' (May 1888).[66] '"How's your room? Mine's 96°." "You're lucky. Can't keep mine below 100°. Any hope of rain?"' (10 June 1884).[67] 'By the way red hot is not such an exaggeration as it sounds. The thermometer is 86°, under the Punkah, 108° away from it and 167° in the sun' (24 April 1883).[68] Despite his effort to 'talk of more pleasant things',[69] the heat of the summer kept coming back to Kipling and left indelible marks on his writing as well.

Working in such a hot temperature was, however, *not* the worst part of the Indian heat. Kipling found the night-time, when there was nothing to do other than sleep, difficult to bear. In one of his letters, he writes, 'The heat here is maddening and gets worse at night. In the day one can force oneself into work and not notice but in the night there is no such relief and so one kicks and knocks about "till the day break"' (May 1888).[70] Kipling is here referring to his own sketch 'Till the Day Break', published in the *Civil and Military Gazette* in the same month, the stream of consciousness of a sleepless man suffering from both heat and fever. Despite the narrator's utmost effort to get some sleep, this very effort soon turns into what he calls 'sick fancies' and 'a helpless knot of doubt, perplexity, argument, re-argument, wonder and pain', while the number of sheep which he is counting in order to fall asleep reaches some nine hundred thousand, enough to fill the whole of Australia by the time day breaks.[71] A sketch called 'From the Dusk to the Dawn', published in the *Civil and Military Gazette* on 14 September 1886 (the year in which Kipling found the heat most unbearable), deals with exactly the same situation. Here the horrors of insomnia are likened to the Chinese punishment for treason, 'death through want of sleep'. Kipling gives us a detailed account of this Chinese torture, followed by a detailed account of a sleepless night. According to him, the latter is as bad as the former. The only difference is that the torture by nature is 'superior in degree' and has 'a refinement of cruelty which even the Chinese would abandon'.[72]

Janet Montefiore has already pointed out that there is a clear dichotomy between day and night in Kipling's Indian stories, the former representing the white man's world of reason and work and the latter the world of natives, which cannot be explained and which threatens to undermine the former.[73] We may also paraphrase this as the contrast between Day's work and Night's sleeplessness; indeed: 'In the day one can force oneself into work and not notice but in the night there is no such relief . . .' Therefore, here we find a less well-known aspect of Kipling's Empire builders: they do their hard day's work not because they are truly devoted to the cause of Empire, but rather because there is no other way to forget the unbearable heat of summer. Work is virtually the only means to escape from it and avoid losing their sanity; as Kipling puts it in 'Wressley of the Foreign Office' (1887), 'without the work and the sense of purpose, however delusional, it gives, they would sit down and kill themselves'.[74] And they have no prospect of resting their tired brains after work. Kipling, in his autobiography, later describes his experience of the Indian night-time in summer as follows: from 'mid-April to mid-October – one took up one's bed and walked about with it from room to room, seeking for less heated air'.[75] This search for cool air was also the quest for a chance to represent India as a journalist and writer, for the hot climate certainly undermined his capability of forming any representation, and Kipling lets his narrator wander throughout the night in search of less hot air, as he himself did in his Indian days.

'"The City of Dreadful Night"', first published in the *Civil and Military Gazette*, 10 September 1885 (later collected in *Life's Handicap*), is the account of an adventure into the city of Lahore by a narrator who has given up the effort to sleep: 'The dense wet heat that hung over the face of land, like a blanket, prevented all hope of sleep in the first instance . . . The heated air and the heavy earth had driven the very dead upward for coolness' sake.'[76] The narrator's attention is repeatedly drawn to the ground, probably because the heat of the night, along with the epidemics it propagates, is prone to drag whomever is within its grasp downwards, that is, to death. The narrator sees hundreds of corpses scattered all around him and 'sleeping men who lay like sheeted corpses'.[77] Literally, 'the ground is covered with them'.[78] The corpses and those who sleep are so alike that the only way to tell that they are not dead is to see the 'lean dogs snuff at them and turn away'.[79] Inside the city, the heat feels even worse, with its 'high house-walls . . . still radiating heat savagely'.[80]

In the middle of the sketch, the narrator finds a way to the top of a minaret, and thereby successfully lifts himself up from the hot ground, which might well batter him together with those whom he observes. It gives him at once a less heated air and a better view of the city. It is in this moment that the narrator gains the full power of description:

> There is the shadow of a cool, or at least a less sultry breeze at this height; and refreshed thereby, I turn to look on the City of Dreadful Night.
>
> Doré might have drawn it! Zola could describe it – this spectacle of sleeping thousands in the moonlight and the shadow of the Moon.[81]

From the top of the minaret, the narrator can now visualize the city as a spectacle, liken himself to masters of realism like Doré and Zola, and even 'watch and wonder over that heat-tortured hive till the dawn'.[82]

This story effectively demonstrates that the hot weather has the effect of localizing the colonizer. Far from freely exercising his omnipresent rule over India, the colonizer looks for a narrow strip of space with less heated air, where some representation is possible. His representation of India is, for this reason, destined to be limited and selective. The climate and the point of view were thus closely entwined in the Raj. As Kipling, when interviewed on the subject of 'Indian Journalism' in 1889, maintains, 'Our local news is comparatively limited. The ubiquitous reporter is unknown with us. It is too hot for one thing, and again he is not needed, and absolutely unknown.'[83] In India where it is too hot, the point of view is likely to become 'local' rather than all-seeing.

The movement up from the heated ground in order to find a place to forge a representation corresponds to the reality of the Raj. Just as the narrator in 'The City of Dreadful Night' goes up the minaret to find cooler air, so the Anglo-Indians escaped the heat of summer by going to the hill stations. The hill station was the only place in which the English could dismiss the supremacy of the Indian ground-effect over them. Kipling represents these hill stations as a panacea for almost any unintelligible problem which the European encounters in the plains, where the heat dominates. For example, in 'Haunted Subalterns' (1887) – a story which demonstrates that the easiest way to see ghosts is to go to 'the hottest Cantonment of all'– a haunted subaltern in the story, Tesser, is released from the ghost playing his banjo only when he obtains a post in the hills: 'The Devil stayed below, and Tesser went up and was free.'[84] In 'The Conversion of Aurelian McGoggin' (1887), an Indian civil servant who tried to play 'bricks with words' against the climate, all of sudden loses control of his speech. The prescription the doctor gives for his aphasia is simply, 'Go up into the Hills for three months, and don't think about it.' He goes into the hills, 'in fear and trembling, wondering whether he would be permitted to reach the end of any sentence he began'.[85]

The hill stations were indispensable for the English because of the illusion of similarity between India and England which they created. As Francis Hutchins puts it, the discovery of hill stations facilitated the 'reconciliation to Indian residence as a permanent condition'.[86] With their less harsh and almost 'English-like' climate, the hill stations 'did give a "hearty English tone" to Indian government'.[87] The Indian climate, especially in summer, would not allow the English to cherish the illusion that India was a larger England – as Kipling expresses in his letter, 'India isn't England and a thermometer at 168° in the sun isn't calculated to bring about a resemblance.'[88] If there was a location where any similarity between India and England could be forged, it was only the hill regions. Kavita Philip points out that colonial narratives construct the hills in India as an English landscape and as 'a home away from Home':[89] they were repeatedly described as very similar to England, compared to the plains, where the climate was oppressive and densely populated by natives. Hill stations, such as the 'Nilgiri district of Madras Presidency where the British colonial government located its summer capital in order to escape the heats of the plains', Philip argues, were 'the object not of those common constructions of the colonized landscape as hostile and barren . . . but of constructions so cloying and rosy that they might seem . . . to assimilate India to the English self, rather than figuring it as radically other'.[90] In fact, the hill regions were, as Dane Kennedy puts it, 'landscapes of memory' through which memories of England were brought back to the Anglo-Indian mind.[91] We may here recall that in 'On Greenhow Hill', 'the bare sub-Himalayan spur' reminds Learoyd of 'his Yorkshire moors'.[92] The resemblance between the two regions is so perfect that it suddenly brings to his mind the memories of his early love and the life at home which he has been forgetting since he left England. Only in the hills can such a psychological identification between India and England become possible.

The importance of the hill regions for the English colonizer cannot be overemphasized. The act of *representing* India – literary as well as political – from the English point of view was never possible without the height of the hills (as is well known, the administrative capital was moved from Calcutta to Simla during the summer). Kipling's narrator tells tales of the plains from the hills, never vice versa. The plains can be represented only from the hills or, when the weather is a little cooler, as a picture or as a glimpse. If one dares to tell stories about the Indian plains, as Kipling does, it should be done in a few strokes; otherwise, the picture will be caught in the ground-effect and will be damaged. Here again, speed is needed, just as it was needed in the Siege of Delhi. We may say that this is why most of the stories in *Plain Tales from the Hills* are very short. 'Writing back' from the plains – all that was excluded from the safe representational space constructed as Home – was impossible rather than impermissible, and tales told from the hills should be by all means plain; otherwise the Indian climate relentlessly takes off all the false embellishments.

Kipling spent seven summer seasons in India, of which he says in one of his letters, 'I like it less each year.'[93] In *Something of Myself*, he writes, 'I felt each succeeding hot weather more and more, and cowered in my soul as it returned.'[94] It was 'one hot-weather evening, in '86 or thereabouts' that he felt that he had 'come to the edge of all endurance': 'As I entered my empty house in the dusk there was no more in me except the horror of a great darkness, that I must have been fighting for some days. I came through that darkness alive, but how I do not know.' Encouraged by a novel by Walter Besant, which 'dealt with a young man who desired to write . . . and who eventually succeeded in his desire', Kipling decided to try his literary talent at home in England: 'I was certainly, I argued, as well equipped as the hero and – and – after all, there was no need for me to stay here for ever.'[95] He left India in 1889, never to return. To be precise, he did once go back to India, but he chose to go at Christmas-time, when the heat of India was absent.[96]

5

There are two noticeable differences between Kipling's writing on India before and after he left India. Firstly, the hot weather disappears from these stories. Secondly, the narrator becomes more and more omnipresent and all-knowing. We can see both changes consummated in *Kim*. The detrimental effect of the Indian ground thus seems to disappear from his bricks of words in his later writings about India. It is as if the narrator's bodily presence in India (without which the heat cannot even be felt) diminished, as the author removed himself from the effect of the Indian climate.

The omission of the weather is all the more interesting considering that the heat of the summer is most prominent in the earlier stories. In 'The Daughter of the Regiment' (1887), it is the 'bitter, burnin' sun'[97] which kills Mother McKenna, who has overworked herself nursing the soldiers of her regiment dying of cholera. In 'With the Main Guard' (1888), Mulvaney has to talk through 'a stifling June night' in order to keep Learoyd in his senses, for, 'feeling the heat acutely, being of fleshly build', he is 'half mad with the fear of death presaged in the swelling veins of his neck'.[98] 'In the Matter of a Private' (1888), it is the oppressive heat of the summer – 'eight hours a day in a temperature of 96° or 98° in the shade, running up sometimes to 103° at midnight'[99] – which is solely responsible for a murder in the Irish regiment.

Of course, Kipling cannot completely do away with the hot Indian weather, without which his writing would have sounded less oriental. Yet he seems to be less willing to leave his characters at the mercy of the Indian climate in his later Indian stories. These are therefore preferably told 'at the beginning of the hot weather'[100] ('My Lord Elephant',1892), instead of the middle of it, or in autumn[101] ('His Private Honour', 1893), or when '[m]ercifully the hot weather was yet young'[102] ('Love-O'-Women', 1893).

Furthermore, the change in his representation of the Indian summer seems to directly affect his presentation of what is true and/or real. In his early Indian stories, the heat of the summer often entails 'hallucinations', but Kipling does not present these as false or illusory, but rather as the most crucial part of the Indian experience. There is little point in questioning the validity of the phenomena, because they are perfectly real as long as they kill and destroy people and, what is more, there is no truer experience available outside them. However, in Kipling's later Indian stories, the reality or truth (of the British Empire) which cannot possibly be affected by the Indian summer suddenly emerges. The heat of the summer, now associated with hallucinations or madness rather than with reality, becomes a convenient excuse to cover up a truer reality. In 'The Incarnation of Krishna Mulvaney' (1889), Ortheris says, 'You lie! . . . You're mad or sunstrooke,' to which Mulvaney answers, 'Then my lie an' my sunstroke is concealed under that lump av sod yonder.'[103] In 'His Private Honour', Ortheris defends a lieutenant who hit him, saying that the latter 'has been in the sun too long'.[104] 'Reeking heat', which triggers a tragic murder in 'In the Matter of a Private', is reduced to a mere setting and the possible explanation of a murder by a sergeant in 'Love-O'-Women', which masks the true reason, namely that his wife had an affair with one of his corporals, whom he shot down.[105]

As the hot weather loses importance in Kipling's later writing on India, so the omnipresent and omniscient narrator who can occupy any narrative position emerges, which was not possible under the tremendous summer heat. Many critics argue that one of the characteristics of Kipling's writing is his pretence to 'know all' about India, and as K. Bhaskara Rao, for example, suggests, this quality can be seen in Kipling's use of the omniscient and omnipresent narrator, 'I'.[106] Rao's comment is true as far as his later stories on India are concerned – especially those written after 1890, including *Kim*. His earlier Indian stories, however, especially the ones written in India, do not necessarily have an omniscient and omnipresent narrator. There is a narrator 'I', to be sure, but we can see that this narrator is physically present in the stories and sometimes even intervenes in the course of events. He plays the role of a witness and often, though not always, tells us how he got to know the story he narrates, rather than being an omniscient and omnipresent narrator about whom nothing is known – neither where he is narrating from nor how he obtains all his information. This is especially true of the stories about the Soldiers Three. We find the narrator, for example, sitting beside the soldiers with his notebook, in order to write down what they tell him. This is the kind of narrator who is proud of knowing his characters personally and who informs us how he comes to know the story. He buys some drinks for his characters in order to encourage them to tell him more stories, and sometimes even takes part in the course of the events which he is narrating.

These changes in tone concerning the climate and the role of the narrator can be observed in the Mulvaney stories. In the later collections, written after Kipling left India, the emphasis mainly falls on presenting the reader with a solid picture of the British Empire, in particular how it has a safe network even throughout India. This change is already seen as early as *Life's Handicap*, the first collection published after Kipling returned from India. Here the narrator is no longer a conscientious writer scribbling down in his notebook whatever the soldiers tell him, so je can make a stories out of his notes. Now whatever Kipling's Tommy Atkins does has to be seen in a bigger framework, that is, that of the British Empire. 'The Courting of Dinah Shadd' (1891) begins by providing 'a bird's-eye view' of the British army in India: 'Thirty thousand troops had, by the wisdom of the Government of India, been turned loose over a few thousand square miles of country to practise in peace what they would never attempt in war.'[107] The narrator's friendship with the privates has itself been recognized by the officers of higher rank: 'I bundled several things into Mulvaney's haversack before the major's hand fell on my shoulder and he said tenderly, "Requisitioned for the Queen's service. Wolseley was quite wrong about special correspondents: they are the soldier's best friends. Come and take pot-luck with us tonight."'[108] He is no longer an innocent friend of the Three Musketeers who by sheer luck is accepted among their company. In 'The Incarnation of Krishna Mulvaney', he even knows the conversation that has taken place between the colonel and his 'much-trusted adjutant', who recognizes Mulvaney as 'worth a couple of non-commissioned officers when we are dealing with an Irish draft'.[109]

In *Kim*, written ten years after Kipling left India, the Indian weather and climate are, as Rukmini Bhaya Nair has already pointed out, almost absent: '*Kim* is an outdoor novel that prances all over Upper India for several years during the hero's adolescence, but is it ever drenched by the monsoons, oppressed by the heat, frozen in the snowy Himalayan passes? No. Just two fleeting references to rain occur in *Kim*.'[110] Nair rightly argues that the inclusion of the weather would have spoiled Kipling's picture of the efficient and successful Raj. Firstly, the description of the Indian climate would be embarrassing in *Kim* where everybody is 'frightfully energetic', because the reality is probably that 'the Indian climate enervates its masses so that they loll about all day long, unable to bestir themselves at any cost'.[111] Secondly, she suggests that Kipling has to check 'the metamorphosis of (destructive) weather into (dangerous) crowd':[112] Kipling's fear of Indian nationalism and democracy results in the omission of the weather, for it may trigger again the tragedy which Great Britain had once gone through – the Indian Mutiny. In order to make the Raj and the Indian climate compatible, Kipling has to eliminate the latter to the extent that his India does not seem to correspond to the reality. We may also say that Kipling felt the need to make his Irish regiment more manageable, owing to growing concerns about the Irish question. In 'With the Main Guard', an uneasy issue to which Kipling cannot possibly give an appropriate response unexpectedly slips into the text through the mouth of Mulvaney in the terrifying heat of a June night: the reason why the Irish have to be in India. 'Mary, Mother av Mercy, fwhat the devil possist us to take an' kape this melancolious counthry? Answer me that, sorr.'[113] The story begins with this exclamation, as if the narrator, startled by an insurgent voice coming from the darkness, immediately puts Mulvaney under his narrative control. Here we may also recall that the Irish mutiny in India in 1920 broke out in Jullundur, a military station 'situated in an immense fertile plain where the climate is oppressively hot during the summer months'.[114]

The two changes, that is, the gradual disappearance of the ground-effect typically embodied in the hot weather and the narrator's transformation into a god-like omnipresent being, come together in his last Indian narrative, *Kim*, which seems to me to reflect the colonizer's desire to do away with the effect of the ground by achieving the speed of light so that there is no delay any more, and one can even be 'in two places at the same time'. *Kim* seems timeless and even *ground*less, because Kipling in *Kim* pushes this colonial desire further away and presents India as the place least bound by the earth's gravity. *Kim* almost achieves what Virilio terms 'telepresence', that is, meeting at a distance, 'here and elsewhere, *at the same time*', thus opening up 'a communicative elsewhere that no longer has anything to do with our "concrete presence" in the world'.[115] The state of being telepresent is possible solely in the open sky, away from actual geographical spaces and distances. As Virilio puts it, a 'secret perspective is, in fact, hidden on high'.[116] So there is a movement *up*, as far away from the ground as possible, in the way a narrator narrates, as well as *speed* in describing quickly rather than fiddling around with details.

Kipling's imperialism became, as he left India, more and more a search for this hidden and therefore yet to be discovered perspective, up in the open air. This secret perspective of the know-all narrator is significantly shared by what Thomas Richards calls 'the imperial archive' – the fantasy that the British were capable of 'superintending all knowledge, particularly the great reams of knowledge coming in from all parts of the Empire'.[117] The search for telepresence therefore takes the form of an information war in *Kim*, supervised by the Raj's high archivist, Colonel Creighton, an 'archive superman'[118] who can comprehend and superintend the immense Empire without being defeated by a mass of incoming information. While the Russian spies have to struggle on the Indian ground and against delay in order to smuggle out the important information they have acquired ('We have not time. We must get into Simla as soon as may be'.[119]), the British intelligence system, in which numerous spies, who recognize each other by a certain password, form a wide network to exchange and relay necessary information, seems to function on a more real-time basis (thus, indeed, 'there is no hurry for Hurree'[120]). All the colonies of the Great Empire 'meet at a distance' in this information network, to be united into one, rather than in a representation of the actual Empire 'in geographic correctness'. Kim, a friend of all the world, is both an archivist and an archive of this know-all Empire, embodying also the unique association between India and Ireland, which must be catalogued. Through Kim, India and Ireland, the two separate places, truly meet, under the sky-high supervision of the British Empire.

Chapter Three

Exiled Home

The Voice of the Irish Soldiers

It is difficult now to imagine that Kipling was once best known as 'the man who made Mulvaney' rather than Kim.[1] At the height of his popularity in the 1890s, Private Mulvaney was undoubtedly the people's (and the author's) favourite, 'a truly attaching character from his strength and his little weakness'.[2] 'Mulvaney the Multivagant, who holds the picture place in the Kipling pantheon, takes our love the first, and, perhaps, will hold it longest,' writes G. F. Monkshood in 1899: 'A masterpiece is this man. Theseus of free-lances, a pipe-clayed belted musketeer of the masses, and as adventuresome and amorous as those much-harassed men of Dumas . . . he shines well always, even in his misdeeds.'[3] In 1897, the *Academy*, on behalf of a girl in Arizona, implored Kipling to arrange for Mulvaney to die a worthy death on Indian soil, adding that 'the request is one which all who know and honour Terence Mulvaney (and who does not?) will join'.[4]

Significantly, Mulvaney was loved for almost the same reasons as Kim is now, for his playfulness, resourcefulness and for his many colourful and successful adventures. Both are masters of improvisation, and many of Kim's famous adventures remind us of Mulvaney's. If Kim instantly transforms the native spy E23 from a mahratta to a saddhu by painting his body,[5] Mulvaney has Ortheris (who is a taxidermist) change a white dog into a fox terrier by painting marks:[6] in both cases the change is just 'skin-deep' and the cunning scheme is assisted by modern technology, namely, the speed and anonymity of train travel, allowing the enemies of the Empire only a momentary chance of inspection – in Kim's case, Russian agents in pursuit of E23, in Mulvaney's, a Eurasian woman eager to steal a pedigree dog belonging to the colonel's wife. Even though Mulvaney does not have Kim's comprehensive knowledge of Indian tongues, we often see him admirably deal with natives by resorting to 'all the sweet talk [he had ever] learnt in the bazars',[7] and his fluent mixing of Irish accents with Indian words is undoubtedly the most fascinating (and also the most visible) representation of the Irish merging into India. If Kim is most famous for his chameleon-like ability to transform himself into any of the castes and races of India, Mulvaney has already demonstrated a similar talent in 'The Incarnation of Krishna Mulvaney' (1889) – indeed, 'in what does not Mulvaney shine?'[8] In this story, Mulvaney is carried into a temple of Benares in a palanquin, being mistaken for 'an estimable old queen of the Central Indian States', where he witnesses 'a big Queens' Praying', a fertility rite in which 'the wives and daughters of most of the kings of India' come and pray to Prithi-Devi.[9] Mulvaney thus finds himself inadvertently peeping into the most secret and sacred part of India – women of the royal zenanas, praying, crying and throwing themselves about, all consumed by their deepest passion to be blessed with children – which Mulvaney, as a white man, should not see. He could have been killed if caught, but Mulvaney escapes from his difficulties by acting as Krishna, and the Irish song he sings is taken for the divine song of the great god himself. This episode sounds very much like one in which Kim might have been involved,[10] and the likeness is not confined to Benares as the setting and to the theme of Irish access into the hidden life of India. Mulvaney disappears from the army during this adventure, but the colonel simply laughs at the rumour that he might have deserted. The disappearance of Mulvaney is known to, and approved by, his seniors, who have faith in him as the ablest soldier, just as Kim's occasional disappearance into the Road is considered essential if he is to learn the Game.[11] Indeed, when the colonel says of Mulvaney, 'I like him and believe he likes me,'[12] this uncannily echoes Lurgan Sahib's remark about Kim, 'he is very fond of Mahbub, and of me a little',[13] given as a reason why the boy can be trusted; in both cases, the homosocial bonds of friendship are formed not only laterally but hierarchically, ensuring the firm foundation of the colonial administration.

Mulvaney is certainly Kim's predecessor, an Irish character given a leading role in Kipling's Indian stories. However, despite many structural similarities, Kipling presents them in strikingly different manners. Mulvaney is an adult and a married man, Kim a boy (for '[t]he younger the better'[14] for the Great Game). Mulvaney is a soldier, while Kim escapes this more predictable fate of being enlisted as a soldier, thanks to the lama's contribution to his education (the lama expresses his satisfaction that Kim is entering into the government as 'a scribe' and '[n]ot as a warrior'[15]). Most importantly, while Mulvaney is strongly marked by, and identifiable with, his Irish accent, Kim, an Irish boy, does *not* have an Irish voice. Instead, Kim speaks English with a distinctively *Indian* accent.[16] It is almost as if Kipling, by writing *Kim*, radically revised Mulvaney and his representation of the Irish in India, and Kim has now certainly overshadowed Mulvaney as Kipling's most famous Irish character in India.

The reincarnation of Terence Mulvaney as Kimball O'Hara is indeed significant, and this change closely corresponds with Kipling's own changing status from an Anglo-Indian writer to an uncrowned laureate, and also with the shifting politics of the British Empire at the turn of the nineteenth century. Through Mulvaney, Kipling presents one kind of representation of the Irish in India, which he later replaces and makes obscure by the creation of a new character to take his place: Kim. Simply put, Kipling grants Mulvaney an Irish voices, which he firmly denies to Kim. In order to understand the full implications of Kim's fated aphasia as Irish, I would like to look more closely at the ways in which Kipling represents Mulvaney's voice, or more precisely Mulvaney as an Irish voice, alongside those of other soldiers in British India, and what kind of 'Irish' stories Kipling allows this voice to tell us.

1

According to Linda Dowling, there emerged a new interest in spoken dialects in the late nineteenth century, owimg to a strong sense at that time that 'written language, the literary tongue of the great English writers, was simply another dead language in relationship to living speech'.[17] The identification of written language with national spirit typically seen in Coleridge's 'lingua communis', the idea that written language can hold people together who are otherwise widely different and allow men to 'conceive of themselves as belonging to a larger cultural and historical whole',[18] was now felt to be artificial and inauthentic, and needed to be supplemented by the living spoken voice. Thus, songs, ballads and local dialects started to be discovered and incorporated into literature. Although Dowling dismisses Kipling and prefers to discuss other 'Counter-Decadent' poets such as William Ernest Henley and John Davidson, we may say that Kipling's work can be seen as a perfect example of the incorporation into literature of newly discovered spoken dialects in the Victorian *fin de siècle*. In fact, Andrew Lang, one of the earliest proponents of Kipling, was himself a well-known folklorist, who collected and studied myths and folktales from all quarters of the world. In his article on 'Ballads' for the *Encyclopaedia Britannica*, Lang writes,

> Ballads sprang from the very heart of the people, and flit from age to age, from lip to lip of shepherds, peasants, nurses, of all the class that continues nearest to the state of natural men . . . Ballads are a voice from secret places, from silent peoples, and old times long dead; and as such they stir us in a strangely intimate fashion to which artistic verse can never attain.[19]

Kipling not only brings new voices into literature, but also gives life to the representation of the British rule in India, which had been reduced to written documents of the Indian administration and numerous books on the subject covered with dust and buried in the library.

If the 'voice' of the subaltern, the silenced Other who is deprived of the power of self-representation, and the (im)possibility of their speaking for themselves is at stake in recent criticism, we may be made to feel a little uneasy by the fact that Rudyard Kipling, regarded by many as a racist, seems to pay special attention to such voices too.[20] If we are not to push 'the subaltern' too much into the margin, making of it a repressed and almost esoteric sign which only a chosen elite can decode, we may argue that the British soldiers serving outside the 'British Isles' in the nineteenth century can be called, in more ways than one, the subaltern. They were 'real-life' soldiers, mostly privates who had no hope of being promoted to the rank of commissioned officer. As we have already seen, many of them were from the lower class and/or Ireland, the dangerous and unmanageable excess which would have disturbed the peace of the Empire if kept at home. Compared to those who emigrated to, for example, America and gained a voice as 'Fenians', the British soldiers sent abroad seem to have been more quiet. Their voices are not well known to us, and not only because they were placed geographically too far away from England to make themselves heard. They were not supposed to complain – no matter what their circumstances were – after all they had agreed to take the royal shilling and fight for the British Empire; therefore, they should keep whatever grudge they might have against Great Britain to themselves, for it might endanger the order of the army and that of the Empire. It is these 'silent' soldiers, especially in India, to whom Kipling lends his ears.

Much has been written on the politics of seeing in Kipling's work. Even from the very start of his literary career, he was praised as 'an Englishman with eyes, with a pen extraordinarily deft, an observation marvellously rapid and keen' who 'has the power of making us see what he sees'.[21] The narrator's eyes are also given the power to frame what would otherwise have been lost in the margin of the Western representation, as can be seen in 'The Man who would be King' (1888). Carnehan, on the threshold of sense and madness, asks the narrator to keep him under his gaze ('Keep looking at me, or maybe my words will go all to pieces. Keep looking at me in my eyes and don't say anything'), while he narrates 'everything from beginning to end' of what happened after he and Dravot went beyond the territory of the Raj.[22] Thus it is interesting to observe that Kipling's narrator seems to resort to his ears rather than his eyes when he represents his Irish soldiers. In fact, it is very difficult to visualize 'Irishness'. It was Charles Kingsley who, in a letter, famously expressed his desire to see blackness in the Irish: 'to see white chimpanzees is dreadful; if they were black, one would not feel it so much, but their skins, except where tanned by exposure, are as white as ours . . .'[23] The whiteness of their skin disappoints the narrator's desire to fix the racial inferiority of the Irish to the English as visual images. The red hair, a stereotypical racial marker of the Irish, does not always help, for in reality not all Irish have red hair and those with red hair still possess white skin.[24] In this sense, the Irish body does not exist. However, when he resorts to the ears, the missing racial difference starts emerging: it is difficult not to notice the Irish accent. That is to say, the voice is the only bodily component which can truly be called Irish. Some of the stories are narrated at night in the dark, when the narrator can easily concentrate on the voices he is listening to without being tricked by the speakers' appearances.[25] Kipling does not, for instance, give us a detailed account of Terence Mulvaney's body. We only vaguely know that he is 'the tallest man in the Regiment'[26] and has black hair (that is, he is not visibly marked as possessing the red hair typically attributed to the Irish). Nevertheless, Mulvaney is rather superfluously visible in the text on account of his Irish accent. Furthermore, the narrator, always present in Mulvaney's stories, listens and controls the potential rebelliousness of the Irishman. His presence also helps visualize the 'corruption' (or degeneration) of Mulvaney's English by contrasting it with the narrator's standard English. In this way, Kipling succeeds in retrieving the visual body of the Irish (as 'misspellings') on his pages.

At first glance, there are striking similarities between the world of the Soldiers Three and that described by Mikhail Bakhtin. Kipling's transcription of different voices – an Irishman, a Yorkshireman, a Cockney mixed together – could be seen as a perfect practice of Bakhtinian polyphony and dialogism as multivocality. As Michael Holquist writes of Bakhtin's use of musical metaphors like polyphony and orchestration:

> Music is the metaphor for moving from seeing to *hearing*. For Bakhtin this is a crucial shift . . . Within a novel perceived as a musical score, a single 'horizontal' message (melody) can be harmonized vertically in a number of ways, and each of these scores with its fixed pitches can be further altered by giving the notes to different instruments. The possibilities of orchestration make any segment of text almost infinitely variable.[27]

'The Three Musketeers' (1887), the first story of Mulvaney & Co., presents the speeches of the three soldiers as if in a scene from an opera. The soldiers take turns to play a solo, occasionally mixing in some Indian words which give an exotic flavour to their tune. In the middle of the story, Mulvaney and Ortheris speak together, this being described as a 'duet'.[28] The narrator even tells how the soldiers perform their parts ('Mulvaney leading',[29] 'Here Ortheris, slowly, with immense pride',[30] 'Here the Three Musketeers retired simultaneously into the beer'[31]). The narrator's notebook in which he scribbles down the soldiers' conversation becomes a musical score, in which the name of their troop, '*B* Company of a *Line* Regiment'[32] may look like a part of the musical notation.

Recent postcolonial and feminist critics have, in their readings of texts, found Bakhtin's dialogism. For example, Mae Gwendolyn Henderson points out black women's writing's 'interlocutory, or dialogic, character, reflecting not only a relationship with the "other(s)", but an internal dialogue with the plural aspects of self that constitute the matrix of black subjectivity'.[33] Or, as Michael Bernard-Donals puts it, 'there is a subaltern effect even in the most monologic of utterances'.[34] The association between Kipling's soldiers and dialogism, or the so-called 'subaltern', is, however, rarely made. This is because the voice of the soldiers in Kipling's work is usually considered to be the complete opposite of dialogism or multivocality. Regardless of the seeming similarity with multivocal orchestration, in which various voices are given a chance to vertically subvert the single 'horizontal' melody, Kipling's soldiers' chorus seems to accentuate the 'horizontal' melody, namely, the ideology of the British Empire. Kipling's narrator listens to the soldiers and lets them speak, to be sure, but as soon as they open their mouths, they start speaking not so much for themselves as for the Empire. Supposing that the soldiers serving the army were indeed a silenced Other of the Empire, it is as though their voices were discovered only to justify the very cause of their distress. The voice which Kipling grants his soldiers is, to borrow Robert Buchanan's phrase, 'the Voice of the Hooligan': 'a wild carnival of drunken, bragging, boasting Hooligans in red coats and seamen's jackets, shrieking to the sound of the banjo and applauding the English flag'.[35] Kipling thereby fixes the subaltern as knowable, and therefore manageable, stereotypes, or, worse still, 'silences' the real voices of the subaltern by forcing them to speak in a false voice, the voice which 'univocally' speaks for the glory of the Empire.[36] Kipling's methods for making the soldiers mouthpieces of the Empire met the taste of the time, probably because they succeeded in presenting an image of the Empire which Kipling's audience wanted; that is to say, an image of the Empire as being supported by the very lowest stratum of society, proud to serve as soldiers despite the harshness of their living conditions in the colonies.

Indeed, Kipling's transcription of different voices *cannot*, in itself, be seen as equivalent to Bakhtin's dialogism or multivocality, especially because it is closely related to the highlighting of the native English-speakers' ability to detect different accents. This is a powerful policing technique shared by native speakers as the masters of the English language, allowing them to guess the origins and identities (including races and classes) of whatever unfamiliar faces they come across. In Kipling's work, some 'Indian' characters (for example, Kim and Namgay Doola) are detected as 'Irish' owing to their voicing of some English phrases, and we see Kipling himself indulge in this art of spotting his countrymen while travelling abroad (for example, he detected that a 'Mormon' lady he met in Salt Lake City was English, for '[t]he dropped "h" betrayed her'[37]). In 'The Three Musketeers', the reader is asked to distinguish one voice from another – 'You must pick out the speakers as best you can.'[38] This is Kipling's call to his fellow English-speakers to join in the detective work of hearing different voices and accents; Kipling thereby selects and 'creates' a truly 'English' audience, who rejoice in being able to discern the play of subtle differences.

We cannot therefore wholeheartedly resort to Bahktin's concepts of dialogism, heteroglossia and multivocality when looking at Kipling's representation of the British soldiers as many different voices. Yet, as far as the *Irish* voice is concerned, it seems to me that these Bahktinian concepts still might hold some relevance; Kipling, by representing the Irish as subversive voices which need constant controlling, seems to have inadvertently given some kind of 'autonomy' to these voices, which are always represented with a sense of unpredictability, and alertness on the side of the narrator. In *Stalky & Co.*, the enraged Irish boy M'Turk candidly speaks to an Irish landlord in the 'Irish dialect' which Stalky and Beetle 'had carefully kicked out' of him during their four years of being together in school.[39] This is a moment in which the English boys witness in their best friend a deep-seated 'Irishness' that neither an English education nor his friendship with them can wipe out, and they also see 'the Irish dialect' function as a secret code which immediately connects one Irishman with another, excluding them and leaving them powerless. It is true that M'Turk's bond with the Irish landlord is that between two landed men – M'Turk being the doted son of an Irish landlord of 'four thousand naked acres'. However, it is important to note that this association between two Irish landlords is nevertheless represented here as *Irish*. M'Turk's adventure ends with his 'crooning' a line from 'The Wearing of the Green', which is, under other circumstances, 'barred utterly – anathema – the sin of witchcraft', but on this particular occasion the two English boys 'danced round him in silence, waiting till it pleased him to touch earth',[40] for M'Turk has just wrought something that they never could have: turning a potential Irish enemy (the landlord) into a formidable ally, and he did so by appealing to shared Irish identity and love for 'the Old Country'. Of course, Kipling's representation of 'subversive' Irish voices is by no means real, but is rather the projection of his anxiety about Irish 'rebellions' and nationalist movements which is given expression through his Irish characters. However, the effort of containment sets up an interesting polarity in his representation of Irish voices, split between those loyal and reliable ones which the narrator wishes to hear and the suppressed, rebellious and nationalist ones which nevertheless come back to haunt the former.

In fact, if we look at the Mulvaney stories a little more closely, we will soon notice that the voices of the three soldiers are not treated equally. That is to say, they do not even sing a univocal chorus for the imperial cause, for Kipling, especially in his later stories, seems to give more credence to the English voice of Learoyd than to the Irish voice of Mulvaney, even though the latter would not speak against the Empire. Interestingly, the narrator is always present in the text (either as a listener or as an omnipresent narrator) whenever Mulvaney speaks, while he allows Learoyd to speak on his own, without being interrupted by the narrator, in 'Private Learoyd's Story' (1888).[41] The gesture of silencing the disturbing voices of the Other and letting the English monologue be heard undisturbed is consummated in 'On Greenhow Hill' (1890). The story opens with a native voice which invites the Indian soldiers to desert and 'fight against the English'.[42] It is the voice of a deserter from a native corps, whom the Three Musketeers go out to hunt. While they wait for the deserter to come out, Learoyd starts telling a story of his life in England. This story soon turns into a monologue, for he takes 'no heed' of Mulvaney's comments (thereby refusing to interact with any other voices) and the Irishman only gives '[s]ympathetic grunts'[43] and nods 'sympathy'[44] to the Englishman's story. In this way, the Englishman's representation of England as a sacred Home (as I characterized the story in Chapter 1), is completed without being disturbed by the voices of the Other. At the end of the story, another Englishman, Ortheris, shoots the deserter, whereby not only Mulvaney's Irish voice but also the native Indian voice is successfully silenced. The same hierarchy of voices can be seen in 'My Lord the Elephant' (1892), in which the narrator doubts the authenticity of the story of Mulvaney who, in his opinion, has 'a profligate imagination', and decides to 'wait till Learoyd comes', since he does 'not tell lies', before believing the story.[45] At the very end of the story, Learoyd appears and gives his word that the story is true.[46]

In contrast, the voice of Mulvaney is always framed by that of the narrator, who lets Mulvaney speak and even uses every possible means to get as many tales as possible out of him. The narrator is by no means a passive audience, but plays a great part in shaping Mulvaney's narratives into stories. In 'The Courting of Dinah Shadd' (1891), for example, he insists that Mulvaney 'begin at the very beginning',[47] just as the narrator in 'The Man who would be King' encourages Carnehan to tell his tale from the beginning. The constant presence of the narrator as a listener in Mulvaney's stories makes these stories 'dialogic', with verbal contests, collaboration and exchange between the narrator and Mulvaney playing a crucial role in shaping the latter's narratives. Though they seem to have agreed to tell these loyalist stories together, Mulvaney is nevertheless represented as forever eluding the narrator's attempt to frame him and his stories completely. Indeed, if we focus on *what* Mulvaney tells, we are likely to hear the most imperialist remarks. However, when we focus on *how* Mulvaney tells his stories, there seems to be some incongruity between the content and the form of his speech; Mulvaney speaks for the Empire, to be sure, but his speech is not necessarily as disciplined as he claims himself to be. His tale tends to become larger and digresses – in the manner of Tristram Shandy. In 'The Big Drunk Draf' (1888), Mulvaney, now time-expired and a civilian, tells the narrator how he came to help a new young officer of the Ould Regiment to restore order when a 'Home draft' of this regiment became too drunk and started 'knockin' red cindhers out av ivrything an' ivrybody'.[48] Here, we find that the course of his story is as out of control as the drunk draft which he, in his story, controlled. Mulvaney himself realizes that, as soon as he starts talking about the draft, he is 'digresshin' and complains to his wife, Dinah Shadd, 'You and your digresshins interfere wid the coorse av the narrative.'[49] Thus the story of the ex-Irish soldier who disciplined an unlawful draft of his old regiment is in truth that of the taming of the Irish voice (which might have become even more chaotic because Mulvaney has been away from the military discipline for so long) with the help of the English narrator. Mulvaney's narrative, even under the close inspection of this narrator, shows a resemblance to Bakhtin's dialogical concepts: the narrator's single horizontal narrative is vertically and infinitely disturbed by that of Mulvaney whose story, despite his best loyalist intention, tends to digress.

Significantly, 'The Big Drunk Draf'', in which Mulvaney's story clearly becomes most unruly and digressive, is narrated throughout around the 'taboo' theme – that of the Irish returning home. Not only is it a draft who were about to sail back home which Mulvaney puts back in order – without him, Mulvaney boasts, 'the last time-expired wud be still pullin' hair on their way to the sea'[50] – but also this story of the Irish soldiers' near failure to sail back to Ireland is narrated alongside Mulvaney's own failure to return and make Ireland his home. The story begins with a poem from *Barrack-Room Ballads* as an epigraph, in which a time-expired soldier cheerfully sings, 'We're goin' 'ome, we're goin' 'ome'/Our ship is *at* the shore/An' you mus' pack your 'aversack/For we won't come back no more . . .'[51] Then we are told, at the very beginning of the story, the shocking news that Mulvaney *did* go back to Ireland time-expired (an episode which we have already discussed in Chapter 1): 'The fact was that the Mulvaneys had been out here too long, and had lost touch with England.'[52] Mulvaney then plays a role in assisting his fellow Irish soldiers to go 'Home' – Ireland, called 'England' – which he himself could not rediscover nor freshly settle in after going back time-expired. What is more, the theme of the Irish homecoming brings in another grand narrative of the British Empire, namely, that of Irish nationalism, characteristically marked by its desire for Ireland as Home, a land from which so many Irish people had to emigrate, a lost origin that was waiting to be liberated from its long subjugation to English rule. It is then only natural that the drunken Irish draft, refusing to obey their officer, call themselves 'a bloomin' Republic', to which Mulvaney retorts, 'thin I'm O'Connell the Dictator':[53] Irish nationalist contexts are readily at hand, should any of the Irish children wish to deviate from loyalist ideologies. The taming of the drunken Irish home draft involves not simply its suppression as a subversive voice; it also has to be put back on the 'imperialist' narrative course leading them safely back to 'England', against the pull of the Irish nationalist narrative, with its longing for Ireland as Home. Mulvaney's is itself just such an Irish voice under imperial control, redirected away from its origin lest it should gain sufficient momentum to speak for itself: though faithfully echoing the ideology of the Empire, he nonetheless suffers the same fate as the Irish, the wandering away from home while being deprived of the possibility of his voice having a firm origin in its homeland.

According to Graham Pechey, Bakhtin's dialogical concepts, such as polyphony, heteroglossia and carnival, all refuse the kind of narratives 'that seek to pull these concepts back to a primary instance or origin'.[54] In this sense, Mulvaney as an Irish voice, whose reminiscing of his past always digresses and becomes fragmentary, is markedly Bakhtinian. Caught between two grand narratives, both of which urge him to return 'Home', Mulvaney tries but never succeeds. Unlike Homer's hero, who eventually goes back and successfully reclaims his home space, Mulvaney, as a 'very wise Ulysses', is trapped on one of the mythical islands along the way, which is called India. His journey homewards as Irish is forever deferred and interdicted.

2

> 'My first rig'mint was Irish – Faynians an' rebils to the heart av their marrow was they, an' *so* they fought for the Widdy betther than most, bein' contrairy – Irish. They was the Black Tyrone. You've heard av thim, sorr?'
>
> Heard of them! I knew the Black Tyrone for the choicest collection of unmitigated blackguards, dog-stealers, robbers of hen-roosters, assaulters of innocent citizens, and recklessly daring heroes in the Army List. Half Europe and half Asia has had cause to know the Black Tyrone.[55]

When the narrator meets the Soldiers Three in India, Terence Mulvaney already belongs to his last regiment, the 'Ould Regiment'. According to the narrator, Mulvaney served with 'various regiments from Bermuda to Halifax'[56] before joining the 'Ould Regiment'. Interestingly, Mulvaney, though he tells us many episodes of his younger days, gives away surprisingly few clues as to when he served with which regiment, and even when he does, the details about his past, spread across the eighteen separate stories, sometimes contradict each other. Thus it is almost impossible to construct a precise chronology of Mulvaney's military career.[57] It is as if his past becomes more distanced and mystified as he tells us more about it. In this way, he gives to himself the almost mythical status of a loyal soldier in the British army – 'old in war, scarred, reckless, resourceful, and in his pious hours an unequalled soldier'[58] – out in India.

Hence, it is worth paying special attention to the 'Black Tyrone', the only regiment which Mulvaney names and which is therefore identifiable in his military career, apart from the 'Ould Regiment'. In fact, the presence of the 'Black Tyrone', a piece of his past which somehow keeps coming back to haunt Mulvaney's narrative, makes his stories something other than the 'cornucopia of memories and adventures' with an obscured social background which Keating characterizes them as.[59] What we have instead is a series of stories about a loyal British soldier who tries to come to terms with his rather Fenian past by narrating it. At one level, Mulvaney's career as a soldier, starting with the 'Black Tyrone' and ending with the 'Ould Regiment', can be read as his transformation from rebellious Irish to law-abiding British through his service in the British army in India; the voice of Mulvaney is not only the representation of the Irish accent and character, but functions as an apparatus through which the political 'reality' of Ireland seeks to be represented among the discourses which constitute the British Empire. In this sense, it is significant that Mulvaney defines his first regiment, the Black Tyrone, first and foremost as 'Irish'. The 'Black Tyrone', which is, according to Mulvaney, recruited from 'here, there, and ivrywhere'[60] in Ireland, can be seen as representative of Ireland itself, in contrast to, for example, the Mavericks in *Kim*, in which Irish Protestants are the large majority[61] (Mulvaney himself is a Catholic). Or, to be more precise, Mulvaney's stories show that a 'true' representation of Ireland is possible only if it is spatially and temporally mediated by narrative devices, that is to say, only in the form of the reminiscences of an old Irish soldier who serves in India.

Let us take a closer look at Kipling's reference to Mulvaney as a 'very wise Ulysses', a comment made by the narrator in 'Private Learoyd's Story'. This reference goes beyond simply evoking the general attributes of Ulysses, such as those of traveller, trickster and married man.[62] *The Odyssey* starts with a plea to the Muse to tell the story of Odysseus, and the narrator then characterizes his journey as the struggle to 'preserve his life and bring his comrades home'.[63] In other words, Odysseus' journey is not solely by and for himself, but rather a journey to take his people back to Ithaca. Odysseus and his countrymen, like the Irish people in the nineteenth century, are driven away to wander from one foreign land to another, but cannot give up their desire to go home, which unites them and keeps the long journey going. The peaceful Lotus-eaters become formidable enemies only in this context, for their lotuses make his crew 'forget all thoughts of return' and 'think no more of home'.[64] It should be noted here that unlike Odysseus, Mulvaney has to move geographically away from his home (Ireland) so as to sail ideologically towards Home (the Empire), and this causes a painful separation from his crew, whose destination – Ireland – somehow differs from his own.

Indeed, the striking similarity between Mulvaney and Odysseus becomes more apparent when we remember that both stories tell us how the heroes come to part from their own countrymen who violated society's laws. Just as Mulvaney confronts the Fenian side of the other Irish soldiers, so Odysseus has to deal with his crew, who turn out to be by no means law-abiding. The opening paragraph of *The Odyssey* reveals Odysseus' failure to take home his comrades, who broke a rule and angered a god:

> he fails to save those comrades, in spite of all his efforts. It was their own transgression that brought them to their doom, for in their folly they devoured the oxen of Hyperion the Sun-god and he saw to it that they would never return.[65]

Odysseus, in his reminiscence, recalls that his men often refused to obey his orders, as if to confirm the statement of the opening paragraph which condemns his men for their transgression and to cleanse himself of any further charge. For example, when Odysseus raided the city of the Ciones, he urged his men to escape with all possible speed, but they refused and 'kept on drinking and butchering sheep and shambling crooked-horned cattle by the shore',[66] which gave the Ciones the time to ask for help and attack them. Also, it was their fear of hunger, Odysseus recalls, which made them disregard his order not to eat the sacred cattle of Hyperion. Many times, Odysseus has to delay the smooth course of his journey in order to save his crew, who, for example, are easily turned into pigs by the magic of Circe, which suggests that they have more in common with chaos and animal nature than with civilization and laws. Only Odysseus does not transgress the law of the gods, and therefore survives to tell the story. In Mulvaney's case, it is the law of the Empire that he observes through his long journey as a soldier, which in turn ensures that Mulvaney's story is perpetuated by the bard of the Empire, Kipling – even though it costs him the tie with his Fenian countrymen whose intention was to overturn the Empire.

It is worth noting that both in Mulvaney's stories and in *The Odyssey*, the hero's encounters with monsters, as well as his dealings with the countrymen who transgress the law, is never told in the third person, but only in the first person as the hero's recollection of the past. Odysseus' twenty-year-long wanderings are retrospectively narrated by Odysseus himself at the very end of his journey, a flashback which occupies only four out of the twenty-four books of *The Odyssey* (Books 9 to 12). The famous monsters, such as the Cyclops, the Wandering Rocks, Scylla and Charybdis and the Sirens, all appear in this personal reminiscence. It is not until he finishes looking back on his journey that Odysseus can embark upon his last journey home to reclaim his homeland and wife. Likewise, in Mulvaney's stories, the lawless Black Tyrone figures only in his reminiscence. It is interesting that in the above quotation from 'With the Main Guard' (1888), the Black Tyrone is shown to be a chimera: it is the most unlikely combination of the loyalist Irish and the Fenian Irish – at once 'Faynians an' rebils' *and* the most courageous heroes of the war. That is to say, the encounter with monsters – those which are fully inexplicable yet which the hero knows to be threatening to his own existence and identity – as well as the transgression of the law by his own countrymen, are confronted only in fictional form, in a reminiscence already rendered safe enough for the hero to tell – or retrospectively reconstructed (or even invented) to perform the psychological justification of the narrator.

In my view, the theme of transgression in *The Odyssey* has a special resonance with Kipling's work, for some of his major stories are written around the primal scene of violence, the moment when the laws and taboos of the community are violated and the world is, as a consequence, irretrievably transformed. Kipling does not write directly about these primal scenes, but only *around* them, as if direct treatment of the subject might release further violence and disturb the order of the Empire as well as that of his narrative. The best example of this is the Indian Mutiny, the turning-point of British history in India, which Kipling rarely touches upon, though all his Indian stories are mostly about a post-Mutiny world deeply marked by the impact of that event. In *The Jungle Books*, there is the original sin committed against Man by the First of the Tigers, which, echoing the Mutiny, broke a taboo and let loose chaos and fear into the world.

In both *The Odyssey* and Kipling's stories, the primal violence which broke society's law, though safely mediated in a personal reminiscence, still seems to be powerful enough to disrupt the entire narrative structure. Just like *The Odyssey*, which is marked by temporal disruptions and a lengthy flashback, *The Jungle Books* do not follow a chronological order, and in addition are separated from each other by other animal stories. For example, 'Tiger! Tiger!', which describes Mowgli's hunt for Shere Khan, the tiger, precedes 'How Fear Came', in which Shere Khan is still alive and in which the reason why the tiger has a rightful claim on Mowgli is revealed by Hathi the elephant and Master of the Jungle. The primal scene of violence (the First of the Tigers' killing of Man) is introduced into the narrative only *after* daily scenes of violence (Mowgli's hunt for Shere Khan), for which some kind of justification is always found to be necessary.[67] It is only in *Kim* that Kipling finally succeeds in representing the violence of the Indian Mutiny without letting it interfere with his grand narrative of the Empire: the novel achieves a long, consistent narrative and the single point of view of an omnipresent and omniscient narrator, though here again the Mutiny, 'the first evil' through which a 'madness ate into all the Army',[68] is narrated only by being framed within a personal reminiscence, that is, through the mouth of an old Indian soldier who fought for the British and was duly rewarded for his loyalty.

In the world of Terence Mulvaney, the primal scene of violence takes place in Ireland, when an Irish regiment took up arms against the English.

The incident is told in 'Belts' (1890), a poem in *Barrack-Room Ballads* which describes a 'row' between 'an Irish regiment an' English cavalree' in 'Silver Street' in Dublin.[69] This fictitious event is narrated by an Irish soldier who was himself involved in the row. Though the fight seems to have been precipitated by an excess of drink ('The English were too drunk to know'), it is unambiguously portrayed as an 'Irish' version of the Indian Mutiny against England. The English call the Irish 'Delhi Rebels' and the narrator portrays himself as a staunch Fenian whose 'uniform' is 'A *Freeman's Journal Supplemint*'. 'There was a row in Silver Street – it might ha' raged till now', but the fight suddenly draws to a close when an Irish soldier, Hogan, is accidentally killed, and as a consequence half of the Irish regiment, including the narrator himself, are punished. Kipling dare not let an English soldier die in the row, which would have meant the success of the Irish Mutiny. In other words, the row is subdued when the Irish regiment kills an Irish soldier; it is not only the primal scene of the Irish rebellion against England, but also the original moment in which the Irish turn their weapons against themselves, and let violence loose within Ireland.[70]

'Belts' has been associated with Terence Mulvaney, mainly because of the uncanny intertextuality it has with another poem, 'The Way Av Ut', composed two years before, which is about the Black Mountain Expedition of 1888 – the military operations carried out against 'hostile' hill tribes of the Black Mountain, adjacent to the Hazara district in the north of the Punjab.[71] In this poem, Mulvaney responds to the news that the 18th Royal Irish Regiment has been sent out to the action without drink; though admitting that ''Tis cruel on the Oirish', he nevertheless gives his assent to this temperance strategy of the Commander-in-Chief 'Bobbs', for the regiment would certainly make 'bloody war' if 'their liquor's cut', desperate to have the job done quickly and drink again. Mulvaney speaks as an expert on the matter, not solely because as an Irishman he knows the Irish, but also because, we are told, Mulvaney once belonged to the 18th Royal Irish Regiment in Dublin, revealing – at least in this poem – the official name of the Black Tyrone:

> I lay wid thim in Dublin wanst, an' we was Oirish tu,
> We passed the time av day an' thin the belts wint *whirraru*:
> I misremember fwhat occurred but, followin' the shtorm,
> A *Freeman's Journal Supplemint* was all *my* uniform.[72]

The last three lines of the stanza above are later recycled in 'Belts' with amazing precision, almost merging the two poems. The scene of the Irish Mutiny in Dublin and the Irish military service in India indeed overlap in three lines, the Irish fighting against '*naygur*-log' being an inverted image of them as 'Delhi Rebels' in Dublin – Fenianism, demonized and orientalized, which is redirected into the fighting force against Indians.

The trouble is that there is no definite evidence that the narrator of 'Belts' is indeed Terence Mulvaney, and the poem can be read independently of the other works featuring the Three Musketeers. After all, the connection between 'Belts' and Mulvaney is only sustained by the above three lines, a momentary glimpse of an Irish soldier fighting against the English in Dublin. Mulvaney does not mention anything about 'the Silver Street' or the murder of an Irish soldier in 'The Way Av Ut'. However, the way in which Kipling suggests the connection between 'Belts' and Mulvaney's stories, while determined not to reveal the true link between them, makes us even more suspicious of Mulvaney's involvement in the row in 'Silver Street'. According to the narrator in 'Love-O'-Women', Mulvaney 'had never given the tale in full', though he does admit that there was an incident related to 'a belt and a man's head'[73] in his past, on account of which he was 'caressed an' pershuaded to lave the Tyrone'.[74] The connection is more clearly stated in 'With the Main Guard', in which Mulvaney says, 'I cut a man's head tu deep wid me belt in the days av me youth, an', afther some circumstances which *I will oblitherate*, I came to the Ould Rig'mint, bearin' the character av a man wid hands an' feet.'[75] Here, Mulvaney admits that he deliberately wipes out the true connection between his Fenian past in Ireland and his loyalist present in India. That is to say, his stories are not so much the trustworthy recollection of what happened as the process through which the Irish past is edited and translated into a more acceptable form for the Empire.

Indeed, 'Belts', if viewed in the context of Mulvaney's other stories, is an exceptional text in many senses. Nowhere else does Kipling represent an Irish regiment in Ireland, or allow the Irish to rebel against the English. It is also the only piece in which the past is directly presented by a narrator who was also in the fight between the English and the Irish; by contrast, in the world of the Soldiers Three, Fenianism belongs to the past rather than to the political present, and the same incident concerning 'a belt and a man's head' is, in Mulvaney's stories, doubly (by Mulvaney and by the narrator) mediated as if to mitigate the violence released in the primal scene. Mulvaney, as he talks about his days with the Tyrone, offers us a slightly different version of 'Belts'. For example, he more than once stresses that the man whose head he broke did not die,[76] whereas in 'Belts' the murder does take place; this turns the Irish soldiers into 'murderers' and the murdered Hogan into a 'poor dumb corpse'.[77] However, even more obscure are the true reasons why Mulvaney, then a Fenian, hurt and 'nearly' killed another Irish soldier in their 'row' against the English soldiers. Mulvaney's characteristic silence over the matter seems to imply that it was more than an accident; some story is left untold, that is, the true story of how Mulvaney, a 'Delhi Rebel' in Dublin, transformed himself into a loyal Irish soldier in India, and why it had to happen.

The rewriting of Mulvaney's Fenian past is most clearly shown in 'Black Jack' (1888) when he talks of his old days with the Black Tyrone:

> Now there are Irish an' Irish. The good are good as the best, but the bad are wurrse than the wurrst. 'Tis this way. They clog together in pieces as fast as thieves, an' no wan knows fwhat they will do till wan turns informer an' the gang is bruk. But ut begins agin, a day later, meetin' in holes an' corners an' swearin' bloody oaths an' shtickin' a man in the back an' runnin' away, an' thin waitin' for the blood-money on the reward papers – to see if ut's worth enough. Those are the Black Irish, an' 'tis they that bring dishgrace upon the name av Ireland, an' thim I wud kill – as I nearly killed wan wanst.[78]

We can see that initially there is little distinction between the two types of Irish; on the contrary, they are identical – 'Irish' and 'Irish'. It is the next sentence, however, which introduces discrimination and judges one as good and the other as bad and 'Black'. Mulvaney goes on to tell us that he had to protect himself from the 'dog's thricks' of twelve 'Black Irish' with whom he had to share a room: 'I dhrew a line round my cot, an' the man that thransgressed ut wint into hospital for three days good.'[79] Here Mulvaney physically and symbolically distinguishes himself from the 'Black' Irish, in order to define himself as a good Irish. The circle, once drawn, turns into a boundary between the self and the other, creating an immune system by means of which the self fights against being contaminated from the outside and restores its identity according to the plan of what the self is supposed to be. His narrative becomes almost a ritual act of inventing a line between 'Irish an' Irish', making it visible and real, to the extent that it gains power over the reality outside. I would like to point out here that in Bram Stoker's *Dracula* (1897) a holy circle is also drawn around Mina Harker in order to keep the vampire away from her. Van Helsing writes in his memorandum: 'I drew a ring so big for her comfort, round where Madam Mina sat; and over the ring I passed some of the wafer, and I broke it fine so that all was well guarded.'[80] The similarity of the two circles in function and purpose seems to me striking: both are drawn to protect the loyal British subjects from the outer forces which try to assimilate them. This may allow us to interpret *Dracula* as the story of the loyalist Irish who struggle hard not to be influenced by Fenianism.[81] It seems to me that the circle which Mulvaney draws around his cot also symbolizes the split national identities and loyalties in Ireland: it is a fight to keep a piece of ground in Ireland which would belong to the Empire for ever.

It is interesting to note that Mulvaney uses the word 'black' to describe the Fenian Irish. Blackness is associated with the potential rebelliousness of ruled races, as can be seen in *Kim*, in which the year of the Mutiny is called 'the Black Year'.[82] Mulvaney, a Ulysses who has travelled the two worlds of the 'black' Fenian and the 'white' loyalist, becomes something of a borderline being between black and white, as well as between East and West. In 'The Incarnation of Krishna Mulvaney', Mulvaney as a border is given a different role from the English Learoyd and Ortheris. A boxing match, a typically English national sport, is held between two Englishmen, Learoyd and Dearsley, with Ortheris as referee. The fairness (considered to be an English quality) of the match is emphasized: 'the fat man in the red coat [Learoyd] fought with Dearsley Sahib after the custom of white men – with his hands, making no noise, and never at all pulling Dearsley Sahib's hair'.[83] Mulvaney does not directly participate in the match, though it is initially he who finds out that Dearsley has been exploiting the wages of his coolies by forcing upon them a raffle which does not give back any profit, and provokes him into a fight to win a palanquin, the prize for the raffle. Mulvaney, however, asks Learoyd to take his place in the fight, and places himself between these three Englishmen and the coolies in order to protect this purely English space from being disturbed by the interference of the natives. The match is narrated by an Indian who witnesses it, to whose eyes the racial differences among the white races do not exist:

> some fifty of us made shift to rush upon the red-coats [Learoyd and Ortheris]. But a certain man [Mulvaney] . . . ran upon us, and of us he embraced some ten or fifty in both arms, and beat our heads together, so that our lives turned to water, and we ran away. It is not good to interfere in the fightings of white men.[84]

The use of a native narrator is interesting, especially because this is the passage where Kipling clearly separates the English and the Irish. The reader has to reconstruct what the native eyes fail to see, which reinforces whatever subtle racial stereotypes exist.

The blackness of the Irish, which easily turned them into 'Delhi Rebels' in Ireland, is, when relocated in India, denied its association with the blackness of Indians. It is indeed significant that in 'With the Main Guard' Mulvaney recalls one fierce battle in which the Ould Regiment and the Black Tyrone fought side by side against Pathans. Through fighting against racial Others, loyalist and nationalist Irish become united as soldiers in the British army, leaving their differences and mutual hatred behind them. The possibility of the Fenian Irish reaching out to Indians to form a network of cross-colonial resistance is thereby firmly denied by Kipling. This was therefore a significant battle for Mulvaney, in which his new life in the Ould Regiment and his Fenian past in the Tyrone could mingle to overcome their discontinuity. The significance of the battle was further underscored by the fact that Mulvaney together with '[h]alf the Tyrone' proposed to name the place 'Silver's Theatre', after the music hall in Dublin which they used to know well.[85] By the act of naming and commemorating this new battle of unification, Mulvaney and the soldiers of the Tyrone disown 'Silver Street', a public space in which they, as Fenians, once raged against the English. Their new public arena is a 'theatrical space' where every performance, every battle to defend the Empire, can be watched and censored, and rendered as a safe representation. Such a place for the Irish can only be found in India.

3

> Kim's hybridity, simultaneously Indian, Irish, and English, crystallizes Kipling's response to the dangers threatening British rule in India and the wider Empire: the hybrid Irish, who are both colonizers and colonized, and thus 'maverick', will defend the borders of the Empire at the same time as they challenge its integrity and must themselves be contained.[86]

Recently, various attempts have been made to read in *Kim* the imperial anxiety about emerging Irish and Indian nationalisms in the late nineteenth century. A good example of such readings is Tim Watson's 'Indian and Irish Unrest in Kipling's *Kim*', from which the above quotation is taken, which beautifully sums up the implications of Kim's hybrid identity as an Irish boy in India educated to be English. However, these critics read Indian and Irish unrest only in *Kim*, thereby dismissing Terence Mulvaney, Kim's Irish predecessor also trapped in India, in relation to whom the same points can easily be made. Indeed, it is not in Kim but in Mulvaney that we see Kipling's immediate response to 'the dangers threatening British rule in India and the wider Empire'; Mulvaney made his first appearance in 1887 – a time when the presence of both Irish and Indian nationalisms was strongly felt as a result of the foundation of the Indian National Congress in 1885 and the presentation of the first Irish Home Rule Bill in 1886. It was also the period in which Kipling, as an editor of Indian newspapers, was every day closely engaged with discourses surrounding these political events, in the context of which we may say that the character Mulvaney was formed. As a representative of the Irish soldiers in India, he speaks to guarantee transcolonial imperial loyalty against the potential danger of transcolonial resistance. Nevertheless, Mulvaney's is an Irish voice contained in India far away from Ireland, as if its homecoming would be injurious to the integrity of the Empire, and, as we have seen, this voice is always put under the narrator's control – just like Kim, whose 'hybridity' has to be subjected to constant ethnological surveillance. The roles of these two in Kipling's representation of India, Ireland and 'the wider Empire' seem to be almost identical. If Mulvaney was Kipling's immediate response to the combined threat to the Empire from India and Ireland, Kim, invented almost a decade later, should be seen as his renewed attempt to contain it.

This time, Kipling successfully invented an Irish character who would not miss Ireland as home. Kim is also doubly deprived of his Irish voice – physically, by not having an Irish accent, and politically, by not being in touch with any type of Irish nationalism back home. While Mulvaney's Fenian past and his Irish voice could at any time resonate with Indian grievances, Kim, devoid of the Irish voice, may be taken to express a safer combination between India and Ireland as a cornerstone of imperial unity.

Kim, towards the end of the novel, all of a sudden experiences that '[t]hings that rode meaningless on the eyeball an instant before slid into proper proportion': 'They were all real and true – solidly planted upon the feet – perfectly comprehensible – clay of his clay, neither more nor less.'[87] He feels the ground between his toes, with his palms, feeling that 'Mother Earth [is] as faithful as the Sahiba'.[88] This sudden sense of belonging to the ground seems to put a stop to his agonizing search for identity. This ending sharply contrasts with not only the British colonizer's inability to settle in India, but also with Kipling's alleged failure to make Mulvaney stand on his feet, expressed in his lesser-known 'The Last of the Stories'.

Written as the last story for the *Week's News* in 1888, 'The Last of the Stories' is, in the words of Hugh Haughton, 'a kind of playful, self-conscious coda to the fiction he wrote and published in India'.[89] The narrator, caught in hot weather and under the influence of 'the brain-fever bird',[90] was offered by a Devil to take him to 'the Limbo of Lost Endeavour', where stay the souls of all the characters that 'are in any way created by anybody and everybody who has had the fortune or misfortune to put his or her writings into print'.[91] None of the characters in this Limbo, including his own, stand on their feet: '[L]ameness . . . seemed to be almost universal in the Limbo of Lost Endeavour'.[92] The narrator finds it difficult to face his own creatures, for they are nothing but marionettes which awkwardly limp, stutter, mouth and stagger around him. Mrs Hauksbee, the wittiest woman in Simla, turns out to be a 'limp-jointed staring eyed doll . . . hirpling towards [him] with a strained smile of recognition', and the narrator steps back and exclaims, 'I never made *that*!'[93] The distorted picture of his characters is nightmarish enough, but the real nightmare begins when the Devil, by some kind of magic, makes his characters stand on their own feet and turns them into what the narrator initially intended to create. However, the characters, as soon as they recover their firm contact with the ground, start expressing the truth which the narrator does not want to accept: 'You didn't understand.' Every single character of his repeats the same phrase, 'You didn't understand,' pointing out the narrator's complete failure in creating real characters. The narrator despairingly turns to the Three Musketeers, 'dearest of all [his] children', who 'would not turn against me as the others had done'. However, Mulvaney gives the same answer in his Irish accent:

> Savin' your presence, sorr, an' it's more than onwillin' I am to be hurtin' you; you did not onderstand. On my sowl an' honour, sorr, you did not onderstand.[94]

The narrator, horrified by the accusation of his characters, tells the Devil to change them back into disfigured dolls.

The narrator then turns to François Rabelais, 'the Master of the Limbo', for advice on how to create real characters instead of paper dolls, only to be given a piece of advice which he already knows: 'The First Law is to make them stand upon their feet, and the Second is to make them stand upon their feet, and the Third is to make them stand upon their feet'[95] – *how* to make them stand upon their feet is never revealed to the narrator. In this surprisingly Bakhtinian story, in which the characters are given the chance to subvert the narrator's narrative, Kipling bluntly admits that the voices of his own characters in India are no more than a misrepresentation. The narrator's desire to create real characters conflicts with his fear of letting them stand on their own feet – that is, of having their own voices and speaking for themselves – which would make them 'beyond control as soon as they are made'.[96] Mulvaney's loyalist Irish voice should not be taken at face value, for Kipling secretly knows that Mulvaney is not made to stand solidly on his feet – he is banished from his own ground of Ireland and its ideologies, trapped in India as a mythical imperial fairyland and, what is worse, as an Irish subject he is denied the power of self-representation. Kipling later achieved this impossible feat of making his Irish character stand through his new character Kim, but the magic is wrought only in the fashion of 'The Little Mermaid' – Kim's feet on the ground at the cost of his Irish voice.

Chapter Four

Shamrocks in the Veldt
Two Types of Aphasic Empire

> If aphasia is a language disturbance, as the term itself suggests, then any description and classification of aphasic syndromes must begin with the question of what aspects of language are impaired in the various species of such a disorder . . . To study adequately any breakdown in communications we must first understand the nature and structure of the particular mode of communication.[1]

Alfred Austin (1835–1913), the now-forgotten laureate, published *Songs of England*, a collection of poems throughout which he resorts to the word 'England' in order to inspire imperial subjects with patriotic feeling, in 1898, shortly before the Boer War, at the low price of one shilling, to 'place it within the reach, at least, of the many'.[2] For Austin, 'England' is still a magic word which unites 'not only Great Britain and Ireland, but Canada, Australia, South Africa, India, and every spot of earth where men feel an instantaneous thrill of imperial kinship at the very sound of the Name'.[3] The book is dedicated to his friend Lord Garnet Wolseley (1833–1913), a distinguished Irish officer who 'fought and bled for England'[4] in the colonies, and the poet asks the reader to follow Wolseley's example, namely, '[t]o live and die for England'.[5] Despite the profuse use of the word 'England', however, it appears that this volume was received rather coolly by his audience. One of the reviewers sarcastically notes that 'the Laureate at any rate has done his duty. He has written songs which are undoubtedly about England – the name occurs in almost every stanza . . . If every man now does not do his duty as England expects, it is not the fault of Mr. Alfred Austin.'[6]

The unpopularity of his book was, of course, due in large part to Austin's reputation as an untalented poet. Austin was an unfortunate laureate, unfavourably compared to his great predecessor Alfred Tennyson, overshadowed by Rudyard Kipling as the true bard of the Empire, and said to be 'essentially a lyric poet' and 'most successful when he writes untrammelled by the course of political events'.[7] Nevertheless, that his repeated use of the word 'England' could not impress the reader as much as he hoped seems to me to symbolize the loss of prestige which 'England' suffered at the turn of the century. The good old Victorian period that Austin and Wolseley had lived through was beginning to end. It is true that the old familial model of the Empire – England as the Mother and its colonies as her children – was still used, but many of her children had already grown up and were ready to leave their mother's protection, if we follow the logic of the metaphor. In fact, when the Boer War began a year later, England was not the one to give protection but appeared rather as the one to be rescued by her colonies. A gap was looming between 'England' and the British Empire – the synecdochic use of 'England' to represent the entire Empire was no longer to be taken for granted. It is not so much that the concept 'England' had become less important as that it had lost some of its power as the bonding force of the British Empire.

It is, then, interesting to observe that Rudyard Kipling, widely recognized as the voice of the Empire, rarely evokes 'England' with a view to inspiring patriotism. England is, as Kipling writes to Cecil Rhodes, 'a stuffy little place mentally morally and physically',[8] too small to train soldiers into Empire builders. He promotes the image of the 'Five Nations' instead, an ideal alternative to 'England', the great federation of Britain, South Africa, Canada, Australia and New Zealand (note that, in this way, differences within the 'British Isles' are silently obliterated), suggesting a sibling relationship between England and her self-governing settler colonies, rather than the mother–children relationship implied by the word 'England'. Kipling powerfully endorsed a new vision in which England now speaks to each of her settler's colonies as 'A Nation spoke to a Nation'.[9] Kipling's poem 'The Young Queen' (1900) clearly articulates this shifting ideal of the Empire, and was written to commemorate the inauguration of the Commonwealth of Australia, to be proclaimed on New Year's Day 1901. In this poem, England, 'the Old Queen', crowns Australia, 'the Young Queen', in the Hall of 'the Five Free Nations'. The Young Queen then asks the Old Queen for 'a mother's blessing', in answer to which England addresses Australia as 'Daughter no more but Sister'.[10] If this poem sealed the vision of the Five Nations as bonded in sisterhood, the same ideal was more forcefully promoted by its 'male' version – the 'White Man' – the brotherhood of the English-speaking white nations, an image more suited to Kipling's world full of imperial boys, which even suggested a wider Anglo-Saxon network spread beyond the 'Five Nations'. Apart from his famous 'The White Man's Burden' (1899), which was Kipling's call to the United States to join in the imperial mission, Kipling composed 'A Song of the White Men' (1900), a poem in which the phrase 'the White Men' is, just like Austin's 'England', obsessively repeated, seven times in the three-stanza poem.[11] This was Kipling's new slogan to unite the Empire, calling out to White Men all over the world to share the same Burden.

This chapter is about the Boer War. However, its focus is not on the actual battles but on the ideological ones fought around 'the British Empire'. During this war a new image of the Empire as a worldwide federation of white colonies became central, and, at the same time, became the very site where imperial supremacy was contested by the tropes of cross-national resistance against the Empire. In both cases, the seeming downfall of 'England' as the hegemonic power was given as the pretext for a new transcolonial model of the Empire. Kipling and the 'imperialist' camp resorted to this model to secure maximum support from the colonies, while the Irish nationalist camp attacked the very idea of 'England' as the imperial centre – for 'England's difficulty is Ireland's opportunity'[12] – by forging discursive analogies between the 'enslaved' Ireland and the two Transvaal republics under attack. What is more, the two visions both featured 'Ireland' as an important nexus of such transcolonial connections: while Irish nationalists played a leading role in forming anti-imperial alliances with the Boers and beyond, the Irish contribution to the war became the representative image of the solidarity of the Empire.

Two different versions of the 'Irish' Empire therefore fought during the Boer War, and they were both deeply 'aphasiac', if we are to follow Roman Jakobson in defining aphasia as a 'breakdown in communications'. Despite the fact that the two visions were apparently created against each other, almost in the manner of open letters, constantly citing each other and referring to the same events, these two discourses did not seem to communicate at all, nor to understand each other. Furthermore, their battles of propaganda crucially centred on the representability of the 'true' Irish voice, of Irish soldiers who 'silently' fought and died for the Empire, rendering the disagreement over what constituted 'the Irish' at this period emphatically 'aphasiac'; whatever 'Irish' voices were heard or imagined to be heard in the veldt were denounced by the other side as a misrepresentation. Taking my cue from Jakobson, I will analyse the nature and structure of both imperialist and Irish nationalist modes of transcolonial analogies, in the hope that this might help us to better understand the difficulty of communication between the two sides, which was to leave a fatal schism within Ireland even after 'the Empire' was successfully thrown out. Later in this chapter, I will look at Kipling's representation of the network of cross-national and anti-imperial resistance in his Boer War writing, in which he characterizes this as 'colonial rebellion' rather than nationalist struggle. He thereby defines the *Irish* voice as exclusively one which supports the Empire, denying the very existence of a contest between two Irish voices.

1

Whatever the extent to which 'resistance' contributed to subverting the image of Empire, there was certainly a change in this image which made it easier for resistance to be seen, and we see rather unsettling versions of the

British Empire publicly articulated both by imperialists and by (Irish) nationalists during the Boer War. Let us look at the imperialist version of the Empire first. This not only represented the 'Empire in crisis', fighting a difficult war against the two South African republics, but also the 'Empire adrift' or 'the Empire falling apart', threatened by the very possibility that the imperial union might dissolve during the crisis of the war. This image of the Empire falling apart is usually followed by another vision of the Empire as more closely united through overcoming the crisis together: the Boer War was supposed to 'weld the Empire together' more firmly than it had been before the war started. A speech by Alfred Milner is one good example of how this rhetoric works:

> The struggle with the Boers demonstrated for the first time the solidarity of the British Empire. Many continental critics had long believed that the moment Great Britain found herself in difficulties, her Colonies would seize the opportunity to throw off their allegiance to the Crown. The fact was 'very otherwise'. From Australia, Canada, India, New Zealand, and every portion of the Empire, came help and offers of help in men, money and material. The spirit thus demonstrated and fostered by the experience of a brotherhood in arms, rendered it possible later on to take steps in the direction of organizing the defence of the Empire, based upon a co-ordination of its immense resources. And having thus fought in the cause of a united Empire against the threat of dismemberment, the self-governing Dominions not only helped greatly to preserve it, but also themselves took a forward step in their political status and relation with the Empire.[13]

Or Hallam Tennyson, the Governor of South Australia and eldest son of the late laureate, writing in a letter to Queen Victoria:

> The war has done an infinity of good on this island-continent, and has welded Australia to the Empire in such a way that the bond of union will, I feel convinced, be henceforward indissoluble. Before the war there was a party for the separation of Australia from Great Britain, but such has been the earnest and impetuous loyalty of the labouring classes all through the country, that the demagogues have been compelled to give up the utterance of their unpatriotic sentiments, and now are among the most patriotic speakers at public meetings.[14]

In both cases, voices wanting to break away from the Empire are identified, in order to create an image of the 'Empire adrift', only to be contained within a renewed sense of imperial kinship. However, would the inclusion of these voices within the text, rather than in the footnotes or in the margins, inevitably turn the imperialist text itself into *their* frames and annotations?

Roman Jakobson, in 'Two Aspects of Language and Two Types of Aphasic Disturbances' (1915), establishes a distinction between metonymic and metaphoric modes of language, which respectively correspond to the axes of combination and selection. The metonymic mode of language creates a context by *combining* different elements in a state of spatial or temporal *contiguity*, while the metaphoric selects parts from all the available vocabularies and links them according to 'various degrees of *similarity*'.[15] Aphasia is caused by the disorder of either of these two linguistic aspects. For example, the aphasic subject with a similarity (or metaphoric) disorder has to rely on spatial or temporal congruity, or a context, when forming a message, while the aphasic subject with a contiguity (or metonymic) disorder lacks the ability to combine words into contexts, so that his sentences are likely to degenerate into a 'word heap',[16] the words linked to each other only by similarity in the code. Interestingly, Jakobson draws a parallel between his framework and Freud's theory of dreams: a metonymic mode of language, which forces different elements into one context, corresponds to Freud's 'displacement' and 'condensation', and a metaphoric mode of language, in which the subject appropriates an aspect of the other through some kind of similarity, corresponds to Freud's 'identification and symbolism'.[17]

Here I will propose that the tropes used to justify imperialism are metonymic, whereas the nationalist discourse which aims at undermining the Empire is metaphoric. Of course, there are exceptions which do not fit well within this framework: for example, the analogy between the Roman Empire and Great Britain frequently drawn during the nineteenth century may be said to be more metaphoric than metonymic. Nevertheless, the image of the British Empire was constructed primarily using the metonymic mode of language, for it was by definition the combination of the various colonies (which were not necessarily similar to each other) within the context of Empire, or with imperialism as a pretext. This may explain why phrases such as 'to weld the Empire together' and 'to draw the colonies closer together' were obsessively used when the Empire was thought to be in crisis. The more the colonies were imagined to be in a state of spatial or temporal contiguity, the stronger was the solidarity of the Empire felt to be. In this respect, the achievement of the British Empire was most successfully symbolized in the Great Exhibition of 1851, which, according to a contemporary observer, William Whewell, brought 'within [man's] field of view the surface of the globe, with all its workshops and markets, and produce[d] instantaneously a permanent picture, in which the whole were seen side by side'.[18] Modernization and imperialism went together well, because the former's tendency to work towards economizing time and space greatly contributed to greater congruity among colonies. Whewell writes, 'it is not a mere picture of things which are found standing together that we have had presented to us; the great achievement was the bringing them together . . . By annihilating the space which separates different nations, we produce a spectacle in which is also annihilated the time which separates one stage of a nation's progress from another.'[19]

In fact, the Boer War, in which, to use Milner's phrase, from 'every portion of the Empire, came help and offers in men', was the best occasion to see all the imperial subjects together in close proximity. Kipling, who impatiently dashed to South Africa in order to offer help along with countless other British patriots, Arthur Conan Doyle, Winston Churchill, Erskine Childers among them, was immediately represented as the centre of this closely knit 'metonymic' Empire. For example, H. A. Gwynne, in *The Friend*, a newspaper experimentally published at the special request of Lord Roberts for his army during their occupation of Bloemfontein, welcomes the participation of Rudyard Kipling on the editorial board, stating that he 'has contributed more than any one perhaps towards the consolidation of the British Empire', and writing:

> His visit is singularly appropriate. He will find encamped round the town not only his friend Tommy Atkins, but the Australian, the Canadian, the New Zealander, the Tasmanian, the volunteer from Ceylon, from Argentine, and from every quarter of the globe. He will see the man of the soil – the South African Britisher – side by side with his fellow colonist from over the seas. In fact, Bloemfontein will present to him the actual physical fulfilment of what must be one of his dearest hopes – the close union of the various parts of the greatest Empire in the world.[20]

Gwynne then goes on to write, 'His visit, therefore, will have in it something of the triumph of a conqueror – a conqueror who, with the force of genius, has swept away barriers of distance and boundary, and made a fifth of the globe British, not only in title, but in real sentiment';[21] here again, the metonymic magic is to overcome time and space so that all the elements of the Empire can be seen together. Moreover, Kipling's background is also said to symbolize 'Anglo-Saxon unity, a possession of Greater Britain'. The *Bookman* notes that the office of the next poet laureate-to-be after Tennyson should be 'something more than a petty insular distinction' and singles out Kipling for the post:

> Mr. Kipling represents not only in his verse, but in his personality, at once the extension and unity of the race. Born in India, of English stock, he is closely identified in his life and works with the greatest of England's possessions, whose strange life he, in many cases, first revealed to the wondering world; his knowledge of the other British colonies is almost equally minute. By ties of marriage he is in some degree American, and his home for a number of years has been in the most homogeneously English portion of America. He is not, therefore, a mere Englishman, nor a mere Anglo-Indian, nor a mere American,

> but something above and beyond all these distinctions – an Anglo-Saxon.[22]

S. B. Cook, in his *Imperial Affinities: Nineteenth-Century Analogies and Exchanges Between India and Ireland*, emphasizes the role of colonial officials in the formation of analogies: 'They shared common adolescent experiences and some were connected by ties of blood or marriage. Scattered throughout the empire, contact was fostered by the *esprit de corps* of their chosen service and facilitated, from the 1870s, by a global communication system. With a limited knowledge of local conditions, they sometimes attempted to govern in the light of recent experience in other colonies.'[23] The colonial officers who located themselves at the intersection of all aspects of colonial experience were themselves metonymies of the Empire; apart from representing the imperial administration, their function, within the dream-work of the British Empire, can be seen as analogous to Freudian *condensation*, that is, the creation of composite figures by uniting or superimposing various elements – colonies – into one single image of a smooth imperial administration. The transferral of the officers from one colony to another and their repeated use of the same methods and policies in different colonies can also be likened to Freudian *displacement* – the dream exchanges one figure with others through a chain of associations – for it helped to detach the officers from too close an involvement in the local problems of the colonial encounter, which might undermine their control. The exchanges of policy and personnel among colonies was necessary, so that the officers could draw analogies in the light of their former experiences and therefore make the uncanniness of the new colonial encounter familiar and manageable. As I have already mentioned, Jakobson's metonymic mode of language corresponds to Freud's *condensation* and *displacement*, which are, according to Freud, the two governing factors in the dream-work: they operate together to produce distorted forms of the unconscious dream-wish, in order to 'escape the censorship imposed by resistance'.[24] The objectionable contents of imperialism – complicated colonial situations and the grievances of the colonized – had to be censored, condensed and displaced into more palatable dreams which did not interfere with the image of British imperialism. The intra-imperial analogies which these colonial officials embodied were such dreams, protecting the innermost working of Empire.

In a similar way, Kipling in the Boer War came to represent 'successful' connections between old and new colonies by turning to his former colonial experience in India in order to make the Transvaal seem more familiar and accessible. South Africa was, Kipling writes, 'the nearest approach to Anglo-Indian in many of its ideas that I know',[25] and, what is more, '*in all things* life is a heap easier, I think, than India. There is no hot weather; no one goes to the Hills'.[26] When entering into the 'editorial dust bin' of *The Friend*, Kipling, according to Julian Ralph, 'sniffed the mingled odours of ink, wet paper, and dust, and said, "It's quite like old times in India."'[27] When Lord Roberts was appointed Commander-in-Chief of the Boer War, it might have seemed like a realization of Kipling's own literary world. Roberts, just like Kim, embodied a magic combination of the Irish and the Indian. An illustration from *Punch* shows that Roberts's reliability as the guardian of the Empire was widely imagined by the British public as the peculiar combination of India and Ireland which he personified: here we find Lord Roberts, fondly nicknamed as 'Bobs', depicted in Indian attire, with his sword symbolizing the valour and loyalty of the Irish soldiers. Note that Roberts as the Indian *and* Irish idol is enshrined in a 'museum', a highly transnational and transcolonial space designed to visualize the Empire as a whole. The Indo-Irish connection was indeed the 'property of the British Nation', which would save the Empire even in the most difficult time of the Boer War. Gandhi also reports an interesting rivalry between the Indian community and the Irish Association in South Africa over the right to welcome the Commander-in-Chief. [28] With his identity as Anglo/Irish-Indian and his 41-year-long experience as an officer in India, it was expected that Roberts would surely extinguish the fire set in the veldt both by the Boers and by Irish nationalists.

While the imperialists sought to wedge the colonies back into the Empire by employing the metonymic mode of language, Irish nationalists were resorting to 'metaphoric' analogies in order to free Ireland from the yoke of Empire. In fact, the history of Irish nationalism can be seen as a persistent effort to associate Ireland, an island uneasily floating close to England, with other countries through a certain similarity, so as to annul its proximity to England as a natural reason to be ruled. For example, during the American War of Independence and the French Revolution, Ireland sympathized respectively with America and France. The Union followed immediately after, as if England were afraid that Ireland should draw a connection with any nation other than herself. Thomas Moore, as Javed Majeed has pointed out, declared that 'the spirit that had spoken in the melodies of Ireland found itself at home in the East', when writing in his orientalist epic poem *Lalla Rookh* (1817) of 'a fierce struggle' of the ancient Persians against 'their haughty masters', the Muslims:[29] here the voice of Ireland was found by identifying the struggle of Persians against Muslims with that of the Irish against England. Another interesting example can be found in the political writing of Daniel William Cahill (1796–1864), a prolific Catholic preacher and lecturer who became famous for his vigorous attacks on the British government and the Church of Ireland. Cahill, at the beginning of the Indian Mutiny, celebrated the defeat of the English in India by the harsh climate and the numerous native forces.[30] The English defeat in India immediately meant Irish liberation for Cahill, for in the modern world where nations and their interests are 'so closely interwoven', '[s]uccessful tyranny in one kingdom often establishes slavery elsewhere, and *vice versa*, the overthrow of despotism in one locality elevates into liberty the neighbouring peoples'.[31] He attributes the outbreak of the Indian Mutiny to 'an overwhelming and an irresistible feeling of hatred, amounting to horror, against everything English', which was derived from such causes as the insolent and unfair treatment of the natives, the cruel collection of rent, 'the persecution of the Catholic soldiers'[32] and, above all, the mistreatment of Ireland:

> this item [the mistreatment of Ireland], perhaps more than any one or all the other causes taken together, has awakened the most hostile feelings in India towards England . . . Whatever may be the result of our struggles in India, the historian must own, that in any country which English power has ever conquered, she has never made a friend to her constitutional policy or a convert to her creed . . .[33]

Note here that Cahill calls the Indian Mutiny '*our* struggles in India'. It is not difficult to see that the 'overwhelming and irresistible feeling of hatred, amounting to horror, against everything English' which Cahill argues to be the very reason for the Mutiny is in fact the Irish feeling towards England. Through his identification of the Indian hatred towards the ruler with that of the Irish, the sepoys now fight for the sake of Irish liberation, and the Irish, according to this logic, fight alongside the Indian soldiers.

The similarity which Irish nationalists evoke by identifying Ireland with other countries, though, may not always be immediately obvious to those who are not well versed in their code. 'It is difficult to understand,' Byron Farwell writes concerning a series of attempted invasions by American Fenians into Canada from Vermont around 1870, 'how the Fenians reasoned that they could free Ireland by attacking Canada, but attack they did – and more than once.'[34] Similarly, Irish nationalists during the Boer War drew a powerful comparison between Ireland and South Africa. In the House of Commons, speeches were made by the Irish MPs which express the secret tie of sympathy which unites Ireland and South Africa. Michael Davitt, before resigning from the House of Commons and going to South Africa to assist the Boers, said, '[I]n conclusion, let me say that we Irishmen are compelled to give our sympathies to the Boers because they are absolutely in the right in heroically defending with their lives the independence of their country.'[35] John Redmond, in his speech on 7 February 1900, more clearly emphasized the metaphoric connection between the two countries: 'The sympathy of Ireland is with the Boers.'[36] Many Irish interpreted the Boer War as 'the struggle for liberty against England', and used it to articulate their own colonial situation. Redmond specified the main source of sympathy towards the Boers to be 'antagonism to England',[37] and the Irish unionist Michael J. F. McCarthy also observed that '[h]atred of "England", distrust of the English Sassenach, the memories of "treasured wrongs"' were 'the mainsprings of the sympathy felt for the Boers':[38] South Africa is suffering from British imperialism, *just as* Ireland has been. Those who held the imperialist point of view refused to see the logic of this identification. J. B. Robinson, in his article in the *Contemporary Review*, wrote, 'The notion that we might have a second Ireland in the Transvaal is simply absurd. I have known the country and the people intimately from my childhood. They have no similarity whatever to the Irish in their character or their ways of thinking.'[39] And Dr Clark declared in the House of Commons, 'The Boer position in this country is entirely different from that of the Irishman. Why does the able and learned Gentleman come before the House of Commons to offer us an argument of that kind?'[40] Even Kruger, the President of the Transvaal Republic, though gratefully accepting the help offered by the Irish,[41] could not fully acknowledge this identification, telling Maud Gonne that the Irish had to know the country and speak the local language to be of real use to his republic in their fight against England.[42] Nevertheless, we witness here a symptomatic manifestation of imperialists' similarity disorder, and their difficulty in seeing the opponent's point of view which, according to Jakobson, originates in '[l]oss of bilingualism and confinement to a single dialect variety of a single language'[43] – an inability to speak the Other's language and to understand outside his own context. It was against this stubborn refusal of understanding that Irish nationalists had developed their own aphasia, namely, an inability to work within the imperialist context.

2

We have already examined Kipling's representation of the Irish soldiers in India, especially in the form of Terence Mulvaney, who invariably speaks for the Empire. During the Boer War, the figure of the Irish soldier, silently serving the cause of Empire, was fiercely contested, as both Irish nationalists and imperialists used it in their attempts to articulate an authentic Irish voice on their own behalf.

We see some words exchanged on the subject of the 'true' Irish voice after John Redmond in the House of Commons expressed the Irish sympathy towards the Boers on 7 February 1900. Redmond, it was suggested, 'has spoken of Ireland's voice on this question',[44] whereas J. H. M. Campbell argued that his speech was nothing but a 'discordant note' which could have little effect on 'the harmonious chorus of loyalty and patriotism which has been re-echoed to the furthermost corners of the world in which are gathered the subjects of the Queen'.[45] Campbell quoted a passage from the *United Irishman*, without explaining its full context, which said that the complaints of the Irish were 'merely the popular grumbling – a little exaggerated, being Irish', and Irish loyalty is testified to not in words but by deeds – by the fact that the Irish fight for England.[46] Here, he not only forced the *United Irishman*, the recognized organ of Irish nationalists, to speak in favour of the imperial cause, but also interpreted the silence of the Irish soldiers – the ones literally made aphasiac by their imperial service – as the best proof that a majority in Ireland supported the Boer War. The Irish nationalists, on the other hand, sought to undermine this representation of the Irish soldier as the 'Servant of the Queen'. In fact, the strongest demonstration of anti-imperial sentiments was found when John MacBride organized an Irish Brigade in the Transvaal to fight against the British force. In the *United Irishman* there appeared almost every week a strong appeal to the Irish people not to enlist, along with articles denouncing the Irish involvement in the British army as treason against Ireland. This appeal, composed by the 'Irish Transvaal Committee', reads:

> The Irishmen in England's Service who are sent to South Africa will have to fight against Irish Nationalists who have raised Ireland's flag in the Transvaal, and have formed an Irish Brigade to fight for the Boers against the oppressor of Ireland . . . In preventing recruiting for the English Army you are working for Ireland's honour, and you are doing something to help the Boers in their Struggle for Liberty.[47]

Identification and substitution, founded on a secret 'similarity' between the Boers and the Irish – both are fighting against the same oppressor for liberty – strongly colours the rhetoric of this passage, in which the Boers and the Irish become almost synonymous. Thus, it is no wonder that the Boers in the veldt suddenly turn into the Irish Brigade: to fight against the Boers is, for the Irishmen, to fire at their own country folk. Moreover, to help the Boers is to work for the Irish cause, 'in their Struggle for Liberty'.

The war of representation centring on the 'true' Irish voice of the Irish soldier was not only fought in the House of Commons. Queen Victoria herself strongly and publicly acknowledged the bravery of the Irish soldiers at the front, and authorized the formation of a regiment of Irish Guards, reasserting that the Irish Army was her loyal army, as a counter-representation to the Irish Brigade on the Boer side.[48] Moreover, the Queen, instead of going for her spring holiday in Italy as she had first intended, paid a visit to Ireland in 1900 (from 4 to 26 April), which she had not visited since her last rather unsuccessful visit with Prince Albert in 1861. Although it was announced that the nature of this visit was non-political, the Irish nationalists interpreted it as nothing less than the 'clearly political' attempt 'to misrepresent Ireland as being "loyal to the Empire"'[49] in order to enlist more soldiers from Ireland; the Queen, to use George Moore's phrase, 'comes to do the business which her recruiting sergeants have failed to do'.[50] According to W. B. Yeats, 'It has been announced that the Queen will leave Windsor for Ireland on April 2nd. That is a remarkable day, for on that day a hundred years ago the Act of Union, having been pushed through the Irish Parliament by bribery, was introduced into the English Parliament.'[51] Maud Gonne invented the image of Victoria as 'the Famine Queen' in order to 'counteract the poisonous lies which the English Press agencies will spread abroad about the Queen's visit'.[52]

Irish nationalists unanimously interpreted the Queen's gestures as powerful impositions of 'fictions of the Union' which they had to demystify at all costs.[53] This interpretation, albeit true, has made it difficult to see that the Queen's primary aim was to represent the Empire by highlighting the transcolonial intersections between Ireland and South Africa and by offering herself as the focal point. Ireland was, to quote the Queen visiting Dublin, 'the motherland of those brave sons who have recently borne themselves in defence of my Crown and Empire with a cheerful valour'.[54] Thanking Ireland was also the most effective way to acknowledge assistance from the colonies, many of whose inhabitants physically and nostalgically retained emotional ties with their homeland. Moreover, the Queen's tributes to her Irish soldiers tellingly acknowledged Ireland, a colonial periphery, as an integrated part of the imperial centre, and this reassured all her colonies (including non-settler colonies like India) that their contributions to the war, far from being wasted, strengthened and even created the British Empire. Indeed, the settler colonies, Canada and Australia in particular, enthusiastically welcomed the Queen's gifts to Ireland: St Patrick's Day was proclaimed a holiday in many towns and cities and shamrocks were worn 'as a token of appreciation of the gallantry of the Irish troops'.[55] *The Times* special correspondent in Sydney summarized a public speech by Earl Beauchamp, the Governor of New South Wales, delivered on St Patrick's Day, as follows:

> [H]e said that never before had the Empire been so united. The Imperial forces had received great assistance from Australia. He was proud of the British Empire, in whose concerns Australia was playing such an important part. In conclusion, he said he was glad to see the people of Australia so anxious to do homage to the people of Ireland in recognition of the heroic conduct of the Irishmen serving in South Africa.[56]

Here Australia's contributions to the war, together with her enthusiasm for the Irish gallantry in South Africa, demonstrated that Australia was 'an important part' of the British Empire. The link between Ireland and South Africa was thus made to represent the imperial solidarity itself, and the characterization of the Irish voice as loyalist was crucial in securing the thus newly constructed 'Irish' Empire, even if this automatically ruled out any possibility of the 'true' Irish voice being otherwise.

In her journal, the Queen registers the patriotic voices of her Irish subjects which her own visit aroused:

> We went all along the quays in the poorer parts of the town, where thousands had gathered together and gave me a wildly enthusiastic greeting. At Trinity College the students sang 'God Save the Queen', and shouted themselves hoarse. The cheers and often almost screams were quite deafening. Even the Nationalists in front of the City Hall seemed to forget their politics and cheered and waved their hats.[57]

Among the 'screams' which the Queen heard, there must have been nationalist ones, but in her account of the loyal chorus they are not allowed to make any noise. We have to look somewhere else to supplement the noises which were not included in her text; for example, as Elizabeth Longford puts it in her biography of the Queen, 'there were few flags in the back streets of Dublin where she did not drive, and these few caused scuffles. The Dublin Council voted to present an Address provided it did not mention loyalty to the Crown. Copies of the *United Irishman* were seized before she landed, Home Rule meetings broken up and Dubliners arrested for tearing down decorations and smashing shop windows adorned with Union Jacks. The French newspaper *Charivari* published a cartoon of British bayonets forcing the cheers from Irish throats. . .'[58] Maud Gonne also describes the 'true' Irish voice on the Boer War as it reached her ears, when Trinity College was conferring Honorary Degrees on Joseph Chamberlain 'to show Ireland's loyalty to the British Empire': 'Pat O'Brien called for cheers for the Boers, which was responded to wildly by the crowd. The noise and the cheering must have considerably marred the dignified proceedings within the College and made Chamberlain doubt about the love and loyalty of the Irish nation of which he was being assured.'[59]

If the Irish soldiers were deprived of the ability to speak, and their service at the front was to be univocally interpreted as silent approval for the imperial cause, the wearing of the shamrock on St Patrick's Day, the symbol of national identity on the Irish side, was the only possibility left to the soldiers to proclaim their Irish identities. 'Wearing of the green' had been, therefore, a punishable offence in the army: the Irish soldiers were 'ordered and compelled to remove the shamrock'[60] from their helmets, and it was possible, for example, to be 'sentenced' to '48 hours imprisonment'[61] for such an offence. In 1899, a paragraph was introduced into the Queen's Regulations 'to the effect that no officer or soldier is to wear unauthorised ornament or emblem when in uniform'.[62] Thus, it was somewhat surprising when the Queen, prior to her visit to Ireland, marked her appreciation for her Irish soldiers by ordering them to wear the shamrock on St Patrick's

Day. The following order was promulgated to the army a week before St Patrick's Day:

> GALLANTRY OF IRISH REGIMENTS IN SOUTH AFRICA – DISTINCTION TO BE WORN ON ST. PATRICK'S DAY.
>
> Her Majesty the Queen is pleased to order that in future, upon St. Patrick's Day, all ranks in her Majesty's Irish regiments shall wear, as a distinction, a sprig of shamrock in their head-dress, to commemorate the gallantry of her Irish soldiers during the recent battles in South Africa.[63]

The Queen herself, when landing in Ireland, wore 'bunches of real shamrocks', with her bonnet and parasol also 'embroidered with silver shamrocks'.[64] Lord Roberts also wore the shamrock on 17 March to show that asserting Irishness and loyalty to the crown no longer contradicted each other.[65] Lady Roberts chose St. Patrick's Day to sail to the Cape to join her husband, and her cabin was, 'in honour of her ladyship', 'tastefully' decorated with 'garlands of shamrock' and 'the time-honoured Irish harp'[66]. To quote the *Annual Register*, 'a periodically recurring source of irritation between Irish soldiers and their commanding officers was converted by the Queen's intuitive perception into an occasion for the innocent gratification of national feeling'.[67] The *Irish Figaro* also welcomed the new use of the wearing of the shamrock; it turned 'an emblem of discord into an emblem of reconciliation and of peace': '[T]he green immortal shamrock will henceforth be connected with sentiments of love and loyalty, and form a fresh link in the chain that binds us to our English brethren.'[68] The *Academy* went so far as to print the special order from the Queen side by side with lines from 'The Wearing of the Green', declaring that the former had destroyed 'the significance of a popular song written in 1798'.[69] The Queen, in this way, tactfully created a context in which the wearing of the shamrock was no longer a rebellious act, but nothing less than the demonstration of the most loyal sentiment towards her.

Kipling also passionately welcomed this 'personal' gift from the Queen to her Irish soldiers. He composed a one-stanza poem called 'St. Patrick's Day' at the Cape Town telegraph office and sent it off at once, so that it would be in time for the second issue of *The Friend*, on 17 March, 1900.[70] The fuller version of the poem was published a week later; it lengthily praises the gallantry of the Irish soldiers at the front in the added four stanzas. In this poem, Kipling again lets his Irish soldiers enthusiastically speak for the Empire, and he does so by appropriating 'The Wearing of the Green':

> Oh! Terence dear, and did you hear
> The news that's going round?
> The Shamrock's Erin's badge by law,
> Where'er her sons be found.

From Bobsfontein to Ballyhack
'Tis ordered by the Queen,
We've won our right in open fight,
The wearing of the Green.[71]

'The Wearing of the Green', which was 'by law forbid' and for which men and women were hanged according to the original song,[72] is now 'Erin's badge by law', ordered to be sung by nobody else but the Queen. This happy news is passed first and foremost to Terence Mulvaney, Kipling's most famous Irish soldier in India, by another Irish soldier, creating, and testifying to, the network of loyal Irish soldiers whom Kipling knows to be the real Irish: the 'news' is going all around the Empire, even to India where Mulvaney serves, inspiring patriotic sentiment in every Irish soldier's heart. Mulvaney here again operates as a 'metonymic' nexus of the Empire, through which Kipling superimposes the Irish-Indian connection on South Africa and weaves the Boer War into his literary world. At any rate, Kipling's 'St. Patrick's Day' was by no means the only 'imperialist' revision of 'The Wearing of the Green'; to the Irish nationalists' dismay, 'Queen' and 'Green' rhyme perfectly. Significantly, many such revisions were in fact made by the Irish themselves. For instance, Alfred Perceval Graves (1846–1931), an Irish poet famous for his compilation of Irish and Celtic songs, wrote a new lyric for 'The Wearing of the Green', which was duly arranged to the tune of the original song by the renowned Irish composer Sir Charles Villiers Stanford (1852–1924). This song vividly depicts the Irish soldiers' action at the Relief of Ladysmith, in which Ireland is transposed onto South Africa by the evocation of place names like Dublin and Ulster, and the poem ends with the news of the Queen's visit thanking the Irish gallantry.[73] And a pair of Irish ladies, Isabel Sullivan (lyrics) and Alicia Adelaide Needham (music), collaborated to produce a patriotic 'By Order of the Queen', dedicated to 'The Irish Regiments at the Front, South Africa, 1900', whom they call in the song 'Sons of the Empire': 'She, our Queen, well knows their worth / Her tears for them are shed / And the shamrock's doubly sacred / That means honour to our dead . . .'[74] Kipling's 'St. Patrick's Day' was one addition to these 'authentic' Irish approvals of, and their full-hearted support for, the Empire as a federation of colonies, and was made possible only through the evocation of his Irish double, Terence Mulvaney.

The Irish nationalists were keenly aware that the Queen's new order was an ingenious 'transvaluation' of the meaning of the wearing of the shamrock. It is interesting to observe how this new use of the shamrock is received in the *United Irishman*: 'The shamrock, Ireland's emblem of Faith and fatherland, we regret to say has been grossly outraged.'[75] It is converted into 'the emblem of murder', 'the emblem of a lost nation', the 'symbol of our thanks for Butcher Service', which has made the Irish soldier into 'a slave who is praised and patronised, who wears his chain as a badge of honour'[76] – all of which testifies to the importance of restoring the 'true' meaning of the wearing of the shamrock, which has been stripped away. 'England has taken everything she could take away from us save the Faith, a remnant of our Language, and the National Emblem. It rest with us to guard these three heritages, and we can do it if we are true to our principles and firm in our love for our motherland',[77] and according to Moore, '[T]he shamrock is an emblem which can only be worn by Irishmen who believe that Ireland is a nation with a special destiny to fulfil.'[78]

W. B. Yeats sent a letter to the Irish newspapers (*Freeman's Journal*, *Irish Daily Independent*, *Daily Express*) a day before the Queen's arrival, which argued that the Queen's visit to Ireland should be received in silence:

> Whoever is urged to pay honour to this Queen Victoria to-morrow morning should remember this sentence of Mirabeau's – 'The silence of a people is the lesson of kings'. She is the official head and symbol of an Empire that is robbing the South African Republics of their liberty, as it has robbed Ireland of hers. Whoever stands by the roadway cheering for Queen Victoria cheers for that Empire, dishonours Ireland, and condones a crime.[79]

In this letter, Yeats draws two metaphorical identifications: liberty in Ireland is unjustly suppressed, just as it was in France before the French Revolution and as is currently occurring in South Africa. And through these identifications, Yeats seeks to give back to the Irish their speech. The Irish should not any longer be coercively silenced nor conditioned to chant univocally whenever the English monarch passes by. However, this deliberate silence, to be written into the univocal imperial chorus, inevitably entailed the risk of being taken for silent approval of the Empire. Therefore, Yeats goes on to ask the Irish people to go to the meeting of the people, in order to use their voice *to protest*. Silence is one powerful form of protestation, but it has to be followed by the real voiced protest so as not to be mistaken for docile acceptance of English rule. To speak for the Boers, by appropriating the suffering of the Other, was one way for Ireland to recover from its chronic metonymic aphasia.

Thus it was 'Ireland', rather than 'England', which figured centrally in war propaganda during the Boer War. When 'England' was in difficulty, 'Ireland' was summoned to create fresh imperial discourses, pointing to a new direction in which the colonies, no longer excluded or discriminated against, would take an active part in imperial affairs as competent Empire builders. It would be true to say that Kipling was the (uncrowned) bard of this 'Irish Empire', a federation of colonies built and maintained by white colonists, the majority of whom were also Irish immigrants. The two types of Empire which fought during the Boer War were 'aphasic' Empires, for each denied and lost part of the Irish voice, in the course of representing what they firmly believed to be the 'true' voice of Ireland.

3

With the representation of the Irish soldiers being publicly contested between imperialists and Irish nationalists, it might be reasonable to assume that Kipling would write many stories and poems to contribute to the victory of the imperialist representation of the Irish soldiers in the Boer War, as he had already done in his Indian stories. However, 'St. Patrick's Day' is virtually the only piece in which Kipling directly represents the Irish soldiers in the Boer War. As the Irish soldiers became publicly more conspicuous, they seem to have gradually receded from Kipling's text. It is true that there are several characters with Celtic surnames in Kipling's Boer War stories. However, the characters such as McManus ('Folly Bridge' (1900)), McGinnies ('The Outsider' (1900)) and Allen ('A Burgher of the Free State' (1900)) are all civilians, not soldiers. The only Irish soldier is McBride, 'the professional humorist of D Company'[80] in 'The Comprehension of Private Copper' (1902), whose name peculiarly coincides with the name of the leader of the Irish Brigade serving on the Boer side, John MacBride; it may be interpreted that Kipling, by using the same name, reclaims the Irish regiments from the 'misrepresentation' of the Irish nationalists. Equally interesting is the fact that Kipling did *not* write about the Irish conspiracies to strike at the Empire during the crisis of the Boer War, even though the Irish nationalists' pro-Boer campaign in the midst of general Irish support for the war almost looked like the realization of the anti-imperialist plots appearing in 'The Irish Conspiracy' (1889) and 'The Mutiny of the Mavericks' (1891). As the Irish soldiers disappear from Kipling's stories, so do their anti-imperialist counterparts: *Irish* rebels. However, rebellion itself does not totally disappear, quite the contrary, for the question of colonial rebellion looms large in his Boer War writing. It is interesting to note that, unlike in his earlier pieces, where Kipling acknowledged the nationality or ethnicity of rebellion (often as Irish), the colonial rebels of the Boer War seem to be collectively forming a new 'breed' – a 'lesser [breed] without the Law'[81] if you like – corrupted and degenerated, full of hatred and often easily bribed. The contest between the imperialist and anti-nationalist models of transcolonial connections therefore does not exist in Kipling's world, because the Irish, if they decide to support the Boers, can no longer be called 'Irish'.

'The [Cape] Colony's world is a large and growing one,' Kipling writes in his political prose 'The Sin of Witchcraft' (1900), 'the circle of her acquaintances today runs from Edmonton to Invercargill, from Perth to Halifax.' The war has brought 'mud-coloured' men from other colonies, who do not speak the language of the book, but are better suited to deal with South Africa's peculiarities, for they have also known 'the life that is lived out between a horse and a verandah'. There, Kipling witnesses new transcolonial connections being formed, *not* via England as the imperial centre:

> Move a mixed colonial contingent fifty miles here across country, and Winnipeg, Quebec, Canterbury, Wellington, and Brisbane are also moved. Over and above that, they will write to their papers; these men's letters will be read and re-read at cross-road stores, in railroad round-houses, in way-side dossers' camps, at up-country race-meetings, little Masonic lodges, along the wharves of big exporting houses, and in the clubs of all the White Man's world.[82]

Kipling represents the Empire in the light of this 'White Man's world', whose opinion of the Cape Colony – and her 'sin of witchcraft' – 'matters a great deal – not today, but the day after tomorrow'. The phrase 'the sin of witchcraft' signifies rebellion (1 Samuel, 15:23), whereby Kipling means the treachery of colonial rebels in the Cape Colony who 'preach sedition under guise of abject loyalty'. These rebels are 'registered voters' but enemies within, 'who had been firing at you as you blundered desperately across barbed-wire fences'. The 'strange men from the ends of the earth', who came all the way to fight for the Empire, would regard them with contempt, and their verdict is 'to turn up double-leaded in a journal of 80,000 circulation on the other side of the world'. In reality, these so-called 'rebels' mainly consisted of the Boers in the Cape Colony, who assisted the Transvaal republics because of familial and cultural ties. However, Kipling in this essay does not specify the rebels as Dutch, preferring to call them 'disloyalists', who believe that it no longer pays to be loyal. In this way, Kipling downplays the possibility of the Cape rebellion as an ethnic and nationalist struggle. They are 'veritable rebels, neither Free Staters nor Transvaalers', who signal to the enemies to shoot the British, while legally protected by the Empire.[83]

'The Sin of Witchcraft' was first published in *The Times* on 15 March 1900, in the midst of the heated public discussions as to the nature of the Irish loyalty, following the Queen's new order to her Irish soldiers to wear shamrocks on St Patrick's Day and shortly before her visit to Ireland in April. Considering the contemporaneity of the Cape Rebellion and the Irish nationalists' vocal support for the Boers, and also the fact that Kipling had the year before used the exact phrase 'the sin of witchcraft' to describe the song 'The Wearing of the Green', and thereby Irish nationalism, in *Stalky & Co.* (see p. 56), his *not* mentioning the 'Irish' Rebellion looks like a denial, as if the analogies with the Irish situation might further spread fire in the Cape Colony. Instead, an American 'rebel' figures in 'The Captive' (1902); this story can *almost* be seen as the representation of divided loyalties in the

Boer War, except that it is Americans, not Irishmen or Boers, who are shown to fight on both sides of the front line. Laughton O. Zigler is an American inventor from Ohio who came to South Africa to try his powerful weapons such as 'the Laughton-Zigler automatic two-inch field gun' and 'Laughtite, the new explosive'.[84] He joins the Boers, because '[he] wasn't brought up to love the British for one thing', and also because he wishes to get 'an unbiassed report' on his weapons from British officers, whom he finds worthy enemies.[85] Eventually, Zigler and his Dutch commandant are taken captive by the British, and the story is retrospectively narrated by Zigler, who is now a prisoner of war. All in all, Kipling presents Zigler as a likeable character, a lover of adventure and greatly admiring the British Army.[86] Still, whatever the reasons, Zigler's assistance of the Boers is depicted as a despicable sin, and Kipling gets one of his own countrymen to shame Zigler; an American soldier from Kentucky, who fights for the British, talks to Zigler the captive thus:

> I'm not knowing any man that fights for a Tammany Dutchman. But I presoom you've been well paid, you dam gun-runnin' Yank . . . what *you've done* . . . is to go back on the White Man in six places at once – two hemispheres and four continents – America, England, Canada, Australia, New Zealand, and South Africa.[87]

Zigler takes the insult, which the American finishes off by throwing him half a crown, to heart; he breaks down and cries. It cuts Zigler even harder, because the American soldier immediately labels him as a '[d]amned southern rebel' who willingly 'fight[s] for niggers' for money.

Zigler represents the United States, whose growing power as a nation was becoming a threat to the British Empire ('Laughtite's immense; so's the Zigler automatic'[88]): they could be a strong ally of the Empire or its most formidable enemy.[89] The presence of Zigler's American guns and explosives makes an interesting contrast with the absence of the armed Irish from Kipling's stories, despite the fact that Irish gallantry was a favourite theme in Boer War propaganda. Kipling's representation of a rebel as American and with a very *un*Celtic name can be interpreted as a gesture of repressing 'Irish' rebellion, which is metonymically replaced with that of America, a country in which many of the emigrated Irish turned into Irish nationalists. Zigler is, as it were, Kipling's substitute 'Irishman', representing the rebellious yet manageable violence which the Empire easily puts under control. In fact, Zigler's powerful weapons fail to kill any of the British soldiers (though they 'bagged five Kaffirs'[90]) and Zigler decides to offer them to the British side. The 'real' armed Irishmen, however, are invisible, though no doubt present, in Kipling's Boer War stories, essentialized, denationalized, made into an unnamed part of the colonial rebels who attack from the comfort of the Imperial Home and 'befoul the Colony'.[91]

We therefore see a pattern emerging: the White Man's transcolonial network is constantly at war with the international anti-imperial conspiracy, with 'the colonial rebels' to be found in the nexus of the two networks. These are doubly hybrid agents, deceptively occupying the space of loyal Empire-builders, undermining the very foundation of imperialism. Kipling strongly objected to granting an amnesty to colonial rebels towards the end of the war, describing their actions as 'the severest blow to the colonies' trust in England (I speak here of Australia, Canada, &c.)'.[92] In another political treatise, 'The Science of Rebellion' (1901), Kipling turns the news of the outbreak of plague in Cape Town into a political 'allegory', likening the colonial rebels to the rats fast spreading 'the Plague' – 'one rat infecting the other' – and the only way to subdue 'the Plague' is to 'disenfranchise' the rat.[93] In this piece, 'the Plague', which is a disease called colonial rebellion, is seen to spread biologically, ideologically and analogically to contaminate the bodies of imperial subjects all over the world. Kipling not only hints that the rebels are 'a very low type of Dutch', mixed with 'native blood',[94] but according to him they conspire with 'the Opposition', that is, the Liberal Party, which has been working 'peacefully and honourably towards the disintegration of [the] Empire',[95] especially in its persistent effort to realise Irish Home Rule.

Importantly, a potential Dutch rising in South Africa supported by the Cape rebels is described in 'The Science of Rebellion' as the return of the Indian Mutiny,[96] and what is more, Kipling evokes one piece of the Great Game being fought in India to illustrate his point. Cape Town, 'the headquarters of the enemy's right wing' yet not under 'martial law', is likened to Waziristan, a part of the independent tribal territory created outside British India in 1893 as a buffer zone to protect India from the Russian threat.[97] Its two major tribes, Mashuds and Waziris, periodically raided into British territory, led by the legendary Mullah Powindah, waging jihad against British India. Kipling depicts a scenario in which these insubordinate tribesmen are conspiring with subjects of the Raj:

> If you can imagine a Mashud Waziri rising in full swing with the heads of *jirgas* members of the Peshawur Club; the Mullah Powindah himself playing whist with the Commissioner of Peshawur, and all the priests who have preached the *Jehad* for the past sixty Sundays, calling on the wives of the Civil Service men, you will have some faint idea of the present situation.[98]

Waziristan makes its presence felt in *Kim*, published in the same year as 'The Science of Rebellion', as the tribal territory beyond the frontier – 'the Back of Beyond' – that Mahbub Ali's 'caravans penetrated far and far into' to collect information, being 'ambushed and shot at twice on the way down';[99] Ali dared not stop 'at the insalubrious city of Peshawur',[100] the native city with a British military station which guarded the eastern exit of the Khyber

Pass, because he imagines the city to be swarming with spies and rebels, including 'a Hindu banker'[101] who is financing the Conspiracy of Mullah Powindah, who was described as the 'pestilential priest' by Lord Kitchener, the Commander-in-Chief in India after the Boer War.[102] *Kim*'s India is directly connected to South Africa by the theme of 'colonial rebellion', which spreads through one native body after another, and the imperial 'game' continues to combat it at every juncture.

Colonial rebellions are everywhere in Kipling's Boer War stories – 'They are present, omnipresent' – maintaining 'intimate relations with all sides, with the front, and the far more important "back front" which begins at Pretoria'.[103] Nevertheless, in this South African landscape, *Irish* rebels are markedly absent, and their physical absence strikes us as uncanny, especially because some of Kipling's Boer War stories have eerie echoes of 'Namgay Doola' (1891), in which a rebel in India is successfully named and tamed as Irish. In 'The Captive', the American soldier who insults Zigler as a 'damned southern rebel' declares, 'I know this breed', repeating the final scene of 'Namgay Doola' in which the narrator completes his interrogation of the rebel's identity by boasting 'I know that breed.'[104] The 'half-a-crown' thrown at Zigler also reminds us of 'Namgay Doola', in which the narrator presents the rebel's son with a rupee as a reward for stealing his father's gun. Kipling's colonial rebels would instinctively respond to the sight of money, even if it meant betraying their closest kin. Another story written at the time of the Boer War and echoing 'Namgay Doola' is *Kim*, in which the hero is similarly identified as Irish through the names and items belonging to his father.[105] The biggest difference between the two stories is that Namgay Doola is identified as a rebel *and* as Irish, while Kim is Irish and categorically *not* a rebel. For instance, Kim is tested in a similar way to Namgay Doola's son, when Creighton describes to him an imaginary situation in which he is asked to obtain information in a hostile region. In response to Kim's suggestion that he could nevertheless get the job done, Creighton asks how, holding up a rupee and saying to Kim, 'Tell now.' 'Kim's hand half reached towards it, and dropped' – he refuses to take the money, saying that he does 'not know why the question is asked'.[106] Kim thus proves that he cares for the rules of the Game far more than for the money offered. Earlier in the novel, Kim picks up a rupee which Creighton throws as a reward for the information, entrusted to him by Mahbub Ali, concerning 'the pedigree of the white stallion': 'Swiftly Kim took up the money; but for all his training, he was *Irish* enough by birth to reckon silver the least part of any game'.[107] Here Irishness is described as the quality of becoming excited by the Game, rather than being gratified with monetary reward. To interfere with the Game has ceased to be an *Irish* act, and in this way Kipling successfully represents the Irish as exclusively on the side of the Game, not on the enemy's side.

In the scene in which Kim refuses to take a rupee from Creighton, the latter says to Kim, 'There is a good spirit in thee. Do not let it be blunted at St Xavier's. There are many boys there who despise the black men.' Kim in reply points out the hybrid origin of these 'boys who despise the black men', whom Kim thinks to be half-castes whose 'mothers were bazar-women':[108] he will not be influenced by them because they are a breed apart. Kim's 'non-rebel' identity is ensured by his being allegedly pure-blooded – Irishness here means being 'a Sahib and the son of a Sahib'[109] – in marked contrast to Namgay Doola the rebel, the son of an Irishman and a hill-woman. Kim vehemently denies any blood relationship with the Indian woman who raised him[110] and does not hide his contempt for the Eurasian boys who pretend to be pure white and mistreat the natives.[111] The narrator also takes pains to mention that Kim's mother is, like his father, Irish,[112] and his pedigree as a white man is finally guaranteed by his successful rejection of the Woman of Shamlegh who seduces him.

The Eurasian theme and that of the perplexing identity of a rebel are repeated again in 'The Comprehension of Private Copper', the last of Kipling's Boer War stories. An English soldier, Alf Copper, while scouting across the Colesberg kopjes, is captured by a young man, who, with his gun pointing toward Copper, tells how he has come to hate the English: his father moved to the Transvaal and bought land, believing the words of the British government that 'so long as the sun rose and the rivers ran in their courses the Transvaal would belong to England';[113] however, the independence of the Republic was restored by Gladstone in 1881, after the crushing defeat of the British at Majuba, and his father lost 'everything down to his self-respect',[114] since there were, the captor claims, no provisions made to protect the Uitlanders. The man is determined to torture Copper after he finishes telling the latter all his grievances against the English, but Copper turns the tables and succeeds in taking the man prisoner. Strangely, while Copper is listening to his captor, memories of India, especially those concerning the Eurasians, keep coming back to him, because the man's accent, though apparently the same 'offensive' upper-class English one which he had heard 'the young squire of Wilmington'[115] use, nevertheless reminds him of 'pukka bazar chee-chee'[116] which he had heard Eurasians speak while serving in India two years before. Copper suspects the man to be a Eurasian – he looks like one, being 'dark-skinned, dark-haired and dark-eyed'[117] – and when Copper captures him in turn, the first thing he does is check the fingernails, for Eurasians are said to have blackened nails. It turns out that the man's nails are as clean as Copper's, from which evidence he concludes that the man is definitely not a half-caste.[118] Copper then makes the man pronounce the word 'Pore Tommy' several times – just as Namgay Doola is asked to repeat his father's name 'Timlay Doola' – and confirms that the man does speak in a chee-chee accent. Kipling, however, does not give any reasonable explanation of why the man speaks a 'pukka bazar chee-chee' in the story. Nor is the renegade identified as Irish, and Copper does not even try to find out his name. The reader is left in a certain state of uneasiness, even after order is restored by Copper's capture of the renegade. However, Private Copper is happy just to confirm that the renegade assumes a Eurasian accent and appearance, having degenerated into an inferior race.[119]

Ireland has traditionally and stereotypically been associated with violence, and, as such, paradoxically contributed to the representation of the Empire: as long as one could identify violence with the Irish, both could be seen as still manageable and even part of the system. The occasional identification of insurgent factors as Irish, and the elimination or domestication of them, could help consolidate the unity of the Empire. However, as we have seen, by the time of the Boer War the rebel could no longer be named as Irish. An unidentified renegade is still out in the field, ready to point his gun at any English soldier, which makes the 'comprehension' (or control) of the British Empire in the colonies almost impossible. As more Irish left their own country and spread all over the world, it became more and more difficult to pin down the source of violence – the Irish. Moreover, Irish violence was consciously becoming more elusive and widespread in order to be more effective; as Patrick Ford, in his Irish-American newspaper, *The Irish World*, already urges on 4 December 1875: 'The Irish cause requires skirmishers . . . a little band of heroes who will initiate and keep up without intermission a guerrilla warfare – men who will fly over land and sea like invisible beings – now striking the enemy in Ireland, now in India, now in England itself, as occasion may present.'[120] The Queen's order that all ranks in her Majesty's Irish regiments shall wear shamrocks on St Patrick's Day can be interpreted as an attempt to make all the Irish inside the Empire visible and bring them back under control. The veldt, as well as all the British colonies, were filled with shamrocks, indicating the source of potential violence against the Queen. The trouble was that, by the time of the Boer War, the association of the Irish with violence – they were either soldiers or terrorists – could no longer completely identify the forces which were working against the solidarity of the British Empire. Thus, Kipling's Irish characters do not any longer figure as soldiers, nor can the renegade who points his gun at Private Copper be identified as Irish. Both the violence and the Irish become increasingly widespread and elude the grasp of the Empire; they had completely submerged themselves into the land of the colonies to which they had spread, hidden and undetected within the system of the Empire, ready to overthrow it.

Chapter Five

Kim in South Africa

1

'Have I not said an hundred times that the South is a good land?'[1]

In Chapter 2, I argued that the force of the foreign ground, the potential for the colonizer to intermingle with the native and over time to become physically assimilated by the place, was felt to be threatening to English rule in the colonies, because it would corrupt 'Englishness' and the purity of the race, and thus had to be resisted: the colonizer may enjoy whatever riches the colonies offer him, but has to leave the place for Home before being assimilated. However, with the discovery of gold and diamonds in South Africa, the English now allowed themselves to be fully seduced by the force of this foreign ground, only to find that they were forbidden to have full access to it. The place had already been populated by another white race, namely, the Boers, who labelled the British as 'Uitlander', the outsider to the land. Unlike the British colonizers, who sought to maintain their Englishness out in their colonies, the Boers were represented as having become, after their two hundred years of South African wandering, quite successfully assimilated by the land. They were often referred to as 'the sons of the soil', who, according to Arthur Conan Doyle in his *The Great Boer War* (1900), trained themselves 'in constant warfare against savage men and ferocious beasts, in circumstances under which no weakling could survive'.[2] Paula M. Krebs points out that Olive Schreiner also understood the successful assimilation of the Boers in South Africa in terms of social Darwinism.[3] The ability of the Boers to adapt to a new environment was seen as an example of the 'survival of the fittest'. For instance, Schreiner remarks on the South African Boer's 'astonishing gift for forming new societies, and as it were, instinctively creating for himself a new social structure, under whatever conditions he may find himself',[4] which draws a striking contrast with the notorious inflexibility of the English colonizer, which I have already discussed.

It is true that the Boer War officially ended with victory for the British Empire. However, this war also marked the defeat of British imperialism at a very fundamental level. If the British Empire, as Conan Doyle puts it, obtained her colonies by 'the right of conquest and the right of purchase',[5] these rights, which the Empire had fully enjoyed throughout the nineteenth century, were now challenged by the assertion of other peoples' right to the land. The tie that the Boers had created with the country was the most formidable enemy which the British had to fight against (the right of the native 'black' Africans was, though, never seriously taken into account, either by the Boers or by the British). Thus it is no wonder that neither the relief of the besieged principal towns like Ladysmith, Mafeking and Kimberley nor the seizure of Bloemfontein, Johannesburg and Pretoria could completely terminate the war. Instead, it soon developed into bitter guerrilla warfare. The inhabitants of the veldt demonstrated their rootedness to the place by turning themselves into part of the supportive background through which the guerrillas freely moved: non-combatants such as housewives, children and elderly men participated in the war by providing guerrillas with supplies, information and hiding-places.[6] Against this resistance from the land and its people, the British ruthlessly carried out their 'land-clearance' policy. This meant sweeping the land bare of everything which could be a source of supply to the enemy, thereby eradicating whatever ties the Boers had built up with the ground. The British burned and blew up farmhouses, slaughtered livestock, and herded women and children into poorly run 'concentration camps', where many suffered from undernourishment and illness, which made them easy victims of epidemics.

The Boer War seemed to show that the right of the inhabitants had become a more powerful claim to the land than the right of conquest by the end of the nineteenth century. It was not until the Boers were forcefully uprooted from their land that the Empire could gain real control over it. After the Boer War, the colonial government promoted the large-scale settlement of British colonists in South Africa, in order to solve the British/Boer racial problem, which was expected to linger long after the war. Alfred Milner, the High Commissioner of South Africa, writes in a memorandum, 'I attach the greatest importance of all to the increase of the British population. British and Dutch have to live here on equal terms. If, ten years hence, there are three men of British race to two of Dutch, the country will be safe and prosperous.'[7] In fact, *large-scale* settlement was the only hope for maintaining the British settler as 'British' against the corruptive force of the foreign ground: Milner goes on to write, 'A mere sprinkling is no use. They only get absorbed, and become more Dutch than their neighbours.'[8] The greater importance placed on settlement than on mere conquest is also shown by the fact that Milner considers farmers, rather than 'tommies', to be the ideal settlers: the 'common interest of the British and Dutch in agriculture will go a great way to break down the barriers of separation existing at present between the two races, and which will always exist as long as one race absorbs one set of employments and the other a different set'.[9] The colonizer now had to learn to be a settler. Besides, the Land Scheme was presented as an 'agricultural' enterprise: the settlement was to 'plant' men on 'land of suitable quality' chosen by the colonial government.[10] The imperial government's capacity to disseminate British seeds in a well-scorched land and make them grow alongside the hostile Boer breed was seriously tested.

Kipling's work written at the time of the Boer War responds to the transformation which the body of the English 'colonizer' had to go through as he turned himself into a settler. The motif of racial degeneration is, as we have seen, quite conspicuous in his Boer War stories. For example, in 'A Burgher of the Free State' (1900), Allen, an Uitlander, tries to insult a Boer girl by mentioning the 'purplish moons' which are supposed to appear at the base of the fingernails when 'tainted with native blood',[11] and in 'The Comprehension of Private Copper' (1902), Copper actually checks the fingernails of the 'renegade' to see if he is half-caste. As Philip Holden puts it, the Boers are shown as having become degenerate 'to the point at which they are no longer white';[12] in 'A Sahibs' War' (1901), the Boer family 'who provides cover for the ambush exhibits the features of Nordau's degenerate types'.[13] Interestingly, whereas the degenerate bodies of the non-English are accentuated in Kipling's Boer War stories, the bodies of the Englishmen are, as Holden points out, surprisingly invisible,[14] which Holden interprets as a manifestation of the fear of racial degeneration: Kurban Sahib is talked about, and Private Copper is talked to, but their bodies remain curiously absent from the stories, as if to mask the effect of 'degeneration' or 'hybridization' visible on their bodies as a natural result of their being exposed to the foreign ground. Holden notes that Kipling's hope for the regeneration of imperial manliness 'lies in the new children of Empire, Canadians and Australians'.[15] Racial revitalization takes place in the settler colonies only after Englishness loses itself in the foreign land, far away from Home.

In fact, in his poem 'The Settler' (1903), the body of the Englishman, which had to disappear from view during the war, comes back as that of a farmer. Kipling was also enthusiastic about Milner's policy of encouraging British settlement. In a letter to Lady Edward Cecil, he writes: '[E]ach English county should interest itself in picking out a few of the best class of settlers on the land – yeomen farmers and the like . . . It might be that in time each county might take an interest in its settlers, and their lives in the Colony.'[16] The English settlement is shown to be not degeneration, but regeneration through the act of turning the furrows of the conquered land:

> Here, where my fresh-turned furrows run,
>   And the deep soil glistens red,
> I will repair the wrong that was done
>   To the living and the dead.

Here, where the senseless bullet fell,
And the barren shrapnel burst,
I will plant a tree, I will dig a well,
Against the heat and the thirst.[17]

Here the English settler's involvement with the South African soil is equated with the healing of the split between the land and the people, for which too much blood was shed during the war: the split between the Uitlanders and the land, and then the split between the Boers and the land which the British land-clearance policy created. Only through this interaction with the South African soil can the English reach out to the Boers:

Here, in a large and a sunlit land
Where no wrong bites to the bone,
I will lay my hand in my neighbour's hand,
And together we will atone
For the set folly and the red breach
And the black waste of it all,
Giving and taking counsel each
Over the cattle-kraal.[18]

We can see Kipling conduct a great alchemical work in this second paragraph: the 'I' of the English, which had carefully guarded itself from any hybridization, allows itself to dissolve in the land, in order to be regenerated into the 'we' of South Africa. Even the English 'cattle' are now inside the South African *kraal* (a pen for cattle), fully accepted in the South African land. The rest of the poem consistently uses 'we', and the pronoun 'I' does not return, except when 'old fights' are looked back on, where 'blood on his head of my kin / Or blood on my head of his kin'[19] was shed.

A fusion between the English settler and the 'native' Boer was thought to be the best solution, and moral and racial degeneration was linked only to 'the presence of black men and women'.[20] Indeed, the force of the foreign ground which Kipling's colonizer had to fight against provided in South Africa the only hope of uniting the two races into 'one people under one British flag'; Joseph Chamberlain, in the speech which he made in Cape Town on the eve of sailing for England, said, 'I leave this shore more convinced than ever that the forces – the natural forces which are drawing you together – are more potent than those evil influences which would tend to separate you.'[21] The 'evil influences', he explained, included a 'sentiment which . . . unfortunately in the past, has maintained a distinction of race, has cherished the animosities of the past, has nurtured suspicions which had so baneful a result'.[22] In another speech in South Africa, he even 'reminded' the citizens that the Empire had already seen many successful examples of racial amalgamation, such as that between Scotland and England within the Union.[23] Also, Kipling's true Empire-builders are also not the English but the Uitlanders and people from the settler colonies such as New Zealand and Australia, that is, those who have allowed themselves to become fused with the foreign land. When he focuses on 'England' or 'Englishness', it is rather to admonish England for not living up to the expectation of what it should be. His poem 'The Return', written shortly after the Boer War, refrains the following stanza:

> If England was what England seems,
> An' not the England of our dreams,
> But only putty, brass, an' paint,
> 'Ow quick we'd drop 'er! But she ain't![24]

The very sound of 'England' is repeated, but it somehow reveals itself as a split or hollow sign – its signifier, 'what England seems', does not reflect nor even have what is supposed to be its essence, 'the England of our dreams'.

In fact, Kipling represents an Englishness which stubbornly resists being transformed as unfit for imperial service: it is shown to be an empty form whose inflexibility hinders other more important signs from freely circulating. In 'The Outsider' (1900), Walter Setton, a pure-bred Englishman from 'the Home Counties', is an embodiment of this superficial and inflexible 'England'. His superficiality is shown by his concern for looking like 'an officer and a gentleman', that is to say, wearing the uniforms which his position demands (such as 'tunics, richly laced lined silk £6 14s. 6d.'[25]), and his contempt for the 'unbuttoned' soldiers. In fact, he reminds us of another superficial English officer, Lieutenant Golightly in *Plain Tales from the Hills*, whose only concern also is looking like 'an Officer and a Gentleman'.[26] Unlike Golightly, who instantly loses his appearance when he leaves the hill station and starts behaving like a native, Setton's failure to be a true Englishman comes from his inability to forget his appearance and dignity even in a time of emergency. His excessive adherence to English form extends to his way of thinking. He was educated to despise 'the "outsider" – the man beyond his circle', for '[i]f you got mixed up with an outsider, you ended by being "compromised"'.[27] Setton intervenes when his men are about to finish repairing a bridge which was broken by the Boers, saying that they need to get the orders first. In contrast, Private Thrupp, an Uitlander who has lived on the Rand for ten years and can let 'his shirt [be] torn to the waist in a scuffle to get water for a sick man',[28] is shown to be a true colonizer. Another bridge fails to function because of English red tape in 'Folly Bridge' (1900): McManus, 'head of the Corporate Equatorial Bank of South Africa',[29] who is summoned by Lord Roberts and Alfred Milner to urgently disentangle some financial difficulties in the war, is detained at the foot of the bridge for the purely bureaucratic reason that his pass has not been countersigned, despite the fact that he has a 'pass calling on all officers, civil and military, to assist and expedite R. L. McManus, Esq., by every means in their power'.[30] McManus walks away from the matter, and the colonial office loses potential support from this key figure.[31]

Significantly, the banker in 'Folly Bridge' is given the Celtic name of McManus. This name not only emphasizes the idiocy of 'English' bureaucracy, but also shows that Kipling often represents his Celtic characters as more flexible and competent colonizers, or, to be more precise, as settlers. To give another example, Allen, the 'Burgher of the Free State', who settled and married into a Boer family, is a Scot from Edinburgh, who helps to print Lord Roberts's proclamation for circulation, following the British occupation of Bloemfontein.[32] In fact, 'Folly Bridge', in which the obstruction of a Celtic character's voyage leads to an imperial blunder, makes a good contrast with *Kim*, completed around the same period, where the unhindered passage of an Irish boy as a spy saves India from Russian invasion. The Empire had to be dependent on the Celtic ability to circulate, settle down and transform themselves under various circumstances, while 'England', on the other hand, loomed as an obstacle to the smooth circulation of the Celtic signs and became less and less qualified to function as the nexus of the imperial connections.

2

Paula Krebs, in her book on public discourse and the Boer War, draws attention to the fact that Kipling, who 'created such memorable characters as Mahbub Ali', failed to produce any unforgettable African characters or make literature out of South Africa.[33] 'Kipling did not imaginatively reformulate his sense of the land and people of South Africa in his Boer War stories', she argues, not only because his primary concern was 'empire',[34] but also because he had never had the deep understanding of South Africa which he had of India. The ongoing political, economic and armed conflict made it difficult for him to project the illusion of smoothly operating imperial power onto the region, so that, according to Krebs, 'Kipling did not have the luxury of creating a *Kim* out of South Africa',[35] a remark with which I am inclined to disagree. Although Krebs correctly points out Kipling's failure to create a successful representation of Empire through South Africa, she takes it too much for granted that *Kim* is an 'Indian' novel. Instead, I argue that *Kim*, completed in South Africa during the Boer War, is partially a South African story, only taking the form of 'a long leisurely Asiatic yarn'.[36] *Kim*'s India, made hospitable and habitable, is another 'South Africa', from where, Kipling hoped, a new breed of English – a White Man who 'knows the land and the customs of the land'[37] – would spring. The novel can be read as Kipling's strong affirmation of the settlers' Empire, featuring Kim, born and bred in India and capable of making friends with any of the native population, as an ideal colonist. The boy's Irishness, when severed from the political contexts of Irish nationalism, comes to signify the very condition of a settler, namely, a White Man who is *at once* the colonizer and the colonized in the colonial land. The settlers, just like the Irish under the Union, were not only asked to carry the imperial burden, but also to varying degrees suffered from the whole mechanism of colonization: they were acclimatized, politically and geographically marginalized, and were subjected to an agonizing search for identity in the foreign land, which had primarily belonged to others. Kim's hybridity as white and native, the colonizer and the colonized, together with the novel's engagement with the themes of 'cultural difference and syncretism' and so forth, have contributed to *Kim* being recently characterized as the one narrative of Kipling's which 'looks forward to postcolonial narrative'.[38] Rightly so, and *Kim*'s 'postcolonial' relevance has its roots in the large-scale emigration from the British isles to places scattered across the globe, the scramble for Africa, and the Uitlanders' desperate struggle to settle alongside the Boers. Seen in this context, the characterization of India as 'timeless' in the novel is by no means another oriental stereotype, but the ideal of a colony which the British wished to find in order to successfully weave themselves in as settlers in this place cleared of past history and protesting 'natives'.

Kim's marked adolescence is an expression of Kipling's vision that the next generation of Empire-builders will be settlers – the new children of Empire – embodying the youthfulness which Kipling amply witnessed in Canadians and Australians during the Boer War. Don Randall characterizes Kipling's adolescent protagonists (for example, Mowgli, Stalky, Kim) as a site of cultural hybridity, in which Kipling represents 'a liminal subjectivity situated on the in-betweens of cultures and cultural identities involved in a process of mutual transformation',[39] which can be read as a description of how Kipling might wish to see colonists in their various chosen lands. While Randall defines *Kim* as the only narrative in which Kipling gives full expression to the complexities of cultural hybridity,[40] the subtle differences between Kim and his predecessors should also be read as the Imperial Boy's transformation from the colonizer to the colonist towards the turn of the century. Significantly, Kim is virtually the only Imperial Boy whom Kipling keeps in a state of suspended adolescence. Mowgli as an adult is shown to work for the Department of Woods and Forests in 'In the Rukh' (1893), the first of the Mowgli stories to be published, and prior to *The Jungle Book* (1894).[41] Arthur Lionel Corkran, aka 'Stalky', grows up to become a British soldier in India – 'Koran Sahib' – in 'Slaves of the Lamp, II' (1897), the second story of *Stalky & Co.* to be published. Versed in native languages and customs, also beloved by both Sikh and Pathan soldiers, Stalky there appears very much as a Kim-like figure, except that he is a fully-grown adult, no longer a schoolboy.[42] Even 'Wee Willie Winkie', a six-year-old Anglo-Indian boy and 'the 'future Colonel of the 195th', blossoms 'into his manhood' after rescuing a young Englishwoman from native bandits in Kipling's world.[43]

'In the Rukh' and 'Slaves of the Lamp, II' were published prior to most of their protagonists' childhood episodes, indicating that the 'hybrid' play of childhood was to be understood as preparation for their future work in the service of British imperialism. By transforming these adolescent heroes into adult colonizers, Kipling draws and highlights a border which can be crossed and transgressed, *but only from the one side*, from the side of the adult colonizer. Mowgli leaves the Jungle and Stalky graduates from the College, leaving their primitive selves and savage childhoods on the other side of the border. They can, however, revisit this space and claim comradeship there whenever they wish, while what is left behind – animals, natives, children, etc. – cannot, and are not allowed to, cross the border. In *The Jungle Books* and *Stalky & Co.*, the two worlds of childhood and adulthood, apprenticeship and mastery, natives and sahibs, which have boundaries as clearly drawn as that between beast and man, overlap without merging into each other. Kipling's Imperial Boy is a creature of the two worlds, an amphibian (Mowgli means 'frog' according to Mother Wolf, who names him[44]), which adds to the sense of magic and privilege in his imperial childhood. It is this sense of 'two-worldliness' which Mowgli and Stalky enjoy that Kipling firmly denies Kim. Of course, we know of Kim's future career as a spy in the Indian Secret Service, but Kipling does not depict Kim in that role – he is notably kept on the adolescent side of the border. This puzzled some contemporary readers, who expected to see Kim in the next stage of adulthood. '"Kim" is a work that requires a sequel', wrote G. F. Monkshood and George Gamble in 1902. '[Kim] should be allowed by his author to stand by the side of Strickland. He is a child of romance; one would wish to see him shown as a man of mastery.'[45] A reviewer in *The Times* also writes:

> May we hope that another volume may speedily show us how he fares in the years that follow? 'I must have him with me beyond Balkh in six months,' says Mahbub. Take him there, O scarlet-bearded horse-dealer; and let the chronicler go with you, invisible, but jotting down on those wonderful tablets of his the feats of the northern horsemen and the secrets of the Confederate Kings! Then will Creighton Sahib and Lurgan Sahib gain the greater honour, and there will be joy in the hearts of the watchers of the Game![46]

The novel was felt to be somewhat incomplete, because Kim is not shown in his role as an adult colonizer, while Kipling himself writes elsewhere: 'My own idea is that in the fullness of time we may learn how Kim went on with his somewhat unusual career.'[47]

Kim signals the creation of an adolescent hero as a new type of the white imperial subject, a white 'hybrid' on the same side as the native inhabitants. The theme of remaining on the adolescent side of the border is underlined by the parallel search of the lama, who also decides to stay in this world, by the side of his *chela*, even when the path of enlightenment becomes clear to him. The novel therefore works within a different colonial framework than that of *The Jungle Books* and *Stalky & Co.* The colonial hybridity manifested in Mowgli and Stalky is by no means the 'liminal subjectivity . . . involved in a process of mutual transformation' of Kim. Instead, their transformation into 'racial' others creates and reinforces the border between different races. If Kim is a native *and* a sahib at the same time, in the same way is Mowgli a wolf as well as being a Man, and is chosen as the 'Master of the Jungle', but Mowgli's being Man eventually pushes him to the side of manhood and adulthood, drawing the border which his friends in the Jungle cannot transgress.[48] In *Stalky & Co.*, Stalky's adventure as 'a Sikh'[49] echoes his earlier performance as the Slave of the Lamp in a school production of the pantomime *Aladdin*.[50] The attributes of the other are exotic costumes which Stalky can freely change into.

Kipling, when in India, understood natives as 'men with a language of their own', whose vocabularies and codes the colonizer had to learn to understand, 'quote' and master: 'Then they'll believe in you and do things for you.'[51] This is, as it were, *hybridity by quotation*, by which the colonizer incorporates the others' voices, made to serve within his context, while the safety of the border is protected by inviolable quotation marks. This is closely related to a wider project called Orientalism, the collecting and cataloguing of natives' voices into a textual archive.[52] To know a race was to verify quotations, correctly to identify the origin of each race, and to restore a clear border between quotations and the main text. This attitude is no doubt racist and essentialist, but it should also be noted that this might have ironically reserved a space – as a text – for the colonized, which the colonizer as an archivist could quote and appropriate but nevertheless could not assimilate, having instead to leave it in its place. In contrast, Kim as the colonist signals a new type of the imperial subject, who will *become* the other – Mussalman, Hindu, Jain or Buddhist, anybody he wishes, and partially remains so. As Mark Kinkead-Weekes aptly puts it, Kim, chameleon-like, changes not merely his clothes but 'his voices and mannerisms, his whole identity', longing 'not merely to see and to know from the outside' but 'to get into the skin of many "others"'[53] – under their brown skins while losing his own. He is a colonial (or 'capitalist' even) 'desiring machine', demolishing a 'strategically' essentialist site from which the colonized might have spoken.[54] There is no outside, since 'Little Friend of all the World' is himself an expanding and assimilating border.

Kim is a settler who, to quote Mahmood Mamdani, is 'by definition, rootless, footloose, not tied to any specific territory, always trekking'[55] – Kim is always on the move. Moreover, he is a *white* settler, carrying in his amulet case certificates of privilege as his parental heritage.[56] Importantly, Kipling names this new imperial subject as 'Irish', stereotypically represented as childish, fiendish, friendly and adventurous, no longer hampered by the traditional role of the English colonizer. It is Kim's power as a settler that turns a vile colonial ground, even India which is characteristically a 'Bad Lands' in his author's earlier writing, into 'a good land', his new home. Kim will be a 'chain-man', who not only knows the land thoroughly, but also is the one who functions as a part of the *chain* of the White Man's networks. In South Africa, we see Kipling gladly talk of this chain:

> So I sat joyously on the rear platform while Number Three ran the links of empire through my hands. English of the Midlands, Cockney, Scotch, Irish, Welsh, African-born, Queenslander . . . Victorian, and Canadian, one after another, we picked them up and dropped them with a flying hand. There was nothing wrong with that *chain*, and by the same token, it seemed to have got hold of something at last, for a truckload of Boer prisoners slid by in charge of a few disreputable bearded cornets.[57]

The chain is not simply for measuring and surveying; it connects, takes captives, and helps swiftly to pass on information in the manner of the telegraph and trains. *There is nothing wrong with the chain* – says Kipling, even if we might feel occasionally enslaved by the very chain which makes us part of this privileged imperial network.

3

Lispeth, a hill-girl who is raised by a mission but later goes back to her own people with a total distrust of the English in her heart, is given an important place in Kipling's Indian world, appearing, as has been pointed out, in 'the first story in Kipling's first book about India' (*Plain Tales from the Hills*) and reappearing in 'the last story about India that he intended ever to write',[58] *Kim*. With the dichotomy between the English figure and the Indian ground in mind, 'Lispeth' (1886) seems an appropriate story with which to begin his first collection about India: it tells how the Indians who had been nothing but part of the landscape suddenly emerged as figures to the colonizer's eyes. Lispeth's parents come to the Mission because they wish to be protected from the violence of nature, which holds their lives at its mercy: 'One year their maize failed, and two bears spent the night in their only opium poppy-field just above the Sutlej Valley on the Kotgarth side; so, next season, they turned Christian, and brought their baby to the Mission to be baptized.'[59] Ironically, her parents cannot escape from the harsh Indian living conditions regardless of their conversion, for they soon die of cholera, leaving Lispeth alone with the Mission. Lispeth grows into a beautiful lady just like 'Diana of the Romans'[60] and 'the Princesses in fairy tales',[61] universal characters without any particular background and by no means rooted in India. That Lispeth dissociates herself from the native ground and becomes a European-like figure is conventionally symbolized by the bathing habits she acquires from the education given by the Mission: 'Her own people hated her because she had, they said, become a white woman and washed herself daily'.[62] Here, being a white woman and washing oneself are misleadingly equated, for the concern about bodily cleanliness and the custom of washing oneself developed in Europe only in the nineteenth century.[63] Thus, the European's own unsanitary past is now imposed on the Indian as Other – *dirt*iness meaning being still caught up in the ground – and Lispeth, in order to maintain herself as a white woman, has to wipe off all the dirt which her body takes on daily. The education intended to turn her into a European figure turns out to be too successful; her own people will not accept her and the Chaplain feels the difficulty of placing her in Indian society.

There is still, however, one thing even Christianity cannot 'wipe out' in Lispeth, that is, 'uncivilized Eastern instincts, such as falling in love at first sight'.[64] The tragedy occurs when this hidden instinct is awoken by an Englishman, who, according to the Chaplain's wife, is 'of a superior *clay*',[65] and Lispeth wishes this foreign clay to mingle with the Indian one. Unlike Dunmaya's Phil, who severs every tie he had with England and settles down in India, Lispeth's English lover is one of those 'globe-trotters'[66] who are willing to expose themselves to unfamiliar new worlds and shake off their fixed way of seeing while keeping their roots and family safely at Home; he even has a fiancée in England.[67] The Englishman, encouraged by the Chaplain's wife, falsely promises Lispeth that he will come back to marry her, a promise which he has no intention of keeping. And when he later writes a book on the East, 'Lispeth's name did not appear there'.[68] The native girl who saved his life cannot become even a character in his book – she is wholly consigned to the margin. Lispeth, after realizing that the man and the Chaplain's wife cheated her, goes straight back to 'her own unclean people' and becomes 'infamously dirty'.[69] She will soon be dis*figure*d by her native husband who beats her, and finally becomes 'the bleared, wrinkled creature, exactly like a wisp of charred rag'[70] whom no one can any longer distinguish from the filthy earth.

Interestingly, the idea of following her lover to England to be his bride never occurs to Lispeth. She is single-minded: she wants her white lover to marry her and settle down. In *Kim*, Lispeth, now speaking as 'the Woman of Shamlegh' – a personification of the Indian ground – voices this wish in a more direct way: 'Shamlegh is thine: hoof and horn and hide, milk and butter. Take or leave.'[71] Through this forthright invitation to the colonizer to *settle down* in the land does Lispeth slip into the world of *Kim*, which I characterize as the settler's Empire. The common theme of the colonizer turning into the settler binds the two worlds – in *The Plain Tales of the Hills*, as impossibility, in *Kim*, as desirability. 'Lispeth' thus anticipates *Kim* as the settler novel, and the story is set in the salubrious hill region, a piece of India where the white man could easily settle if he so wishes: 'weak' characters like Phil Garron and Namgay Doola's father thus settle in the hills and marry hill-women.[72] More importantly, the presence of Lispeth in *Kim* connects Kipling's India of his younger days, which he experienced as a colonizer, with the India of memories onto which he projects his vision of the White Man's Empire. While Lispeth's seduction of Kim problematically reinforces the colonial fantasy that India wishes to be taken and appropriated by no one but her White Sahib, Kipling's old India comes back, via Lispeth, to confront and question *Kim*, perhaps inadvertently opening up a moment of aporia – of resistance even – in this novel which is otherwise overly regulated. The Woman of Shamlegh, though by no means unkind to Kim and the lama, overtly interferes with the smooth operation of the Game in her sexuality and desire to have Kim stay. Moreover, despite the fact that she is apparently deceived by Kim's disguise as 'a wandering priest',[73] she can equally sees through his flawless disguise to know that he *is* a sahib: 'Thy face and thy walk and thy fashion of speech put me in mind of my Sahib . . . for awhile I thought it was my Sahib come back, and he was my God'.[74] She thus demands Kim to return her love, which her own sahib cruelly betrayed. Here, Kim's young India is suddenly faced with history, and Kim is even asked to compensate for the crime of his predecessor, which he is yet to commit. Lispeth treats Kim not as a young boy but as a responsible *adult* colonizer, just as Kipling as a teenager in India must have been treated by natives in India (Kipling was there from the age of sixteen to twenty-three). Furthermore, Lispeth is one colonial Other whom Kim cannot become through disguise, or take possession of as his 'trove', as he did the lama.[75] From this position of the absolute Other, Lispeth momentarily halts the Game and demands a response. 'At least she did not treat me like a child,' ponders Kim after parting with Lispeth, 'considering the past'.[76] The encounter with her brings back historicity and temporality into Kim's timeless India and, by rendering Kim a returning ghost of Lispeth's lover, splits 'the White Man' many times over through difference and repetition. It even allows us to question *why* Kim is there (in contrast to 'What is Kim?'), one question which the novel does not ask Kim to ponder on.

In 'Lispeth', the heroine's hatred is exclusively directed at the English: 'You are all liars, you English.'[77] In *Kim*, however, her grudge against the English is cunningly substituted by that against her 'Sahib': Lispeth never describes her lover as English, but only as her 'Sahib'. This is why the *Irish*

Kim can play a role to appease her grudge, without giving the reader any sense of contradiction. This encounter between Kim and Lispeth is not a simple encounter between a sahib and an Indian woman, the colonizer and the native land. It is an encounter between Irish and Indian, a colonized colonizer and a colonized ground, one which would not occur in this way if England had not colonized their respective countries. And, significantly, their compromise is made only in an English way:

> . . . putting his arm round her waist, he kissed her on the cheek, adding in English: 'Thank you verree much, my dear. [...] Next time,' Kim went on, 'you must not be so sure of your heatthen priests. Now I say goodbye.' He held out his hand English-fashion. She took it mechanically. 'Goodbye, my dear.'
>
> 'Goodbye, and – and'– she was remembering her English words one by one – 'you will come back again? Goodbye, and – thee God bless you.'[78]

How should we understand this perfect reconciliation presented by Kipling towards the end of *Kim*? On one level, it is possible to read this as the moment of double colonization: Lispeth's long-standing grudge against the colonizer is finally appeased, and Kim internally colonizes himself by proving himself to be an ideal colonizer. If we see Lispeth as a personification of the ground, this is also the moment in which Kim the chain-man successfully exercises a mastery over the land. Kim's character as English is tried and proven true, by his having successfully resisted sexual temptation.

Both Kim and Lispeth can be categorized as the colonized, but the way they are colonized is by no means equal. Whereas Kim is allowed to assume the identity of a colonizer and a white man, which gives him some sense of freedom and superiority over the natives, the fellow colonized, Lispeth, is only allotted the single role of native woman, who is to be deceived and utilized but is never capable of deceit as Kim is. Nevertheless, there is one thing which Kim and Lispeth have peculiarly in common: the state of having suffered colonization and Anglicization. Neither has a *proper* name – other than the parents' name or the place name, and notably both names are 'corrupt' – Kim being the shorter version of 'Kimball', Lispeth of 'Elizabeth'[79] – as if to show a degree of erosion of Englishness through contact with the colonized ground. It is true that Kim has a birth certificate, on which his name must be written. However, he is given the same name as his father – Kimball O'Hara – not any other name. It is worth remembering that his father was caught and lost in the Indian ground, just like some of Kipling's other 'weak' characters: '[H]e came across the woman who took opium and learned the taste from her, and died as poor whites die in India.'[80] That his son who bears the same name is rescued by the same Irish regiment from among the natives where his father has been lost is a symbolic restoration of the Irish regimental tradition in India, which Kipling counts on as a loyal vanguard of imperialism.[81] 'The pedigree of the white stallion' to be established[82] is also that of the Irish who are loyal to the Empire, to be recovered by the Mavericks, who found the Irish boy. Kim is primarily 'Kim of the Rishti',[83] the combination of his father's name and the Irish regiment. In other words, Kim's name does not designate his identity as an individual, but serves as a code which recovers the lost linkage between his father and the Irish regiment. As for Lispeth, when she discards her identity as 'Lispeth of the Kotgarh Mission',[84] she has no choice but to call herself 'old Jadéh's daughter – the daughter of a *pahari* and the servant of Tarka Devi',[85] and later simply 'the Woman of Shamlegh'. So, it is not an encounter between Kim and Lispeth, but between two nameless persons who are deprived of *proper* names by being colonized, who can only describe themselves by gathering as much information as they can, trying to reconnect themselves with place and tradition.

If Lispeth represents the native ground, she is the ground always already colonized and Anglicized. Kim's case is even more peculiar. Unlike Lispeth, who at least can decide which people and place she belongs to (whether or not this is totally possible), Kim, as 'Kim of the Rishti', has only an Irish regiment as a place of origin, which is not only a colonized location but also a colonizing force of Great Britain. Then, is it possible to read the moment of 'reconciliation' as one in which the two colonized change the stigma of being colonized into a means of communication? The important thing is not so much that Kim can perfectly act like an Englishman as that Lispeth can understand the meaning of Kim's gesture and respond to him in an equally English way. Is it naive to read between the lines a recognition that each is colonized – though in a different way – by the same country, the same culture, and that a secret sympathy is exchanged between them? Maybe it is, for Kim warns us, 'Next time . . . you must not be so sure of your heatthen priests.' We should not trust the Christian mission which colonized the land in the name of Christianity any more than we should that Kim who disguises himself as an innocent heathen priest. Kim is an expert in disguising and deceiving others, and nobody knows what he will turn into next. He even disguises himself as an innocent Irish boy, a poor colonized to us the readers, but what for? And will there be any 'next time' – next colonization – we should be aware of?

4

Kim and Kipling's Boer War stories are intimately intertwined, echoing each other. If *Kim*'s vision of the settler's Empire was overshadowed by the ongoing war in South Africa in which the British fought for the right of settlement, Kipling's South Africa is curiously flooded with Indian motifs, which has puzzled many critics. For instance, Angus Wilson writes,

> What has his old [Indian] theme . . . to do with South Africa's war? Or even the devotion of a Sikh non-commissioned officer to his British officer which takes us back to *Plain Tales*? There *were* Indian troops from the British Indian Army serving in Africa. Kipling may have been right to think that there should have been more. But it is an irrelevance. Of the real and large community of Indians in South Africa he showed no awareness whatsoever. In all his winter stays at the Cape, he never visited Natal where the large Indian trading community now lived – perhaps it was as well, for the advocate of their cause was Gandhi, a Babu lawyer.[86]

The reference to India in Kipling's Boer War stories is indeed recurring and persistent to the point of puzzlement. In 'A Sahib's War', a native Sikh soldier follows his sahib to South Africa to fight against the Boers.[87] In 'The Captive' (1902), Van Zyl, an old Boer 'commandant' who is captured by the British is sent to Umballa in India as a prisoner of war.[88] 'Folly Bridge' figures 'an officer late of the Bengal Army', carrying Lord Roberts's private mail-bag.[89] In 'A Burgher of the Free State', Allen, an Uitlander, keeps asking the British troops who occupied his printing office, 'did ye, or did ye not, use native troops fra' Injia against us?',[90] over and over again, even after they assure him that the news is false, to the extent that they, as well as the reader, feel it difficult to 'see the drift' of his remarks.[91] India also haunts 'The Comprehension of Private Copper', in which an English soldier, when confronted by an English-speaking South African, is suddenly subjected to flashbacks of India and the Eurasians he met there (see Chapter 4). Indeed, C. A. Bodelsen devotes one chapter in his *Aspects of Kipling's Art* (1964) to making sense of this Eurasian theme, which, according to him, gives the story 'the appearance of being very badly put together, in a way that seems quite uncharacteristic of Kipling':[92]

> The theme is far too insistent to be a mere digression, and no one familiar with Kipling's short story technique, whose principal characteristic is an extreme verbal economy, could believe that it was. It is entirely foreign to his practice to introduce something into a story that does not serve a purpose, and in this case the theme appears, at the first glance, to be not merely a digression, but to have nothing whatever to do with the ostensible subject of the tale. It *must* mean something, and it must be explicable, if one could only find the clue, for this is obviously not one of the stories that are *meant* to be enigmatic, like for example, *Mrs Bathurst*.[93]

Bodelsen here encapsulates the peculiarity of Kipling's Boer War stories: they are fraught with details and digressions which do not seem to add up or contribute to the main plotline. At the same time, he points out a very important characteristic of Kipling's work, namely, his 'verbal economy', which gives to his reader the impression that every part does mean something, all working together to create a bigger picture, 'the Empire'; this is why Kipling's text was so treasured at the height of high imperialism. Instead of retrieving the verbal economy which is, according to Bodelsen, supposed to exist, I wish to argue here that this digression on the Eurasian theme can simply be seen as the bankruptcy of a unified vision of the Empire. What appears to be a mysterious leftover jigsaw puzzle piece which does not fit anywhere gives us some idea about what failed to fall into place in the grand picture of the Empire, namely, 'India', or to be more precise, the India palimpsested onto South Africa. We are here witnessing the collapse of intercolonial analogies in Kipling's literary world, with his Boer War stories becoming the failed attempt to superimpose the Indian context onto South Africa. He was, though, more successful in bringing South Africa into India, the product of which is *Kim*, a successful allegory of empire which seems to 'bolster' every aspect of this empire.[94]

A pair reminiscent of Kim and the lama walk in the veldt in 'A Sahibs' War'. 'Kurban Sahib', a young British officer who serves in India, goes over to South Africa to fight the Boer War, accompanied by the elderly Sikh trooper Umr Singh, who acts as his servant. Kurban Sahib, a Kim-like figure in many ways, is endowed with all the qualities which the author thinks would make an ideal colonizer. Born in India, he is versed in native tongues and customs, and is bonded with the old man Umr Singh by the tie of affection. He is flexible and capable of dispensing with the red tape if necessary; he feigns illness and takes sick leave in order to join the war in South Africa. He easily makes connections with people from different backgrounds as he travels; indeed, he seems to perform the metonymic magic of Empire as he immediately makes friends with the Canadians and is 'stolen' by the Australians, who discern his worth.[95] In addition to Umr Singh, who would not leave his Sahib, Kurban Sahib also picks up a Pathan called Sikandar Khan on the way, who becomes attached to him and acts as his cook. But the story tells us how he is killed by Boer treachery, and accordingly the imperial circle beginning to form around him has to disperse. The Indian context – a piece of *Kim* even – is projected onto the Boer War scene in this story, but it fails to bolster the empire there; it is defeated and made redundant, uneasily floating in the South African landscape.

The whole story is narrated by Umr Singh in his native tongue, but we can read the story in standard English, thanks to a 'Sahib' who happens to ride in the same carriage as him and acts as both a listener to and interpreter of this former Sikh trooper's story. Umr Singh's monologue powerfully knits the two colonies together, for he comprehends everything he sees in South Africa through the analogy with India. Thus, Australians are nicknamed *Durro Muts* in his language, and are likened to Pathans, both being professional horse-lifters.[96] 'A country full of little hills' reminds him of the Khyber Pass,[97] and Boer conspirators in the Cape Colony are understood as '*mullahs* (priests) . . . [preaching] the Jehad against us'.[98] Just like Kim, who does not want to appear as a 'hubshi (nigger)' as he disguises as a low-caste Hindu boy,[99] Umr Singh pleads with us not to confuse him with black Africans, whom he calls 'black Kaffirs', '*Hubshis*' or 'filth unspeakable';[100] he is indignant at the racial discrimination, which he has never experienced in his own country, although his 'blackness' is made to serve as a connecting point between India and Africa. He also tells us how 'we of Hind' had been informed of the news of the War through 'box-wallas, pedlars, with Pathans a few' in South Africa, and how Kurban Sahib said to him, 'We shall fight for all Hind in that country round Yunasbagh.'[101]

Umr Singh's India embraces South Africa as its own affair, and his narrative connects the two even more closely, until the death of Kurban Sahib signals the disintegration of all the imperial connections. This rupture is marked by the insertion of an English voice into the Sikh soldier's monologue. Umr Singh, at the end of the story, asks his listener to read aloud the inscription on the tomb of 'Kurban Sahib'. There we are informed of the true name and identity of Kurban Sahib, which have been obscured throughout the story by the use of the Sikh soldier as a narrator: 'In Memory of WALTER DECIES CORBYN Late Captain 141st Punjab Cavalry'[102] – this British soldier who served in India is buried in South Africa. It seems to me significant that Kipling chooses this rather rare word – 'Decies' – as Kurban Sahib's middle name, especially when this is the only moment in the story in which the reader is directly communicated with in standard English, unmediated by Umr Singh. The word can be read as a Latinized form of 'Deise', an ancient tribe in Ireland, which is still used for the name of one of the baronies of County Waterford.[103] This leads us to Lord Roberts, who was often mentioned as 'Roberts of Kandahar, Pretoria, and Waterford', being a member of a county Waterford family. Kipling must have had Lord Roberts in mind when writing this story, for Roberts established his reputation as the Commander-in-Chief of the British Army in India, and later performed the same role during the Boer War: a sahibs' war was then also Lord Roberts's war. At any rate, Kurban Sahib, a young Indian soldier bearing an Irish place name as a middle name, reminds us of the Irish Commander 'Bobs', as well as of Kim the Irish boy, through his attachment to an old Indian man, and it would not be far-fetched to argue that his tomb can be seen as a secret tomb of the Irish and Indian connection, which had been so effective in creating the unity of the Empire. If so, it is interesting that Umr Singh emphasizes the hollowness of the inscription as a sign: the Empire built on the metonymic connection between India and Ireland no longer exists. The inscription ends with a Latin sentence '*Si monumentum requiris circumspice*'[104] – 'If you would see his monument, look around'. Umr Singh interprets this as follows:

> That is the second jest. It signifies that those who would desire to behold a proper memorial to Kurban Sahib must look out at the house. And, Sahib, the house is not there, nor the well, nor the big tank which they call dams, nor the little fruit-trees, nor the cattle. There is nothing at all, Sahib, except the two trees withered by the fire. The rest is like the desert here – or my hand – or my heart. Empty, Sahib – all empty![105]

This scene clearly recalls Shelley's 'Ozymandias', in which the inscription on a shattered monument to the Egyptian pharaoh points to his once mighty empire, which is now reduced to boundless desert.[106] Kipling, in his story of the imperial decay, names 'a proper memorial to 'Kurban Sahib' to be a house. Although it is the house of the Boer family who deceived him, the image of the lost house reminds us of the popular analogy between the Home and the Empire. The imperial Home was gone for ever, leaving only the tomb of the imperial analogies, which were once its powerful signifier. This is even more of a jest, considering that it was the British side that burned down the house and thus made the inscription devoid of its referent.

Chapter Six

The Dynamite War of Analogies

> Has it occurred to you that if you turned up the files of 81–85 on Ireland and India you would find almost verbatim the identical questions which are asked to-day as to lawlessness in Ireland: the identical flippant replies, and the same growth of lawlessness. It seems to me sometimes in reading the Standard, that I am back again in India in the middle eighties, when Ripon was introducing Local Self Government into India, and I suppose it must have been Morley – the Irish Secretary – was veiling and palliating intrigue in Ireland.[1]

1

Rudyard Kipling, in this letter to H. A. Gwynne, specifies one moment in history in which India and Ireland, with 'the same growth of lawlessness', looked almost identical: the early to mid 1880s. It is interesting to see that Kipling, in his recollection of the period, slightly modifies the dates of the three separate incidents in order to emphasize their contemporaneity: Kipling returned to India not 'in the middle eighties' but rather the beginning of the eighties, October 1882; Lord Ripon was Governor General and Viceroy of India from 1880 to 1884; John Morley (1838–1923), whom Kipling remembers 'veiling and palliating intrigue in Ireland' as 'the Irish Secretary' when Lord Ripon was plotting for Indian self-government, was elected to Parliament in 1883 and became Irish Secretary in 1886 – that is to say, two years after Lord Ripon's resignation – and held office till the Liberal government was beaten at the general election of the same year, though he took up the same position later, from 1892 to 1895. The link which Kipling retrospectively forms between India and Ireland, Lord Ripon and John Morley, and the first half of 1880s and 1907 when Kipling writes this letter is not difficult to see: during both periods the Liberal government – the party to which Kipling always bitterly attributes the disintegration of the Empire – was in power, and Lord Ripon and John Morley are both liberal politicians and William Gladstone's strongest supporters.

Kipling in this letter projects his anxiety that the Liberal party might undo the unity of the Empire onto the events of nearly twenty years before. In the 1900s, England had to combat a new surge of nationalisms among her colonies, which gained strength from the decline of the British Empire. Immediately after the humiliating victory of the Boer War, there came the stunning news of Japan's triumph over Russia, which blasted the myth of the invincibility and superiority of the West and drastically restored the self-confidence of the Asian people, the Indian among them.[2] Lord Curzon's notorious measure of the partition of Bengal (1905) was enforced as these new aspirations and exalted feelings about Indian racial and national identity gained ground, and it triggered the Swadeshi movement, the boycotting of foreign goods. In the middle of this revolutionary movement, the Indian Congress split into moderates and militants in 1907, and the latter, led by Bal Gangadhar Tilak (1856–1920), pushed the movement towards terrorism, which quickly spread all over India.

Nevertheless, Kipling's impression that there was a parallel growth of 'lawlessness' in India and Ireland during the 1880s seems to be not totally a product of his imagination. In the 1880s, on Gladstone's return to power, liberal reforms were simultaneously inaugurated in India and Ireland. It was in this period that the prospect of Irish Home Rule looked most promising under the strong leadership of Charles Stewart Parnell. Gladstone made the Irish policy of his third government clear by appointing John Morley, who had gained a reputation as the strongest advocate of Irish Home Rule, as Irish Secretary in 1886. In India, Lord Ripon won the favour of the educated Indians by his policy of 'training Indians for self-rule', even at the expense of administrative efficiency,[3] which made him extremely unpopular among the Anglo-Indian community. Ripon's attempt to give Indian judges jurisdiction over Europeans through the Ilbert Bill (1883) was met with, and eventually defeated by, strong resistance from the white community. Kipling, who was in India at that time, castigated Lord Ripon's policy as the 'swart Utopia': 'nourishing the Babu's pride / On the fairy tales of Justice'.[4]

It was also during this period that Irish and Indian nationalists started self-consciously drawing on each other's example. There was a growing sense of mutual sympathy between Indian and Irish nationalists in the late nineteenth century, which opened up the possibility of helping each other achieve self-government, made it easier to portray both India and Ireland as oppressed colonies which must be liberated and even prompted some attempts to form political alliances. The London Indian Society, formed in 1872 to bring into closer union the Indians residing in England, and a precursor of the London India House 'notorious as a centre of sedition' in the 1900s,[5] was, from the start, haunted by the Irish connection: the Irish MP Frank Hugh O'Donnell (1848–1916) made approaches to this society in the 1870s with a proposal to form an Irish-Indian organization to help each other achieve self-government.[6] Lord Ripon, in the eyes of the Irish nationalists, seems to have represented something of the Irish-Indian connection, not only because his liberal policy was seen as the Indian version of Irish home rule, but also because of his sudden conversion to Roman Catholicism in the 1870s, which caused him to resign as Grand

Master of the Freemasons in England and withdraw from public service till 1880. Frank Hugh O'Donnell expressed his enthusiasm over the appointment of Lord Ripon by assuming the Indian voice: he argued in a letter to the Editor of *The Times* that, despite the apprehension of 'some earnest Protestants . . . at the possible effects of the Marquis of Ripon's appointment as Governor-General of India', the natives of India heartily welcomed Lord Ripon as the new viceroy, whose noble character had been proved by his recent religious conversion. O'Donnell generously quoted from a leading Indian newspaper, *Hindoo Patriot*: 'That the Marquis of Ripon is distinguished by high conscientiousness is evident from the fact of his change of faith. A nobleman and a public man in his position would not have changed his ancestral religion if he had not been moved by high conscientious scruples.'[7] To O'Donnell's eyes, Ripon, by not only breaking with the tradition of Protestant and imperialist rule in India, but also choosing Catholicism as his true religion in accordance with his 'high conscientious scruples' against the British Empire, which he had intimately known as a high official, made a powerful anti-imperialist connection between India and Ireland that nationalists in both colonies could readily identify with. It may be interesting to note here that Maud Gonne MacBride rejected the teachings of the Golden Dawn, suspecting the religious order's association with Free Masonry, of which she states, 'as we Irish know it is a British institution and has always been used politically to support the British Empire',[8] while later accepting the Catholic faith – a personal choice informed by the same Irish nationalist rhetoric.

The subversive association between Irish and Indian nationalists did not go unnoticed. In March 1886, Lord Dufferin, who was appointed Viceroy of India (1884–88) after Ripon's resignation, wrote to the Earl of Kimberley, the Indian Secretary of the day, about the dangerous effect of the Irish example on Indian politics:

> I cannot help having a strong suspicion that the course of events at home in regard to Ireland has produced a very considerable effect upon the minds of the intelligent and educated section of our own native community. Associations and sub-associations are being formed all over the country which are also being furnished with a network of caucuses, who of course work the telegraph wire in the orthodox fashion . . .[9]

That is to say, Kipling went back to India when it resembled Ireland in a most subversive way, and the similarity ignited a sense of alarm among Anglo-Indians. Significantly, he was, at least in retrospect, aware of the resemblance. It should also be noted that Kipling started his career as a journalist when the power of the native press was feared and most strongly felt, mostly due to the fact that Lord Ripon in 1882 repealed the Vernacular Press Act of 1878, which had been passed during Lord Lytton's era to suppress the growth of Indian nationalism, and restored the freedom of speech of the native newspapers. Kipling kept a watchful eye on these native newspapers, which he suspected might grow into a seditious voice of Indian nationalism. One of his poems appearing in the *Civil & Military Gazette* features a chorus of 'Native Editors' in approval of a Liberal politician:

> . . . every journal of native persuasion
> That boasts a two hundred per week circulation,
> That's bought by a *bunnia*, or read by a *reis*,
> That's lithoed in gullies, or sold for a *pice*,
> That's worked by a school-boy on thirty rupees;
> That serves for a wrap for *mussalas* and *ghis*.
> Shall, *nemine contradicente*, proclaim
> Your Honour's just dealing and wisdom and fame.
> Shall hold you on high to the World's admiration ...
> And this is the voice of the Indian Nation![10]

It was this burgeoning 'voice of the Indian Nation', rapidly spreading to every corner of the Indian community through native newspapers, which Irish nationalists identified with and wished to echo their own voices. Through the 'Liberal principles' which Kipling detested, the voice of the Indian Nation easily turned into the voice of the Irish Nation, orchestrating, to his eyes at least, the disintegration of the Empire.

Lord Dufferin, in the letter which I quoted above, notes that the educated class of Indian makes 'associations and sub-associations' by means of the telegraph. The British Empire maintained its huge territory by the improvement of communications (including the propagation of English and European values among the colonized, which facilitated communication with the colonies), and the Indian and Irish nationalists took advantage of the very system which governed them in order to form a subversive anti-imperial network. In this sense, the use of the analogy between Ireland and other colonies can be likened to that of the 'dynamite' invented in 1867 by the Swedish chemist Alfred Nobel and put to extensive use in the late nineteenth century. The word 'dynamite', coined by Nobel in the form of *dynamit* in Swedish, was taken from Greek *dunamis*, 'power'. Indeed, dynamite turned out to be a double-edged 'power' which materialized two opposite discursive effects, which imperialists on the one hand and Irish nationalists on the other sought to create. Dynamite enabled the British Empire to quickly establish their communication networks and bring the vast territory of Empire closer together, providing the infrastructure for the metonymic language of the Empire which I discussed in Chapter 4. As Arthur Mee's *Popular Science* (1912–13) celebrates:

> the invention of dýnamite marked a new epoch in the history of civilization. It enabled men to change, in a single generation, the face of

> the earth. By means of it he flung a network of railways swiftly over the continent; he removed mountains from his path; he mined for miles into the fiery heart of his planet. He brought oceans together by blasting away the rocks and earth that sundered them.[11]

The same power to make a change 'in a single generation' was soon adopted by the Irish nationalists as the tool of terrorism, with which they sought to blow up the British Empire. Jeremiah O'Donovan Rossa (1831–1915), after being released from his eight-year long mistreatment in an English prison in 1871, fled to America and in the 1880s waged the 'dynamite war' against England. Although Rossa's dynamiters – 'skirmishers' – used gunpowder instead of dynamite to blow up public buildings, Rossa consistently used the word 'dynamite' in his newspaper, the New York version of the *United Irishman*, in what came to be known as 'dynamite journalism'.[12] Rossa's terrorist tactics were more successfully pursued by another Fenian organization, Clan na Gael, whose bombers employed actual dynamite. Public buildings such as Victoria Station, *The Times* office, the Houses of Parliament, the Tower of London, and London Bridge became the targets of Fenian dynamite outrages.[13]

For both the imperialist and the nationalist, dynamite signified the power to create, connect and unite through destruction. Imperialists expanded the Empire by means of destroying nature, native culture and tradition, while dynamite was put to use by nationalists as a supplement to (or even a substitute for) the nationalist/political discourses which otherwise would have been too easily dismissed, as a means of reclaiming their lost tradition and uniting the divided people of Ireland into one.[14] From the 1880s onwards, the intra-imperial analogies, especially those between India and Ireland, took on the same double-edged power as that of dynamite, and were used alongside it. If Ireland, being the oldest colony of England, had been a nodal point of the analogical practice to which any new experience with other colonies could be constantly referred and thereby contextualized, the association with Irish nationalism and dynamite/violence, once established, became a serious threat to the imagined solidarity of the empire woven by intra-imperial analogies. It was therefore important to deny the similarity and emphasize the difference, in order to guarantee that India was, unlike Ireland, free from violence and content with British rule.

Kipling's India, created around this significant period when he worked for the Indian newspapers, inevitably reflects the political analogies between India and Ireland frequently made and rebuked in the contemporary political arena. As a young journalist he was deeply engaged in this discursive war of analogies, and he even carried them over to his literary world in order to better fight this war. In 'The Way Av Ut' (1888), the

'Fenian' Mulvaney in Dublin wears 'A *Freeman's Journal Supplemint*' as his uniform, and in 'The Irish Conspiracy', the narrator, infuriated by the report of a possible Irish mutiny in India in 'the Friday's *Pioneer*', confronts Mulvaney, demanding the real Irish answer.[15] In 'The Mutiny of the Mavericks' (1891), Mulcahy tries to persuade an Irish regiment in India to mutiny by means of 'his copies of the Irish papers and his everlasting beer'.[16] Rebellion in the shape of newspapers also spreads to South Africa, where, in 'The Comprehension of Private Copper' (1902), 'a renegade' armed with the pro-Boer 'Jerrold's Weekly' (i.e. *Lloyd's Weekly News*) condemns the wrongdoings of the British government.[17] It is, then, no wonder that Kipling was again reminded of the parallel growth of Irish and Indian nationalisms as he was leafing through the pages of the *Standard*. Anti-imperial analogies between India and Ireland, real and imaginary, were circulating as newspaper discourses, against which Kipling devised his own version of the same analogies; the evocation of the Irish rebellion in India, for example, had to be matched and defeated by his representation of the Irish soldiers in India. *Kim*, in which the Great Game is fought to combat the international intrigue far deadlier than 'dynamite',[18] can also be read as a newspaper war. The players of the Game, always carrying important 'news', are special correspondents, Kim being a promising addition to the team who are in touch with the bazaar-talk and rumour which function like native 'newspapers' in Kipling's world, communicating news as quickly and accurately as European newspapers and telegraphs.[19] Kim, as an Irishman in India, is perfectly positioned to fight off the Indo-Irish analogies which were secretly undermining the Raj in the form of newspaper discourses. It may not be accidental that in the Jewel Game, which Kim plays to prepare for the Great Game, 'an old newspaper'[20] is used to cover the objects that Kim has to observe and describe. Newspapers cast a shadow on the Great Game, requiring the power to see through diverse, circulating discourses.

2

According to S. B. Cook, the Indo-Irish analogies frequently used and even abused as an aid in the process of inventing and charting a legislative course in India and Ireland suddenly became 'increasingly irrelevant' and were 'made superfluous' once 'official information and scholarly knowledge attained a certain threshold':[21] 'From the 1890s, Indian and Irish legislation assumed increasingly divergent paths and the scope for emulation or adaptation narrowed sharply. After 1900, no Indian tenancy acts were discernibly influenced by the Irish example.'[22] Considering that England had had a very long history of ruling both India and Ireland, however, it seems to be misleading to attribute the sudden disappearance of these

Indo-Irish analogies in the 1890s, which, according to Cook, flourished in the 1880s, solely to the 'fact' that the Indian and Irish legislative courses were finally separately established, especially when it was in the 1890s that the British management of her colonies notably started crumbling. I suggest that the analogy became unpopular at the end of the 1880s because it turned out to be not so much 'irrelevant' or 'superfluous' as dangerous, and something which it was, if possible, desirable to do away with. The frequent use of analogies and comparisons between India and Ireland, the exchange of the colonial experience among contemporaries on both physical and discursive levels, which had greatly contributed to creating a sense of the solidarity and 'reality' of the Empire, proved to be no longer effective and even dangerous to evoke. With the growing demand for autonomy among non-self-governing colonies like India and Ireland, the comparison between colonies started arousing anxiety rather than a sense of unity.

The need to deny any association between the Indo-Irish analogies and nationalist violence can be seen in an article entitled 'The Home Rule Movement in India and in Ireland' published in 1890 in the *Contemporary Review*, which was simply signed by 'a Bengal Magistrate', for Charles William McMinn, the author of the article, requested anonymity when sending it to the editor, Percy William Bunting.[23] It is also a perfect example of the downfall of the analogical practice at the end of the 1880s, for the article, subtitled 'A Contrast', deals with the 'striking and instructive contrasts' between rather than the similarities of the two colonies, drawn from the author's fifty years of experience in both India and Ireland.[24] Most interestingly, McMinn, in the early part of the essay, records an old episode which shows how the British officials made their Indian policy by analogy with Ireland and their former colonial experience.

> Lord Mayo once remarked to the present writer, when we were waiting in our howdahs for the outburst of a family of tigers, that the problems which he had to solve as Secretary at Dublin and as Governor-General at Calcutta, showed a great mutual resemblance. But I would dwell rather on the contrasts which the two countries present, because I consider them more instructive on the question of Home Rule, and more pregnant with emphatic lessons in the art of government.[25]

Here McMinn evokes an exotic picture of two Irishmen in the Indian landscape – on elephants' backs, ready to hunt tigers – talking of 'a great mutual resemblance' between India and Ireland. Lord Mayo was assassinated in 1872, nearly twenty years before the article was written, so we may say that the episode testifies to the good old days in which the imperial affinity – making analogies between Ireland and India, and between the Irish experience and the Indian one, and the physical presence of the Irish on Indian soil – seemed to sustain the reality and success of the Raj in post-

Mutiny India. The 'great mutual resemblance' between India and Ireland noted above is, in fact, ironic, considering that the Irish officials are here depicted with the power to kill (tigers) and control (elephants) Indian nature. It was the same power that Lord Mayo, an Anglo-Irish politician, seeing Ireland in India and India in Ireland, thought it appropriate to exercise over his 'Irish' countrymen.

McMinn admits that both colonies look alike in their nationalist aim and strategy, namely, 'the abolition of bureaucracy and the development of Imperial Federation by means of constitutional agitation'.[26] Nonetheless, he argues that the situations of the two countries are too different to even suggest analogies: they are first of all two different 'units' of the British Empire, differing from each other in size, population, religion, climate and ancient history. British India turns out to be a far more successful colony than Ireland, increasing 'not only in area, but in wealth, strength, and population', while in Ireland all of these have decreased.[27] Moreover, it is the feeling towards the British administration which most decisively separates India and Ireland. McMinn more than once emphasizes that India is, unlike Ireland, free from the 'legacy of national bitterness' towards England. For example, whereas Ireland is 'still garrisoned with 42,000 soldiers and military police', in India '[p]eace has been maintained for many years without a single white soldier'.[28] In India, the discontented are only 'a small minority', whereas in Ireland the people 'dislike with varying degrees of intensity their magistracy, their police, and the Coercion laws'.[29] Indian nationalists are supported by 'very few rupees',[30] whereas Irish nationalists have been financially supported by Irish emigrants scattered all over the world who 'have given of their substance as freely as their sisters in Carthage contributed their hair in order to manufacture bowstrings'.[31]

To do McMinn justice, we have to admit that he, as an Irishman, gives a very sympathetic account of Irish suffering and holds the English government responsible for it. However, when it comes to the Indian situation, his picture of a peaceful India hardly seems to be either a sympathetic or an accurate report. For example, the statement that there was not a single white soldier in India for many years is difficult to believe, for there *were* quite a few white soldiers in India in the nineteenth century. According to the *India Office List for 1889*, for example, the number of European soldiers in British India for the official year 1886–7 is 73,582, while that of native soldiers, 'exclusive of Native Artificers and followers', is 134,492.[32] The contrast between the total absence of white soldiers in the vast territory of India and the overabundance of them in Ireland which McMinn suggests is, however, significant, for in his essay the refusal to make analogies between India and Ireland works in tandem with the disavowal of any violence in India. His comparison between the two countries is purged of the armed white soldiers in India who, if not checked, might at any time turn into

Irish violence in India: thus he concludes by claiming that, even though India also suffered many great famines and scarcities, 'not one landlord or public servant was assassinated, not one dynamite cartridge was exploded in India by the survivors of the great Indian famines, or by the sons of those who perished'.[33]

If, as Cook observes, the practice of making an analogical connection between India and Ireland to create a sense of imperial unity became obsolete by 1890, we may assume that the frequent use made of the Indo-Irish analogy by Irish nationalists together with their use of bombs, which became prominent during the 1880s, subverted the imperial use of the same analogy. In fact, it is probably no coincidence that recurrent Indian motifs in Kipling's Boer War stories have been described as 'irrelevant' and 'superfluous' by Kipling's critics (see Chapter 5), almost in the same way as Cook describes the fall of Indo-Irish analogies which took place in the 1890s, for it seems to me that Kipling's representation of the Empire delineates the same story of the rise and fall of those analogies. The floating Indian memories in his Boer War stories are nothing but the ghosts of these analogies, which Kipling could only reappropriate within the world of *Kim*, and while imperialists like Kipling and McMinn felt the urgent need to exorcise them from their representation of the Empire, both Indian and Irish nationalists started strategically and unrelentingly resorting to the same analogies throughout their nationalist struggle towards independence, leaving a valuable legacy of intercolonial resistance.

It is indeed significant that *Kim*, written and completed in the very last years of the nineteenth century, turned out to be not only Kipling's last Indian story but also his last representation of the Irish in the Indian setting. India was no longer a safe representational space in which the unshakeable solidarity of the whole Empire could be shown through the use of intra-imperial analogies, while Indian officials still looked up to Kipling as the very person to represent the glory of imperial India. When Lord Kitchener, now the Commander-in-Chief of the Indian Army, decided to publish a vernacular newspaper for his Indian Army in 1908 in response to the circulation of nationalist seditious writing, he wrote to Kipling asking for 'a short serial story' for the paper. He hoped that his new army newspaper, *Fauji Akhbar*, would 'prove both interesting and instructive to the native rank'.[34] Kitchener must surely have remembered that Kipling, during the Boer War, composed the famous 'The Absent-Minded Beggar', and energetically participated in the editorship of the experimental army newspaper, *The Friend*. However, disappointing Kitchener's expectations, Kipling did not contribute a new story. Instead, he suggested that the paper translate some of his old Indian stories. He gave a list of four stories, which, according to him, 'all deal more or less directly with the relations between the Sahibs and the natives'.[35] More surprisingly, Kipling gave him 'an absolutely free hand in cutting down or simplifying these tales as he thought best'.[36] His enthusiasm for representing India was already consigned to the past. The gaze of Kipling, the Bard of the Empire, had drifted away from India in search of a more suitable representation of the new imperial situation. Already in 1903, when Lord Curzon invited Kipling to India for the coronation durbar, which was to be 'attended by 100 ruling chiefs and was climaxed by a review of 30,000 troops before Curzon as Viceroy and the Duke and Duchess of Connaught', Kipling chose not to go. He replied to Curzon: '[A]t present I must go down to the Cape this winter when instead of seeing India consolidated I shall have the felicity of watching South Africa being slowly but scientifically wrecked by "the strongest government of modern times"'. Kipling, at the end of the letter, added, 'Thank you so much for remembering us.'[37] India was dethroned from its long-held status as *the* representation of imperial solidarity, left with a legacy of analogies with other colonies, which the nationalists could readily ignite.

3

Kipling must have enjoyed representing his Irish characters because of their seeming malleability: essentially 'white', they are easily 'darkened' according to their degree of hybridization with subversive ideologies. They are especially dangerous when they miss home – Ireland as the Nation – too much, while they can be trusted as the colonizer when they decide to make somewhere else in the Empire their home, incorporating their chosen new land as part of their identity. Therefore Mulvaney settles in India instead of going back to Ireland, and Kim never sets foot in his ancestral homeland. Kipling later praises the white settler colonies, which many Irish immigrants made their new home. To represent the Empire almost meant to conjure up an unproblematic representation of the Irish. Accordingly, Kipling's representation of Empire gradually shifted from the Raj to the federation of self-governing colonies, which he called 'the White Man's world'. This change corresponds to the disappearance of Irish rebels, who were exclusively represented in India, from his later stories. In terms of the Indo-Irish analogies I trace, their disappearance can be interpreted as the deliberate obscuring and depoliticization, in Kipling's later version of Empire, of the anti-imperial analogies which these rebels had embodied.

It should also be noted that the self-governing colonies played a crucial part in the formation of Indo-Irish analogies: India and Ireland were not given home rule, which meant that they were always unfavourably compared to these self-governing colonies. Therefore, Indo-Irish analogies essentially presupposed the failure of intra-imperial analogies between India/Ireland and the self-governing colonies, while on the other hand India and Ireland, for many, made a perfect pair owing to their supposed lack of self-discipline and alleged need to be ruled by the 'better' race. Whenever the issue of home rule surfaced, the comparisons between Ireland/India and colonies like Canada were repeatedly made and were invariably rejected, together with the possibility of Irish/Indian nationalists having their national voices, *separately* from the imperial affairs. Indo-Irish analogies were the voiceless voices of the two colonies, which joined forces in mutual identification and dejection. They were therefore fundamentally aphasiac.

In the nexus of Indo-Irish analogies and the Empire as the network of white self-governing colonies, we find John Morley, who acted as Secretary for Ireland under Gladstone (1886, 1892–5) and was later Secretary of State for India (1905–10, 1911). He was highly sensitive to the intra-imperial analogies surrounding the Irish Question, and this may not be unrelated to the fact that he was, just like Kipling, a journalist before launching his political career, taking up the editorship of leading magazines such as *Fortnightly Review* (1867–82), the *Pall Mall Gazette* (1880–83), and *Macmillan's Magazine* (1883–5). To make a case for Irish Home Rule, Morley repudiates the argument that Ireland lacks the conditions which pertain in self-governing colonies, by attacking the very practice of comparing Ireland to other colonies. Ireland, according to Morley, ought to attain a form of self-government which is free from 'some shy bungling underhand imitation of a Crown Colony':

> They are distant, Ireland is near; they are prosperous, Ireland is poor; they are proud of the connection with England, Ireland resents it. But the question is not whether the conditions are identical with those of any colony; it is enough if in themselves they seem to promise a certain basis for government . . . If the people of Ireland are not to be trusted with real power over their own affairs, it would be a hundred times more just to England, and more merciful to Ireland, to take away from her that semblance of free government which torments and paralyses one country, while it robs the other of national self-respect and of all the strongest motives and best opportunities of self-help.[38]

Morley rightly argues that this 'semblance' with other colonies 'torments' and 'paralyses' Ireland's power of self-representation. Ireland was represented, not by herself, but by others, often with reference to something other than herself – sometimes the dependencies like India and sometimes the Crown Colonies, while being precisely categorized as neither. Irish Home Rule, to be attained within the imperial context, was therefore an attempt to exorcize the ghosts of intra-imperial analogies from Ireland, in order to form an Irish government capable of self-representation.

It is ironic that Morley was later appointed, in 1905, as Secretary of State for India, which Lord Curzon's partition of that colony had left in a state of turmoil: he inadvertently put himself in a perfect position to embody the analogical connection between India and Ireland which his colleague Lord Ripon once embodied. Indeed, his appointment raised expectations which arose from this very analogy between India and Ireland. Ras Behari Ghose, for instance, expressed his hope that Morley 'might be safely trusted . . . to pacify Bengal' as he had 'pacified Ireland'.[39] Morley, who had been 'closely identified with [the Irish] cause for the last forty years'[40] and wished to purge the unnecessary analogies which were making Irish Home Rule difficult, was now forced to confront the rhetoric of Indian nationalists who demanded the same home rule as Ireland was demanding. A man of letters who fought for freedom of speech for Ireland now set about restricting that same freedom in India. In defence of such seeming inconsistencies, Morley stood up in the House of Commons to argue that any identification between the Irish situation and the Indian one was misleading:

> Reference has been made to my having resisted the Irish Crimes Act, as if there were a scandalous inconsistency between opposing the policy of that Act and imposing this policy on the natives of India and supporting the deportation of these two men, and other men who may follow if it should prove to be necessary. That inconsistency can only be established by anyone who will take up the position that Ireland, a part of the United Kingdom, is exactly on the same footing as these 300,000,000 people – composite, heterogeneous, with different histories, of different races, different faiths.[41]

Morley was aware that his coercive measures in India could become a threat to the organic consistency of the Liberal beliefs which he had endorsed throughout his life. He published his Indian speeches to defend his position, and in these we see him explain that the political confusion within the Empire was created less by the inconsistency of the imperial or liberal policy in dealing with Indian and other colonial affairs, than by the political language which drew a parallel between various colonies. In his speech of 21 October 1907, Morley points out 'one tremendous fallacy' in a statement whose logic is based on an analogy between two British colonies: '[W]hatever is good in the way of self-government for Canada, must be good for India.' This concise statement, attributed to a 'British Member of Parliament now travelling in India', contains, according to Morley, 'the grossest fallacy in all politics'. Here the imperial affinity among colonies was officially declared invalid:

> It is a thoroughly dangerous fallacy. I think it is the hollowest and, I am sorry to say, the commonest, of all the fallacies in the history of the world in all stages of civilisation. Because a particular policy or principle is true and expedient and vital in certain definite circumstances, therefore it must be equally true and vital in a completely different set

> of circumstances. What sophism can be more gross and dangerous? You might just as well say that, because a fur coat in Canada at certain times of the year is a truly comfortable garment, therefore a fur coat in the Deccan is just the very garment that you would be delighted to wear. I only throw it out to you as an example and an illustration. Where the historical traditions, the religious beliefs, the racial conditions, are all different – there to transfer by mere untempered and cast-iron logic all the conclusions that you apply in one case to the other, is the height of political folly . . .[42]

At first glance, it might seem that Morley is trying to separate India from the paralysing web of colonial analogies, in the same way as he had earlier sought to disentangle Ireland. However, what is happening here is fundamentally different: Morley, by insisting on differences between India and other colonies, is trapped by intra-imperial analogies, their function being not only to create similarities, but also 'tempered' differences, between colonies. From that position, Morley attacks Indian nationalists' rhetoric of sameness. Morley's predicament of ruling India after Ireland demonstrates the near inescapability of analogical practice within the Empire, even for a conscientious critic of political discourses like Morley, as well as revealing a crucial difference between the imperial analogies made by imperialists and those drawn by nationalists. The imperialist analogies create the space for accommodating 'differences' (by no means real differences, but ones ethnologically regulated and politically manipulated). Kipling celebrated a diversity of colonies and tribes, being proud of his ability to represent subtle differences. On the other hand, the nationalist analogies aim to shatter this Empire of nicely laid-out differences and semblances between colonies by imposing a 'cast-iron' sameness: no matter how different the historical traditions, the religious beliefs, the racial conditions are, all colonies are the same because they are ruled by England. Such discourse demolishes differences and leaves the ashes of sameness – like dynamite – and was therefore deemed extremely dangerous. Kipling's representation of anti-imperial networks acknowledges the power of these nationalist discourses which transform the transcolonial federation – the very foundation of the Empire – into discursive dynamite. Kipling's Empire should be understood alongside this dynamite, which he took such pains to contain.

One example of such nationalist 'fallacies' was undoubtedly Maud Gonne's designation of Queen Victoria as the 'Famine Queen'. This explosive image, connecting India and Ireland through the spectre of famine, emerged in 1900 through the mediation of another colony, South Africa, in the midst of the Boer War. At this time, the visitation of the 'Famine Queen' in India was no fiction, for India was suffering from the 'Great Famine' of 1899–1900, the worst famine on record, breaking out only two years after the catastrophic famine of 1896–7 – India was certainly *not* the colourful playground represented in *Kim* (1901) when the novel was being written.[43] The famines in India and Ireland were notably marked by the *same* image which was crucial to the representation of the Empire, namely, the image of home. If Victorian Britain's self-portrait was of a happy, prosperous Home, both India and Ireland under the famines were represented as its antithesis – a neglected home space, a loss of homes; this image was perhaps more clearly visible in the case of the Irish famines, which were always presented as scenes of eviction. Through the image of Victoria as 'the Famine Queen', Gonne superimposed the two famine-stricken home spaces to create one disparaging image of English misrule. In this sense, 'the Famine Queen' can be seen as a counter to Kipling's representation of the Irish in India, in which the two home spaces – the India to which they immigrate and the Ireland they left behind – are kept safely separate, in order to defend the wholesome image of Empire as Home.

4

In 1847, *The Times* reported that the news of the Irish famines prompted liberal subscriptions for the relief fund from Indians of all ranks and classes, which 'evidences the vital unity of feeling which binds together the members of England's mighty empire'.[44] The *Irish* sympathy for the famine-stricken India was, in turn, also witnessed, for example in 1861, when a relief fund for the Indian famine was raised in Ireland and the Archbishop of Dublin, Richard Whately, expressing sympathy for Indians, referred to 'the Irish famine as enabling the people of [Ireland] to comprehend the terrible nature of their sufferings'.[45] 'These mutual acts of kindness and fellow feeling' among the imperial subjects were, to quote *The Times* again, supposed to 'strengthen the attachment both of the mother country and her dependencies, and are among the best pledges of its perseverance'.[46] The common calamity joined the two British colonies in deep sympathy, and this binding sentiment could be found in plenty throughout the nineteenth century, for both India and Ireland suffered from recurring famines. As Mahatma Gandhi, in an appeal for funds for the Indian famine, made in a letter to the editor of the *Natal Advertiser* dated 30 July 1900, writes:

> The Lord Bishop of Natal has dwelt on the good that the [Boer] War, bad as it is, has done, in that it has brought closer together the various parts of the mighty Empire to which it is our pride to belong. It may be that the threefold scourge in India – viz. Famine, plague and cholera – black as it is, will be the means of forging another link in the chain that ties all together.[47]

Maud Gonne, far less tactfully than Gandhi, called this black imperial tie binding the colonies together 'the Famine Queen'. Her article 'The Famine

Queen' first appeared in her Paris-based paper, *L'Irelande Libre*, and the English translation of the article was published in the *United Irishman* on 7 April 1900, to coincide with the Queen's visit to Ireland. Gonne interpreted this visit as part of a recruitment drive to encourage more Irishmen – 'the victims of the criminal policy of her reign, the survivors of sixty years of organised famine'[48] – to enlist and die at the front. Gonne holds the Queen accountable for '[e]very eviction during sixty-three years [which] has been carried out in [her] name', the fate of 'the poor Irish emigrant girls whose very innocence renders them an easy prey' on foreign shores, and evokes a vivid image of dying Irish mothers and their resentful voices, rarely recorded: '[T]he countless Irish mothers who, shelterless under the cloudy Irish sky, watching their starving little ones, have cursed [the Queen] before they died.' These voices were consciously and unconsciously silenced by the Famine Queen, 'whose bourgeoise virtue is so boasted and in whose name [Irish] homes were destroyed'.[49] Irish mothers' voices and their home space were overridden by Queen Victoria, the imperial Mother.

Though 'The Famine Queen' only addressed the Irish famine, Gonne, in articles which appeared subsequently in the *United Irishman*, repeatedly turned to *Indian* famines to illustrate her point that '[n]o Government has ever systematised the art of draining the life blood of a people as the English Government has done'.[50] Indeed, one of her articles is entitled 'India', and in this she calls the imperial policy 'a famine policy' by which the government creates a chronic state of famine by steadily exhausting the resources of her colonies to make them pay for the cost of the Empire. No drastic measure to relieve the death agony of her subjects would be taken – unless 'their material interest is the bugle-call':

> If the Indian people or the Irish people once realised the true meaning of 'famine policy' they would say 'It is better to die fighting than starving; by fighting perchance we may save the lives of our children, and future generations, delivered from English rule, will bless us.' The people of Ireland and India should realise that if alone they may not attain to ideal freedom, they would be better under the rule of any other power than that of England, for no other power adopted a 'famine policy'.[51]

In her condemnatory description of the imperial policy as a famine policy, the suffering of Ireland became equated with that of India. The official reports of eight million famine deaths in India during 1896–7 and of the catastrophic 'Great Famine' raging throughout India during the Boer War, the details of which Gonne extensively quoted in her article, were all transformed into '[t]he death by starvation of millions of *Irish* and Indians' – Ireland's own death, Ireland's own victimization. This identification of India with Ireland can be seen everywhere in her articles: for example: she said, 'the wealth of India' was 'scientifically [drained] to England, as the wealth of Ireland has been drained . . .';[52] 'We in Ireland, like those in India, have let ourselves be hypnotised by England's *pretended* greatness, and have thus brought about our own *real* weakness';[53] '"[F]amine policy" as practiced in India and in Ireland . . . has built up the prosperity of England';[54] and more succinctly, 'Ireland is bled, much as India is bled.'[55] In doing so, Gonne significantly borrowed and spoke in an Indian nationalist voice. Lengthily quoting, in two of her articles, Dadabhai Naoroji's speeches on the Indian famine, in which he strongly criticizes the systematic drain of Indian wealth to England, Gonne assured the readers that '[a]ll that Mr. Naoroji says of India equally applies to Ireland'.[56] The *United Irishman* itself, in concert with Gonne's attack on the imperial famine policy, published details of ghastly episodes of the Great Hunger in the 1840s, alongside the news of the ongoing Indian famines, letting the two constantly echo each other. Through the Indian famines, the suffering of the Irish Famine becomes accentuated, massively exaggerated and presented as a fatal man-made catastrophe which British rule engendered.

Gonne, by frequently borrowing Indian examples, spoke of the Irish condition, in such a way as to suggest that the Great Famine and other recurrent famines in Ireland were not in themselves powerful enough to raise the alarm about an imperial famine policy. India was utilized by Gonne to overcome the loss of voice which Irish nationalism chronically suffered from, and which the British Empire chose not to acknowledge in order to maintain its self-representation as a benevolent protector of all the suffering subjects under her dominion. The famine-stricken condition in Ireland indeed posed a serious problem for Irish nationalism, since famine narratives, especially those formed concurrently with real-time disaster, are by definition what Thomas Lacqueur calls 'humanitarian narratives', whose detailed descriptions of suffering and death are calculated to prompt spontaneous offers of help, sympathy and, most importantly, money; and the English, the nearest and wealthiest neighbours, were inevitably the first recipients of such narratives.[57] This humanitarian drive repeatedly created for England an opportunity to insert itself as a ministering angel – the Queen as a benevolent mother in particular – within the representation of Ireland. A strong counter-representation was needed, which rejected any motherly gesture as an attempt to smother the autonomous voice of Ireland, and asserted its dream of independence: Gonne's 'Famine Queen', who 'in guise of famine relief . . . organise[s] death',[58] was such a representation. Gonne, by letting the 'Famine Queen' preside over the Indian famines, not only paints a disturbing picture of the British Empire, whose splendour rests on 'the millions and millions of famine corpses',[59] but also questions the legitimacy of British rule in India, where the Queen had been more successful in presenting herself as a merciful ruler.

Significantly, in both India and Ireland the famine deprivation was most graphically represented in the form of helpless and homeless children. Not only were mothers dying of hunger, left with no power to feed their own children, but also the whole starving population was turned into infants – the word etymologically means those 'unable to speak' – due to their intense starvation. If, as Margaret Kelleher argues, the representation of famine and its effects are most prevalently represented 'through images of women', especially with the 'depictions of the failure or collapse of [the] primary shelter, or the mother's inability to nourish or protect her child',[60] the effect of this was not only the feminization but also the infantilization of Famine. The absence of a strong mother figure in such representations thus created a space for the English to intervene and speak for them. India was therefore teeming with many well-meaning Englishwomen, who aspired to take up this imperial burden of playing mother figures to hapless Indian children.[61] One of them was Florence Nightingale, who dedicated the latter part of her life to combating the famine-stricken condition of India. She urged the English to speak on behalf of the Indian people: 'We do not care for the people of India . . . Have we no voice for these voiceless millions?'[62]

It is important to note that the model of Victorian domesticity to be propagated throughout the Empire inevitably assumed a public and masculine character, which set out to liberate the passive and corrupted domestic space of the colonized, typically presented as the zenana or harem. This may be why in Kipling's story of the Indian famine, 'William the Conqueror' (1895), the heroine is nicknamed William and helps the relief work with both determination and womanly care, suggesting that English domesticity advanced to India almost like a conquest in response to the famine outbreaks.[63] Significantly, William and her brother's colleague Scott together conquer the famine by becoming surrogate mothers to the starving Indian babies entrusted to them by their helpless mothers. Thus Queen Victoria, firmly in charge of her home management, may appear masculinized, the fearless Britannia in relation to the image of powerless Oriental mothers and the beautiful and passive Erin, but in her man-like efficiency she became an authentic Mother, with the real ability to feed her imperial children (as well as silence them by stuffing their mouths with food), which the famished and feminized Indian and Irish mothers were incapable of.

Gonne typically presents Ireland as 'our Mother and Queen',[64] who rejects Victoria's claim to her land and her Irish children. Gonne, with her renowned beauty and public charisma, embodied this Irish Queen, challenging Queen Victoria's ability to feed Irish children, assuming this role herself. The proudest moment of her life was in 1897 when she 'had stopped a famine and saved many lives' in Mayo[65] which the 'Famine Queen' idly neglected. Queen Victoria, during her visit to Dublin, organized 'Children's Day', which was alternatively called 'Queen's Day', for which nearly 50,000 children from all parts of Ireland were summoned to Phoenix Park to welcome the Queen, each child receiving a substantial luncheon 'with chocolate and sweets *en route*, and on the ground also'.[66] This image of abundance and Irish children happily fed and gathered around the Queen was the opposite image to that of Victoria as the 'Famine Queen's which Gonne sought to propagate. To wipe out the distasteful memory of Children's Day, Gonne organized a counter-demonstration – 'a Patriotic children's treat to all children who had not participated in Queen Victoria's treat'.[67] In her autobiography, Gonne boasts of the spectacular success of this event, to which 'some twenty-thousand children responded, eclipsing Queen Victoria's children's Treat'.[68] Gonne certainly attempted to eclipse the Queen's event by drastically misquoting the number of children who attended – only 15,000 children instead of the 50,000 officially reported.[69] In her article in the *United Irishman*, thanking Irish children for choosing her treat over the Queen's, Gonne writes that these children, even if momentarily, turned Ireland, the sad 'Shan Van Vocht', into Kathleen the Beautiful, 'bright with hope, and powerful with the wonderful vitality of the Irish race'.[70] Feeding Irish children soon became her principal preoccupation, leading her to campaign for the provision of school meals in Ireland in the early 1910s. Again, the spectre of India repeatedly haunted her attempt to save Irish children from hunger. When in 1901 'the Winter Treat' was organized by Inghinidhe na hÉireann (Daughters of Erin), the women's organization launched in 1900 with Gonne as President, magic-lantern views were shown, including 'various scenes illustrating English Rule, such as the Famine in India and in the West of Ireland'.[71] Gonne's *nationalist* voice as the Irish mother was articulated in the context of England's inability to feed all her *imperial* children: '[T]he strangers brought the blight of famine often upon our land, and by thousands the little ones drooped and died . . . by hundreds of thousands in Ireland, by millions in India, by thousands in the Concentration Camps of South Africa, the English have slain the children.'[72]

It was the scene of the Irish famine in Mayo, 'the awful sum of human misery it contains', which made Gonne determined to break 'the veil of silence' cast over England's misgovernment. As she said: 'I will be the voice of these helpless victims of England's policy, I will speak for them before the world.'[73] In a sense, Gonne, as a well-off upper-class woman, responded to famine narratives as humanitarian narratives in the same way as many Englishwomen in the nineteenth century. However, Gonne's voice for India came not from her moral obligation as the colonizer, but from her keen awareness that her voice as an Irish nationalist was equally suppressed and unheard, *just as* millions of Indians were physically and politically made voiceless. Thus she wrote, 'I am one of the race of the oppressed, my people are too weak to weigh in the world's counsels, my voice is feeble and is drowned in the death-sob of the millions of victims of the British Empire. When will a voice be found strong enough to voice their gigantic suffering, a voice of accusation which will startle the rulers of the world?'[74] In the death agony of millions of Indians and all other oppressed races, she recognized her own voice, the voice of Irish nationalism, equally reduced to the scenes of famine, to the cries of the helpless starving children of the Empire, deprived of the power of speech, smothered and overwritten by the English mother, whose imperial Home interdicts the emergence of any other home space to rival her own. Gonne therefore tries to speak *through* Indians and their sufferings, instead of speaking *for* them. In Gonne's accusatory designation of Victoria as the 'Famine Queen', we hear the echo of Indian famines, even the occasional blast of dynamite, which she approved as a legitimate means of vengeance against the Empire. Her association between India and Ireland through famines was designed to be explosive, a stick of dynamite to blast apart the self-righteous representation of the British Empire. To regain the national voice she chose to speak through each other's misery – after all, is it not possible to speak for *the Other's* pain? The result was a powerful anti-imperial network of suffering 'based on mutual hates',[75] whose sweeping generalization through identification was indeed famine-like – denying any subtleties of different circumstances and individual histories, and turning everything it touched into dying, skeletal bodies – but which nevertheless served as a powerful means to demolish the Imperial Home.

* * *

Kipling, in 'On the Strength of a Likeness' (1887), tells the story of a young Indian official, Hannasyde, who becomes a self-appointed 'special *cavalier servente*' to Mrs Landys-Haggert because she is the living image of his old love, Alice Chisane:

> 'Not only were the face and figure of Alice Chisane, but the voice and lower tones were exactly the same, and so were the turns of speech; and the little mannerisms, that every woman has, of gait and gesticulation, were absolutely and identically the same. The turn of the head was the same; the tired look in the eyes at the end of a long walk was the same; the stoop-and-wrench over the saddle to hold in a pulling horse was the same . . .'

Hannasyde only wishes to see and think about the 'maddening and perplexing likeness of face and voice and manner' between the two women and '[a]nything outside that, reminding him of another personality, jarred, and he showed that it did'. He is shaken from his self-satisfactory delusion when Mrs Haggert demands to know the true reason for his devotion, saying that she is 'perfectly certain' that he does not 'care the least little bit in the world for [her]' and, after listening to his confession of his old love, points out that it is not fair to expect her to act 'as the lay-figure for him to hang the rags of his tattered affections on'. After that, even when he goes back to his station and sees no more of Mrs Haggert, 'he found himself thinking steadily of the Haggert-Chisane ghost; and he could not be certain whether it was Haggert or Chisane that made up the greater part of the pretty phantom'. When he meets Mrs Haggert again a month later, he realizes that the two women are different individuals and that it is Mrs Haggert whom he loves.[76]

This story of a projected semblance can be read as another allegory of the Empire, especially of the Empire built on the strength of a likeness between her colonies. Hannasyde sees the similarities between the women in order to perpetuate and idealize his old love, just as England saw her experience with Ireland as the most successful and primal example, which ought to be repeated. The awakening of the Indian official from a world haunted by similarity is all the more interesting, for the story was written around the time – the late 1880s – when the analogical practice on the administrative level suddenly became obsolete. It is significant to note that the figure that is most familiar to Hannasyde because of its resemblance to his old love turns into a 'ghost' once the legitimacy of his projection is challenged. Here the story reminds us of Sigmund Freud's famous essay 'Das Unheimliche' (1919), in which he shows how the familiar and homely (*heimlich*) could easily slip into and coincide with its apparent antonym, the uncanny and unhomely (*unheimlich*). For Freud, the uncanny is not an encounter with the unfamiliar or unknown, but rather the repeated return of the same and familiar. Thus, in *Die Elixire des Teufels*, the novel by E. T. A. Hoffman, who is, according to Freud, 'the unrivalled master of the uncanny in literature',[77] there is a multiplication of 'characters who are to be considered identical because they look alike': '[T]here is a doubling, dividing and interchanging of the self. And finally there is the constant recurrence of the same thing – the repetition of the same features or character-traits or vicissitudes, of the same crimes, or even the same names through several consecutive generations.'[78] The frequent reference to analogies and former colonial experience by imperialists can be characterized as a desire to see what is the same and familiar in the *foreign* land, enabling the colonizers to repeatedly see through the matrix of what they had already known, and thereby to sweep the incomprehensible under a domestic carpet. To borrow Homi K. Bhabha's phrases, the '*heimlich* pleasures of the hearth' were possible only by repressing 'the *unheimlich* terror of the space or race of the Other'.[79] However, the return of the same never failed to accompany the repressed, turning the British Empire as Home into something like a ghost house.

In 'On the Strength of a Likeness', Hannasyde is released from the Haggert-Chisane ghost only when he comes to perceive two women separately as different individuals. The disappearance of the ghost upon recognition of the difference is, however, one detail which did not happen in the history of Ireland. The Home Rule to exorcise the uncanny resemblance between Ireland and other colonies was attempted, promised but never realized. 'The Empire' was haunted and has been haunted by the ghost of resemblance between India and Ireland even to this day – the partition lines drawn in both countries when they achieved independence opened up a threshold which the ghost would not leave.

Conclusion

Going through the pages of Ian Colvin's *The Life of General Dyer* (1929) makes us realize that the stories of Kim and Terence Mulvaney were not merely wishful representations of Irish loyalty to the British Empire, but could pass as illustrative biographies of the Irish who served in India. Born in India in 1864, Reginald Edward Dyer could speak Hindustani like a native throughout his life and later mastered other Oriental languages such as Urdu and Persian. Following the custom of the Anglo-Indian, he was sent Home – in his case to County Cork in Ireland – to be educated at the age of eleven, then entered the Royal Military College in Sandhurst and joined the British Army in 1885. His first service was in Ireland: he helped subdue the 'factions' which were agitating about Home Rule 'with rivets, brickbats, and guns',[1] which reminds us of the row in Silver Street between the English and the Irish in which Mulvaney became involved.[2] He first served in Burma, as Mulvaney did, and then transferred to the army in India. He fought in the Black Mountain Expedition of 1888, to which Mulvaney's former Irish regiment was sent to fight in 'The Way Av Ut'. He converted to Sikhism, following the example of John Nicholson, the Irish hero of the Indian Mutiny. Dyer was, just like Kim, the friend of all the world, easily making friends and allies with various different people in India, owing to 'his knowledge of their language and their customs, and a certain turn of humour which they found irresistible' and above all there was, according to one of his Indian officers, something 'between the eyes', 'which makes [them] all love him'.[3]

The Amritsar Massacre is a significant moment in Indian history in which the Irish in India showed a firm determination to save the British Raj. On 13 April 1919, Dyer gave the order to fire at an unarmed crowd of Indians at Jallianwala Bagh in Amritsar, killing, according to the official record, 379 people and injuring about 1,200. This was intended to put a stop to the unrest which had lately been building near Amritsar, during which several Europeans were killed and a female English doctor was beaten by the Indians, and which was, to the eyes of Europeans, the potential beginning of another Indian Mutiny. Sir Michael O'Dwyer, an Irishman with a Catholic background who was Governor of Punjab at that time, immediately approved the action of General Dyer. Edward Carson, the Unionist leader, defended Dyer in the House of Commons, arguing that he had tried to prevent 'the conspiracy to drive the British out of India . . . developing into revolution'.[4] Carson also stated that 'I am very proud of him as an Irishman'.[5] To these Irishmen, saving the Raj was equal to maintaining Ireland under the Union.

Would Kim and Mulvaney have made the same decision as General Dyer, if placed in the same situation? Probably yes, for their creator, Kipling, had a strong sympathy towards General Dyer's action. Kiping was one of those who sent a wreath when Dyer died in 1927, 'with a card which read "He did his duty as he saw it"'.[6] His friend Rider Haggard recorded in his diary on 4 December 1919 that 'Kipling believes . . . that the worst thing that is happening to us as an Empire is what he calls "the handing over of India"'.[7] In January 1922, Haggard also wrote that Kipling 'takes a most despondent view of the position in Ireland, Egypt and India, and even went so far as to say that it looks as though the Empire were going to fall to pieces'.[8] In this respect, Kipling's *The Irish Guards in the Great War* (1923) was his homage to the Irish military tradition which had fought for the solidarity of the Empire – 'a wonderful tale', according to Patrick Braybrooke writing in 1926, 'and more so when we remember that in the war . . . Ireland did her best to injure her Motherland'.[9] This book was also written in honour of the memory of Kipling's only son, John, who served in the Irish Guards and was killed in his first action at the battle of Loos in 1915; Kipling was to the end the historian of those now forgotten Irish who were loyal to the Empire.[10] Ironically, though, it was Kipling's Indian connection which eventually brought about John's death in the Irish regiment: John was first rejected as a soldier owing to his poor sight, but his father nevertheless secured a position in the Irish Guards through his old friend and hero Lord Roberts, whom he first met in India.

Kipling was a dreamer – as J. M. S. Thomkins puts it, '[The] power of dreaming, which De Quincey calls one of the inlets of the dark sublime into our minds, was certainly his.'[11] With this gift, Kipling created his literary world, deeply in touch with his unconscious dream life. Not only do many of his stories deal with dreams and the supernatural, but he also used his dream power to carve out a most fascinating vision of the Empire, out of many conflicting realities and out of a colonial space full of alien Others, which, 'like language and the unconscious' needed to be 'controlled, ordered, ruled and colonized'.[12] Indeed, Kipling created the British Empire as resembling a dream – almost a masterful dream-work of condensation, with its colonies, different from each other in history, culture and language, threaded together into one vision, solely by virtue of their belonging to the Empire. The combination of India and Ireland was one of the most crucial pieces of his imperial dream-work, combining Europe and Asia, the West and the East, the Celtic and the Orient, the colonizer and the colonized, and one colony with another, while silently erasing the bitter differences between England and Ireland in the form of the Irish Raj. Kim, an imperial boy who is at once Irish and Indian, and therefore quintessentially 'English', is placed in what Edward Said describes as 'a timeless, unchanging, and "essential" locale, a place almost as much poetic as it is actual in geographic correctness'[13] – in the very dream of Empire. Kipling's dream-work was the tracing of the magic of the British Empire itself, which in reality succeeded in bringing different colonies side by side, annihilating vast time and space. The building of imperial networks was undoubtedly the greatest and proudest achievement of the Empire, the most important element of the imperial dreams, and that is why intercolonial analogies and alliances, made by nationalists, proved to be so subversive as the signs of imperial decline started to show. The pairing of India and Ireland is important, because this is precisely where we find two separate dreams born out of the Empire curiously intersect: the dream of India and Ireland closely united in their unwavering loyalty to the Queen, and that of Indian and Irish nationalists, united in their goal of throwing off imperial rule to achieve their respective independences.

Notes

Introduction

1 Rudyard Kipling, *Kim* (Harmondsworth: Penguin Books, 1987), p. 151; my italics.
2 Ibid., p. 137.
3 Henry Yule and A. C. Burnell, *Hobson-Jobson: A Glossary of Colloquial Anglo-Indian Words and Phrases, and of Kindred Terms, Etymological, Historical, Geographical and Discursive*, second edition (London: Routledge & Kegan Paul, 1986), pp. 93–4. The word is also spelled as *Bilayut*, *Billait*, etc.
4 Kipling, *Kim*, op. cit., p. 151.
5 This translation appears two chapters before, when the old Kulu woman replies to an English officer who has tried to mock her: '*Hai*, my son, thou hast never learned all that since thou camest from *Belait* [Europe]' (Ibid., p. 123).
6 Ibid., p. 134.
7 Ibid., p. 151.
8 Donald M. MacRaild, *Irish Migrants in Modern Britain: 1750–1922* (London: Macmillan, 1999), pp. 58–9.
9 Roger Swift and Sheridan Gilley, 'Introduction', in Roger Swift and Sheridan Gilley (eds.), *The Irish in Victorian Britain: The Local Dimension* (Dublin: Four Courts Press, 1999), p. 13.
10 Ibid., p. 9. As to the large Irish community in Victorian Liverpool, see also John Belchem, 'Class, Creed and Country: The Irish Middle Class in Victorian Liverpool', in ibid., pp. 190–211.
11 Kipling, *Kim*, op. cit., p. 142.
12 William Hamley, 'Ireland Our Reproach', *Blackwood's Edinburgh Magazine* 128 (December 1880), 775–92.
13 For example, Keith Jeffery (ed.), *'An Irish Empire'?: Aspects of Ireland and the British Empire* (Manchester and New York: Manchester University Press, 1996); Michael Holmes and Denis Holmes (eds.), *Ireland and India: Connections, Comparisons, Contrasts* (Dublin: Folens, 1997); Narinder Kapur, *The Irish Raj: Illustrated Stories about Irish in India and Indians in Ireland* (Antrim: Greystone Press, 1997). The recent 'India and Ireland' conference in Galway featured many papers exploring various forms of Indo-Irish connections, testifying well to the critical attention lately paid to this topic (The Fourth Galway Conference on Colonialism: India and Ireland, National University of Ireland, Galway, 2–5 June 2004).
14 Javed Majeed, *Ungoverned Imaginings: James Mill's The History of British India and Orientalism* (Oxford: Clarendon Press, 1992), p. 17.

15 S. B. Cook, *Imperial Affinities: Nineteenth-Century Analogies and Exchanges Between India and Ireland* (New Delhi: Sage Publications, 1993), p. 12.
16 Ibid., p. 16.
17 Ibid., p. 17.
18 Michael S. Silvestri, 'The "Sinn Fein of India": Irish Nationalism and the Policing of Revolutionary Terrorism in Bengal, 1905–1939', *Journal of British Studies* 39 (October 2000), 457.
19 Ibid., 455.
20 Elleke Boehmer, *Empire, the National, and the Postcolonial, 1890–1920: Resistance in Interaction* (Oxford: Oxford University Press, 2002).
21 Boehmer's *Empire, the National, and the Postcolonial* examines the interactions between Tagore and Yeats, Margaret Noble and the Bengali activist Aurobindo Ghose. See also Joseph Lennon, 'Writing Across Empire: W. B. Yeats and Rabindranath Tagore', in Patrick Colm Hogan and Lalita Pandit (eds.), *Rabindranath Tagore: Universality and Tradition* (Madison, NJ: Fairleigh Dickinson University Press, 2003), pp. 213–29; Howard Brasted, 'Indian Nationalist Development and the Influence of Irish Home Rule, 1870–1886', *Modern Asian Studies* 14:1 (1980), 37–63; N. F. Anderson, '"Mother Besant" and Indian National Politics', *Journal of Imperial and Commonwealth History* 30:3 (September 2002), 27–54.
22 Gauri Viswanathan, 'Spirituality, Internationalism and Decolonization: James Cousins, the "Irish Poet from India"', in Clare Carroll and Patricia King (eds.), *Ireland and Postcolonial Theory* (Cork: Cork University Press, 2003), pp. 158–176. See also Gauri Viswanathan, 'Ireland, India, and the Poetics of Internationalism', *Journal of World History* 15:1 (March 2004), 7–30; Catherine Candy, 'Relating Feminisms, Nationalisms and Imperialisms: Ireland, India and Margaret Cousins's Sexual Politics', *Women's History Review* 3:4 (1994), 581–94, and 'Margaret Cousins's Occult Feminism in Ireland and India, 1878–1954', in Mary Cullen and Maria Luddy (eds.), *Female Activists: Irish Women and Change, 1900–1960* (Dublin: Woodfield Press, 2001).
23 Stephen Howe, *Ireland and Empire: Colonial Legacies in Irish History and Culture* (Oxford: Oxford University Press, 2002), p. 217.
24 Ibid., pp. 233–5.
25 For the discussion about the propriety of using postcolonial theories within Irish studies, see also Declan Kiberd, *Inventing Ireland* (London: Jonathan Cape, 1995); Colin Graham and Willy Maley (eds.), Special Issue: 'Irish Studies and Postcolonial Theory', *Irish Studies Review* 7:2 (1999); C. Connolly (ed.), Special Issue: 'Postcolonial Ireland?', *European Journal of English Studies* 3:3 (1999).
26 Joseph Lennon, *Irish Orientalism: A Literary and Intellectual History* (New York: Syracuse University Press, 2004).
27 Glenn Hopper and Colin Graham (eds.), *Irish and Postcolonial Writing: History, Theory, and Practice* (New York: Palgrave Macmillan, 2002).
28 The three essays on Indo-Irish connections included in Carroll and King's collection are Amitav Ghosh, 'Mutines: India, Ireland and Imperialism', pp. 122–8; Joseph Lennon, 'Irish Orientalism: An Overview', pp. 129–57, and Gauri Viswanathan's essay on Cousins, which I have already mentioned above (n. 22).

29 Carroll and King, op. cit., p. 11.
30 David Lloyd, 'After History: Historicism and Postcolonial Studies', in Carroll and King, op. cit., p. 55.
31 Ibid., p. 47.
32 Ibid.
33 F. Max Müller, 'Opening Address Delivered by the President of the Aryan Section at the International Congress of Orientalists, Held in London, 14–21 September, 1874', collected in *Chips from a German Workshop* vol. 4 (London: Longmans, Green & Co., 1880), p. 343.
34 I take this phrase from Benedict Anderson, *The Spectre of Comparisons: Nationalism, South Asia and the World* (London and New York: Verso, 1998). In this and in his celebrated *Imagined Communities: Reflections on the Origin and Spread of Nationalism* (London and New York: Verso, 1991), Anderson explores the way in which the new modern temporality, 'empty, homogenous time', created by the circulation of newspapers and other printed materials, gave birth to the idea of the nation as an imagined community, as well as an international space, in which each nation formed its national identity in relation to others. I will discuss this in more detail in Chapter 2. Though Anderson's *The Spectre of Comparisons* is a regional study centred on South Asia, this title seems to me to be a very fitting one to describe the Irish situation within the Empire.
35 For a discussion of the 'whiteness' of the Irish, or their lack of visible racial markers, see Luke Gibbons, 'Race Against Time: Racial Discourse and Irish History', *Oxford Literary Review* 13:1–2 (1991), 95–117. See also Catherine M. Eagan, '"White," if "Not Quite": Irish Whiteness in the Nineteenth-Century Irish-American Novel', *Éire-Ireland: A Journal of Irish Studies* 36:1–2 (Spring–Summer 2001), 66–81.
36 Scott B. Cook, 'The Irish Raj: Social Origins and Careers of Irishmen in the Indian Civil Service, 1855–1914', *Journal of Social History* 20:3 (1987), 507.
37 Ibid., 514.
38 Peter Karsten, 'Irish Soldiers in the British Army, 1792–1922: Suborned or Subordinate?', *Journal of Social History* 17 (Fall 1983), 41–2. See also Lawrence James, *Mutiny: In the British and Commonwealth Forces, 1797–1956* (London: Buchan & Enright, 1987), Chapter 6, 'Red Coat and Green Flag: Irish Mutinies, 1798–1920', pp. 185–208; and Keith Jeffery, 'The Irish Military Tradition and the British Empire' in Keith Jeffery (ed.), op. cit., pp. 94–122 – both authors trace the tradition of the 'Irish Mutinies' in the British army.
39 Karsten, op. cit., 51–2.
40 Mohandas Karamchand Gandhi, *The Collected Works of Mahatma Gandhi*, vol. 7 (Ahmedabad: Navajivan Trust, 1962), p. 213.
41 In May 1798, Wolfe Tone received a letter from his brother William in India, telling that 'he was in health and spirits, being second in command of the infantry of the Peschwa, or chief of the Mahratta State, with appointments of 500 rupees a month, which is about 750*l.* sterling a year'. Wolfe writes in his journal, 'I cannot express the pleasure which this account of his success gave us all . . . Six years ago he went to India as a private soldier, unknown, unfriended and unprotected . . . he has forced his way to a station of rank and eminence, and I have no doubt that his views and talents are extended with

his elevation' (Theobald Wolfe Tone, *Memoirs of Theobald Wolfe Tone*, edited by William Theobald Wolfe Tone, vol. 2, (London: Henry Colburn, 1827), p. 300). According to the *Dictionary of National Biography*, William Henry Tone joined the East India Company's service in 1792, and in 1796 'went to Poona and entered the Mahratta service. He wrote a pamphlet upon "Some Institutions of the Mahratta People", which has been praised by Grant Duff and other historians. He was killed in 1802 in an action near Choli Maheswur, while serving with Holkar' (Leslie Stephen and Sidney Lee (eds.), *Dictionary of National Biography* vol. 19, (London: Oxford University Press, 1959–60), p. 951).

42 J. Mukherjee, 'The Relevance of the Irish Aspect in Rudyard Kipling's *Kim*', *Literary Criterion* 22:4 (1987), 41–5.

43 T. G. Fraser, 'Ireland and India', in Jeffery (ed.), op. cit., p. 78.

44 Rukmini Bhaya Nair, 'The Pedigree of the White Stallion', in Marshall Brown (ed.), *The Use of Literary History,* (Durham, NC, and London: Duke University Press, 1995), p. 162. A similar comment is made by Gayatri Chakravorty Spivak: 'The heroes of both novels [*Gora* and *Kim*] are Irish orphans of the Indian Mutiny, turned Indian. But there the resemblance ends' ('The Burden of English', in Carol A. Breckenridge and Peter van der Veer (eds.), *Orientalism and the Postcolonial Predicament: Perspectives on South Asia* (Philadelphia: University of Pennsylvania Press, 1993), p. 143).

45 Phillip E. Wegner, '"Life as He Would Have It": The Invention of India in Kipling's *Kim*', *Cultural Critique* 26 (Winter 1993–4), 155.

46 Tim Watson, 'Indian and Irish Unrest in Kipling's *Kim*', in Laura Chrisman and Benita Parry (eds.), *Postcolonial Theory and Criticism* (Woodbridge: D. S. Brewer, 2000), pp. 95–113.

47 Ibid., pp. 107, 111.

48 Ibid., p. 110. (Also Wegner, op. cit., 154.)

49 Ibid., p. 106.

50 Kipling, *Kim*, op. cit., p. 291.

51 Ibid., p. 161.

52 Ibid., p. 49.

53 Ibid.

54 Peter H. Hoffenberg, *An Empire Display: English, Indian, and Australian Exhibitions from the Crystal Palace to the Great War* (Berkeley: University of California Press, 2001), p. 27.

55 Kipling, 'The Three Musketeers' (1887), in *Plain Tales from the Hills* (Harmondsworth: Penguin Books, 1987), p. 89.

56 Kipling, *Something of Myself: For My Friends Known and Unknown* (Harmondsworth: Penguin Books, 1977), p. 66. Kipling wrote two poems in honour of Lord Roberts : 'Bobs', collected in *Barrack-Room Ballads* (London: Methuen & Co., 1973), and 'Lord Roberts', an elegy he wrote on Roberts's death in November 1914.

57 Charles Carrington, *Rudyard Kipling: His Life and Work* (London: Macmillan & Co, 1955), p. 370.

Chapter 1. The Taming of the Irish Afreets

1 Margaret Oliphant, ''Tis Sixty Years Since', *Blackwood's Edinburgh Magazine* 161 (May 1897), 609.
2 Charles Carrington, *Rudyard Kipling: His Life and Work* (London: Macmillan & Co, 1955), p. 105.
3 P. J. Keating, *The Working Classes in Victorian Fiction* (London: Routledge & Kegan Paul, 1971), Chapter 6, 'Rudyard Kipling and Cockney Archetypes', pp. 139–66.
4 Ibid., p. 143.
5 Ibid.
6 R. E. Harbord (ed.), *The Readers' Guide to Rudyard Kipling's Work*, vol. 1 (Canterbury: Gibbs & Sons Ltd, 1961), p. 10.
7 Rudyard Kipling, 'The Daughter of the Regiment', in *Plain Tales from the Hills* (Harmondsworth: Penguin Books, 1987), p. 186.
8 Another example of Irish names combined with Indian is 'Krishna Mulvaney', from an episode in which Indians mistake Mulvaney for the God Krishna ('The Incarnation of Krishna Mulvaney' (1889), in *Life's Handicap* (Harmondsworth: Penguin Books, 1987)). Kim's name, 'Kim Rishti ke', meaning 'Kim of the Irish' in Hindi, can also be seen as an Irish name successfully integrated into India.
9 For the idealization of the Victorian home as a sacred place of love and peace, see, for example, Walter E. Houghton, *The Victorian Frame of Mind, 1830–70* (New Haven: Yale University Press, 1957), pp. 341–8; Eric Trudgill, *Madonnas and Magdalens: The Origins and Development of Victorian Sexual Attitudes* (London: Heinemann, 1976), pp. 38–49. Also see Rod Edmond, *Affairs of the Hearth: Victorian Poetry and Domestic Narrative* (London: Routledge, 1988) for a more critical discussion of the ideologies of this ideal image.
10 Kipling, 'The Madness of Private Ortheris' (1888), in *Plain Tales from the Hills*, op. cit., p. 243.
11 Kipling, 'On Greenhow Hill', in *Life's Handicap*, op. cit., p. 84.
12 Miriam Bailin, *The Sickroom in Victorian Fiction: The Art of Being Ill* (Cambridge: Cambridge University Press, 1994), p. 5.
13 These oriental heroines respectively appear in 'Lispeth' (1886) (Lispeth) and 'Beyond the Pale' (Bisesa) in *Plain Tales from the Hills*, op. cit., 'Georgie Porgie' (Georgina) in *Life's Handicap*, op. cit.
14 Kipling, 'Without Benefit of Clergy', in *Life's Handicap*, op. cit., p. 155.
15 Kipling, 'Thrown Away' in *Plain Tales from the Hills*, op. cit., p. 43.
16 Ibid., pp. 46–7.
17 Abdul R. JanMohamed, 'Worldliness-without-World, Homelessness-as-Home: Toward a Definition of the Specular Border Intellectual', in Jessica Munns and Gita Rajan (eds.), *A Cultural Studies Reader: History, Theory, Practice* (London and New York: Longman, 1995), p. 446.
18 Ibid.
19 'Strickland has finished his Indian Service, and lives now at a place in England called Weston-super-Mare, where his wife plays the organ in one of the churches' (Kipling, 'A Deal in Cotton' (1909), in *Actions and Reactions* (London: Macmillan & Co., 1909), p. 173).

20 Kipling, 'Private Learoyd's Story' (1888), in *Soldiers Three and In Black and White* (Harmondsworth: Penguin Books, 1993), p. 20.
21 Kipling, 'The Big Drunk Draf'' (1888), in *Soldiers Three and In Black and White*, op. cit., p. 28.
22 Francis G. Hutchins, *The Illusion of Permanence: British Imperialism in India* (Princeton: Princeton University Press, 1967), p. 112.
23 Recent studies have criticized this portrayal of the British colonial community as 'socially cohesive, composed mainly of upper middle class' stressed by the 'first generation of historians', including Hutchins (Dane Kennedy, *The Magic Mountains: Hill Stations and the British Raj* (Berkeley: University of California Press, 1996), p. 221), and have shed light on the facts that the British Indian population was in fact made up of 'many occupational, ethnic, and other groups with disparate interests and concerns' (ibid., p. 224) and that there were 'various groups on the margin of British society – vagrants, orphans, prostitutes, the insane, and pushed to the social periphery by their mixed racial origin' (ibid., p. 225). See also Teresa Hubel, 'Tommy Atkins in India: Class Conflict and the British Raj', *Kunapipi* 22:1 (2000), 95–105, which reads Kipling's poem 'Danny Deever' as a representation of the experience of working-class soldiers by a middle-class author, Kipling.
24 As for the colonizers' return home as the loss of prestige of white (mem)sahibs, see, for example, Elizabeth Buettner, 'From Somebodies to Nobodies: Britons Returning Home from India', in Martin Daunton and Bernhard Rieger (eds.), *Meanings of Modernity: Britain from the Late-Victorian Era to World War II* (New York: Berg Publishers, 2001), pp. 221–40.
25 Kipling, 'The Courting of Dinah Shadd', in *Life's Handicap*, op. cit., p. 74.
26 Kipling, 'Private Learoyd's Story', op. cit., p. 20.
27 L. Perry Curtis, Jr., *Apes and Angels: The Irishman in Victorian Caricature* (New Abbot: David & Charles, 1971).
28 Cecil Rhodes, cited in V. I. Lenin, *Imperialism: The Highest Stage of Capitalism: A Popular Outline* (Moscow: Foreign Languages Publishing House, 1970), p. 126.
29 Keating, op. cit., p. 166.
30 A. M. Sullivan, 'Why Send More Irish Out of Ireland?', *Nineteenth Century* 14 (July 1883), 133.
31 *A Kipling Note Book* (New York: M. F. Mansfield & A. Wessels, 1899), pp. 113–14. This originally appeared as an open letter entitled 'The Original Mulvaney', in *Literary World*, 14 June 1895.
32 According to H. J. Hanham, in 1830 the Irish constituted 42.2 per cent of the British army, and '[g]iven the immense popularity of O'Connell's repeal movement, that was an alarming proportion, because it meant that a substantial section of the army had to be regarded as at least potentially disloyal and unsuited for employment in Ireland'. The proportion gradually dropped to 37.2 per cent in 1840, and to 12.2 per cent in 1896 ('Religion and Nationality in the Mid-Victorian Army', in M. R. D. Foot (ed.), *War and Society: Historical Essays in Honour and Memory of J. R. Western, 1928–1971* (London: Elek, 1973), p. 161).
33 Kipling, 'The Irish Conspiracy', *Pioneer*, 18 February 1889, reprinted in Harbord (ed.), The Readers' Guide to Rudyard Kipling's Work, verse section, vol. 1 (Canterbury: Messrs. Gibbs & Sons Ltd, 1969).

34 Ibid., pp. 5256–7.
35 Kipling, 'The Mutiny of the Mavericks', in *Life's Handicap*, op. cit., p. 178.
36 Ibid., p. 179.
37 Ibid.
38 Ibid., p. 186.
39 Ibid., p. 179.
40 Ibid., p. 181.
41 Ibid., p. 193. The possibility of the Irish Mutiny in the British army being funded by the Fenian organization was not totally a product of Kipling's imagination. Jeremiah O'Donovan Rossa, in his Irish-American newspaper the *United Irishman*, encouraged Irish soldiers to desert and murder their officers in the heat of the battle, and to 'avail [themselves] of every opportunity to assist' the enemy who are 'fighting gallantly against the cruel, hypocritical, blood-thirsty nation that for so many years held Ireland in bondage' (K. R. M. Short, *The Dynamite War: Irish-American Bombers in Victorian Britain* (Dublin: Gill & Macmillan, 1979), pp. 219–20). According to Short, 'Free copies of *The United Irishman* were offered postpaid to Irish soldiers in the "English" army anywhere in the world' (p. 220).
42 Rudyard Kipling, *Kim* (Harmondsworth: Penguin Books, 1987), p. 70.
43 Ibid., p. 288.
44 Oliphant, op. cit., 606.
45 Oliphant, op. cit., 616.
46 J. Mukherjee, 'The Relevance of the Irish Aspect in Rudyard Kipling's *Kim*', *Literary Criterion* 22:4 (1987), 43.
47 Murrar G. H. Pittock, *Celtic Identity and the British Image* (Manchester: Manchester University Press, 1999), p. 7.
48 Ibid., p. 11.
49 For the relationship and comparisons between Orientalism and Celticism, see, for example, Lyn Innes, 'Orientalism and Celticism', in Glenn Hopper and Colin Graham (eds.), *Irish and Postcolonial Writing: History, Theory, and Practice* (New York: Palgrave Macmillan, 2002), pp. 142–56; Joseph Lennon, *Irish Orientalism: A Literary and Intellectual History* (New York: Syracuse University Press, 2004).
50 Peter Morey, *Fictions of India: Narrative and Power* (Edinburgh: Edinburgh University Press, 2000), Chapter 1, pp. 21–52.
51 Kipling, 'The Courting of Dinah Shadd', op. cit., pp. 74–5.
52 Kipling, 'The Solid Muldoon', in *Soldiers Three and In Black and White*, op. cit., p. 40.
53 Ibid., p. 37.
54 Ibid., p. 45.
55 Kipling, 'The Mutiny of the Mavericks', op. cit., p. 180.
56 Kipling's letter to Margaret Burne-Jones, 28 November 1885–11 January 1886, in Thomas Pinney (ed.), *The Letters of Rudyard Kipling*, vol. 1 (Iowa City: University of Iowa Press, 1990), p. 100.
57 Kipling, 'On the City Wall', in *Soldiers Three and In Black and White*, op. cit., p. 154.
58 Kipling, *Kim*, op. cit., p. 233.

59 Kipling, 'Namgay Doola', in *Life's Handicap*, op. cit., p. 223.
60 Ibid., p. 229.
61 Ibid., p. 228.
62 Ibid., p. 228.
63 Ibid., p. 230.
64 Ibid.
65 Kipling, 'My Lord the Elephant', in *Many Inventions* (London: Macmillan & Co., 1899), p. 46.
66 Ibid., p. 51.
67 Ibid., p. 52.
68 Ibid., p. 53.
69 Ibid., p. 56.
70 Ibid., p. 57.
71 Ibid., p. 58.
72 Ibid., p. 60.
73 Ibid., p. 56.
74 Ibid.
75 Ibid., p. 58.
76 Ibid.
77 Ibid., p. 60.
78 Ibid., p. 69. The name Malachi reappears in 'The Dog Hervey' (1914), in *A Diversity of Creatures* (Harmondsworth: Penguin Books, 1987), this time as that of the narrator's most loyal and obedient dog. The dog wears a 'collar of gold' (p. 140), which allows us to verify the source of the name 'Malachi' – Thomas Moore's 'Let Erin Remember the Days of Old', in *Irish Melodies* (London: Longmans, 1849): 'Let Erin Remember the Days of Old/ Ere her faithless sons betray'd her; / When Malachi wore the collar of gold, / Which he won from her proud invader . . .' (p. 20).
79 For the representation of the tiger as symbolizing the dangerous Orient, see, for example, Colin Pedley, 'Blake's Tiger and the Discourse of Natural History', *Blake: An Illustrated Quarterly* 24:1 (Summer 1990), 238–46, and John Barrell, *The Infection of Thomas de Quincey: A Psychopathology of Imperialism* (New Haven and London: Yale University Press, 1991), Chapter 4, 'Tigridiasis: Tipu's Revenge', pp. 48–66.
80 Within this context, Kipling's *The Jungle Books* (1894–5) can be seen as a political allegory of how the Irish were 'tamed' into a major force of the British Raj. Hathi, the elephant, by request of Mowgli, the future member of the Forestry Service of the Imperial Government in India, blots out an entire village of unruly natives by eating up all the crops with his three sons and other animals in the Jungle, and leaves the villagers absolutely at the mercy of English charity (Oxford: Oxford World's Classics, 1992), 'Letting in the Jungle', pp. 183–211).
81 Kipling, 'The Courting of Dinah Shadd', op. cit., p. 61.
82 Ibid., pp. 61–2.
83 For the representation of the Irish as the Stage Irishman, see J. O. Bartley, 'The Development of a Stock Character', *Modern Language Review* 37 (1942), 438–47; Declan Kiberd, 'The Fall of the Stage Irishman', *Genre* 12 (1979), 451–72.

Chapter 2. When East Meets West: Kipling's India of Anti-Gravity

1 Jacques Derrida, 'Hospitality', translated by Barry Stocker and Forbes Morlock, *Angelaki* 5:3 (December 2000), 3.

2 Ibid., p. 8

3 Ibid., p. 5.

4 Ibid., p. 6.

5 Rudyard Kipling and Wolcott Balestier, *The Naulakha: A Story of West and East* (London: Macmillan & Co., 1892), pp. 6–7. See also M. K. Naik, *Mirror on the Wall: Images of India and the Englishman in Anglo-Indian Fiction* (New Delhi: Sterling Publishers, 1991).

6 Francis G. Hutchins, *The Illusion of Permanence: British Imperialism in India* (Princeton: Princeton University Press, 1967), p. 118.

7 Rudyard Kipling, '"Yoked with an Unbeliever"', in *Plain Tales from the Hills* (Harmondsworth: Penguin Books, 1987), p. 63.

8 Ibid., p. 62.

9 Ibid.

10 Ibid., p. 64.

11 Ibid., p. 62.

12 Ibid., p. 65.

13 Ibid.

14 W. Somerset Maugham, 'The Force of Circumstance', *The Complete Short Stories of W. Somerset Maugham* vol. 1, (London: Heinemann, 1951), p. 501.

15 Ibid., p. 482.

16 Charles Darwin, *On the Origin of Species* (London: John Murray, 1859).

17 Dane Kennedy, *The Magic Mountains: Hill Stations and the British Raj* (Berkeley: University of California Press, 1996), p. 33. See also his 'The Perils of the Midday Sun: Climatic Anxieties in the Colonial Tropics', in John M. Mackenzie (ed.), *Imperialism and the Natural World* (Manchester: Manchester University Press, 1990), pp. 118–40, in which Kennedy traces the medical and official views concerning the tropical environment, considered the biggest barrier to the colonial settlement of the white race; and Warwick Anderson, 'Climates of Opinion: Acclimatization in Nineteenth-Century France and England', *Victorian Studies* 35:2 (Winter 1992), 135–57.

18 For the colonizer's sexual involvement with native women in the nineteenth century, see, for example, Ronald Hyman, *Empire and Sexuality: the British Experience* (Manchester and New York: Manchester University Press, 1990); and Robert J. C. Young, *Colonial Desire: Hybridity in Theory, Culture and Race* (London: Routledge, 1995).

19 Alan Sandison, 'Kipling: The Artist and the Empire', in Andrew Rutherford (ed.), *Kipling's Mind and Art* (Edinburgh: Oliver & Boyd, 1964), p. 151.

20 Ibid., p. 156.

21 Ibid., p. 155.

22 Ibid., p. 157.

23 Kipling, 'The Conversion of Aurelian McGoggin' (1887), in *Plain Tales from the Hills*, op. cit., pp. 117–21.

24 Kipling, 'To be Filed for Reference' (1888), in *Plain Tales from the Hills*, op. cit.,

p. 271. McIntosh Jellaludin is first mentioned in 'The Gate of the Hundred Sorrows' (1884), in the same collection.

25 Ibid., p. 276.

26 Kipling's letter to Edith Macdonald, dated 30 July 1885, quoted in Charles Carrington, *Rudyard Kipling: His Life and Work* (London: Macmillan & Co., 1955), p. 66.

27 Kipling, 'To be Filed for Reference', op. cit., p. 275.

28 Kipling, 'Miss Youghal's *Sais*' (1887), in *Plain Tales from the Hills*, op. cit., pp. 51–6.

29 Kipling, 'To be Filed for Reference', op. cit., p. 275.

30 F. S. R. Roberts, *Forty-One Years in India, from Subaltern to Commander-in-Chief* vol. 1, (London: Macmillan & Co., 1902), p. 214.

31 According to David Arnold, 'Of 9,467 losses sustained by British forces during the 1857–58 uprising, only 586 soldiers were killed in action or died of their wounds: the rest perished from disease' [David Arnold, *Colonizing the Body: State Medicine and Epidemic Disease in Nineteenth-Century India* (Berkeley: University of California Press, 1993), p. 65].

32 Roberts, op. cit., p. 210.

33 Paul Virilio, *Speed and Politics: An Essay on Dromology*, translated by Mark Polizzotti (New York: Semiotext(e), 1986), p. 22.

34 Quoted in John Kaye, *Kaye's and Malleson's History of the Indian Mutiny of 1857–8*, edited by Colonel Malleson vol. 4, (Westport, Conn.: Greenwood Press, 1971), p. 4.

35 Roberts, op. cit., p. 85.

36 Ibid., p. 87.

37 Ibid., p. 86.

38 Ibid., p. 224.

39 Ibid., p. 227.

40 Ibid., p. 213. Though John Nicholson, an Anglo-Irishman, lost his life during the storming of Delhi, he successfully established himself as a legendary English figure in British military history, whereas many authors on the Mutiny have described Wilson as 'a good soldier but not a man of strong character' (*DNB*, vol. 21, p. 551). It is ironic that many of those who made up for the 'weak' character of Wilson the Englishman were of Celtic origin (for example, Richard Baird Smith was a Scot, and John Nicholson of Anglo-Irish descent), but nevertheless figured far more strongly as English. The Mutiny almost looked like the fight of the Celtic figures defending to the last the only ground in which they could be English.

41 Virilio, op. cit., p. 55.

42 Ibid., op. cit., p. 50.

43 'Report from the Select Committee on Colonization and Settlement (India)', *British Sessional Papers*, House of Commons, 1857–8, VII, pt 1, p. 378.

44 Roberts, op. cit., p. ix. For the impact of the Uprising on the evolution of British intelligence gathering in India, see C. A. Bayly, *Empire and Information: Intelligence Gathering and Social Communication in India, 1780–1870* (Cambridge: Cambridge University Press, 1996), especially Chapters 9 and 10.

45 James W. Carey, *Communication as Culture: Essays on Media and Society* (Boston, Mass.: Unwin Hyman, 1989), p. 203.

46 William Lee-Warner, *The Life of the Marquis of Dalhousie K.T.* vol. 2, (Shannon: Irish University Press, 1972), p. 191. During the 1857 Uprising, thousands of telegrams were sent, providing the British with a strategic advantage. The phrase 'the telegraph saved India' is attributed to John Lawrence, and by which, as Mel Gorman very aptly comments, 'he meant the British Empire' ('Sir William O'Shaughnessy, Lord Dalhousie, and the Establishment of the Telegraph System in India', *Technology and Culture* 12 (1971), 599).
47 Rudyard Kipling, *Kim* (Harmondsworth: Penguin Books, 1987), p. 299.
48 Benedict Anderson, *Imagined Communities: Reflections on the Origin and Spread of Nationalism* (London and New York : Verso, 1991).
49 E. Kay Robinson, 'Rudyard Kipling in India', *Pearson's Magazine* 1 (June 1896), 662.
50 J. H. Fenwick, 'Soldiers Three', in Andrew Rutherford (ed.), *Kipling's Mind and Art* (Edinburgh: Oliver & Boyd, 1964), pp. 244–5.
51 Ibid., p. 244.
52 Ibid., p. 245.
53 For the Edenic theme in Kipling's stories, see Constance Scheerer, 'The Lost Paradise of Rudyard Kipling', in Harold Bloom (ed.), *Rudyard Kipling's* Kim (New York: Chelsea House Publishers, 1987), pp. 75–85; James Harrison, 'Kipling's Jungle Eden', in Harold Orel (ed.), *Critical Essays on Rudyard Kipling* (Boston, Mass.: G. K. Hall & Co., 1989), pp. 77–92.
54 Edward W. Said, *Culture and Imperialism* (London: Vintage, 1994), p. 162.
55 Robert F. Moss, *Rudyard Kipling and the Fiction of Adolescence* (London: Macmillan, 1982).
56 Edmonia Hill, 'Young Kipling', *Atlantic Monthly* 157 (1936), 409.
57 Phillip Mallett, *Rudyard Kipling: A Literary Life* (Basingstoke and New York: Palgrave Macmillan, 2003), p. 29.
58 Benedict Anderson, *Imagined Communities*, op. cit., p. 24.
59 Ibid., p. 25.
60 Irene Tucker, 'International Whiggery', *Victorian Studies* 45:4 (Summer 2003), 689.
61 Benedict Anderson, *Imagined Communities*, op. cit., p. 26.
62 William Howard Russell, *My Indian Mutiny Diary*, edited with an essay on the Mutiny and its consequences by Michael Edwardes (New York: Kraus Reprint Co., 1970), p. 137.
63 Ibid., p. 140.
64 Russell, 'The Climate and the Work', *Cornhill Magazine* 6 (August 1862), 244. For the British experience of the hot summer in India before the advent of air-conditioning, see also Charles Allen (ed.), *Plain Tales from the Raj* (London: Futura Publications, 1975), Chapter 11, 'The Hot Weather'.
65 Russell, 'The Climate and the Work', op. cit., p. 241.
66 Thomas Pinney (ed.), *The Letters of Rudyard Kipling*, vol. 1 (Iowa City: University of Iowa Press, 1990), p. 174.
67 Ibid., p. 67.
68 Ibid., p. 31.
69 Ibid., p. 34.
70 Ibid., p. 194.

71 Kipling, 'Till the Day Break', *Civil and Military Gazette*, 19 May 1888, in Thomas Pinney (ed.), *Kipling's India: Uncollected Sketches 1884–88* (Basingstoke: Macmillan, 1986), p. 287.
72 Kipling, 'From the Dusk to the Dawn' (1886), repr. in R. E. Harbord (ed.), *The Readers' Guide to Rudyard Kipling's Work*, vol. 2 (Canterbury: Gibbs & Sons Ltd, 1963), pp. 1091–2.
73 Janet Montefiore, 'Day and Night in Kipling', *Essays in Criticism* 27 (October 1977), 299–314.
74 Kipling, 'Wressley of the Foreign Office', in *Plain Tales from the Hills*, op. cit., p. 260.
75 Kipling, *Something of Myself: For My Friends Known and Unknown* (Harmondsworth: Penguin Books, 1977), p. 64.
76 Kipling, '"The City of Dreadful Night"', in *Life's Handicap* (Harmondsworth: Penguin Books, 1987), p. 283.
77 Ibid., p. 283.
78 Ibid., p. 284.
79 Ibid.
80 Ibid., p. 285.
81 Ibid., p. 286.
82 Ibid., p. 288.
83 Kipling, 'Indian Journalism', repr. in R. E. Harbord (ed.), *The Readers' Guide to Rudyard Kipling's Work*, vol. vii (Canterbury: Gibbs & Sons Ltd, 1972), p. 3323.
84 Kipling, 'Haunted Subalterns', in *Plain Tales from the Hills*, op. cit., pp. 107–11.
85 Kipling, 'The Conversion of Aurelian McGoggin', op. cit., pp. 117–21.
86 Hutchins, op. cit., p. 104.
87 Ibid., p. 105.
88 Pinney, *Letters*, op. cit., p. 34. William Russell also writes, 'There is a sun, indeed, which tells us we are not in Kent' (Russell, *My Indian Mutiny Diary*, op. cit., p. 141).
89 Kavita Philip, 'English Mud: Towards a Critical Cultural Studies of Colonial Science', *Cultural Studies* 12:3 (July 1998), 305.
90 Ibid., 303.
91 See Dane Kennedy, *The Magic Mountains*, op. cit., Chapter 3, 'Landscapes of Memories', in which Kennedy traces the Anglo-Indian representations of the mountainous regions as similar to the English highlands.
92 Kipling, 'On Greenhow Hill', in *Life's Handicap,* op. cit., p. 83.
93 Pinney, Letters, op. cit., p. 130.
94 Kipling, *Something of Myself*, op. cit., p. 71.
95 Ibid.
96 Kipling went back to India in December 1891. He recorded details of this visit in his article titled 'Home', *Civil and Military Gazette*, 25 December 1891, repr. in R. E. Harbord (ed.) *The Readers' Guide to Rudyard Kipling's Work*, vol. 5 (Canterbury: Gibbs & Sons Ltd, 1970), pp. 2488–504.
97 Kipling, 'The Daughter of the Regiment', in *Plain Tales from the Hills*, op. cit., p. 189.
98 Kipling, 'With the Main Guard', in *Soldiers Three and In Black and White* (Harmondsworth: Penguin Books, 1993), pp. 46–7.

99 Kipling, 'In the Matter of a Private', in *Soldiers Three and In Black and White*, op. cit., p. 61.
100 Kipling, 'My Lord Elephant', in *Many Inventions* (London: Macmillan & Co., 1899) p. 44.
101 Kipling, 'His Private Honour', in *Many Inventions*, op. cit., p. 136.
102 Kipling, '"Love-O'-Women"', in *Many Inventions*, op. cit., p. 264.
103 Kipling, 'The Incarnation of Krishna Mulvaney', in *Life's Handicap*, op. cit., p. 54.
104 Kipling, 'His Private Honour', op. cit., p. 149.
105 Kipling, '"Love-O'-Women"', in *Many Inventions*, op. cit., pp. 261–2.
106 K. Bhaskara Rao, *Rudyard Kipling's India* (Norman: University of Oklahoma Press, 1967), p. 162.
107 Kipling, 'The Courting of Dinah Shadd', in *Life's Handicap*, op. cit., p. 56.
108 Ibid., p. 58.
109 Kipling, 'The Incarnation of Krishna Mulvaney', op. cit., p. 45.
110 Rukmini Bhaya Nair, 'The Pedigree of the White Stallion', in Marshall Brown (ed.), *The Use of Literary History* (Durham, NC, and London: Duke University Press, 1995), p. 181.
111 Ibid., p. 182.
112 Ibid., p. 183.
113 Kipling, 'With the Main Guard', op. cit., p. 46.
114 Anthony Babington, *The Devil to Pay: The Mutiny of the Connaught Rangers, India, July 1920* (London: Leo Cooper, 1991), p. 2.
115 Virilio, *Open Sky*, translated by Julie Rose (London: Verso, 1997), p. 10.
116 Ibid., p. 2.
117 Thomas Richards, *The Imperial Archive: Knowledge and the Fantasy of the Empire* (London and New York: Verso, 1993), p. 6.
118 Ibid., p. 30.
119 Kipling, *Kim*, op. cit., p. 286.
120 Ibid., p. 273.

Chapter 3. Exiled Home: The Voice of the Irish Soldiers

1 Katherine Fullerton Gerould, 'The Man Who Made Mulvaney', *Harper's Monthly Magazine* 172 (1936), 531–8. According to Gerould, a New York newspaper in 1899 composed a poem in honour of Kipling, affectionately calling him 'the man who made Mulvaney and the Road to Mandalay' (p. 531).
2 *The Times*, 25 March 1890, 3a.
3 G. F. Monkshood (W. J. Clarke) and George Gamble, *Rudyard Kipling: An Attempt at Appreciation* (London: Greening & Co., 1902), p. 106. This book was originally published in 1899 (with 'G. F. Monkshood' as a sole author). A new chapter is added to this third edition, which makes reference to Kipling's more recent works like 'The Absent-Minded Beggar' and *Kim*.
4 *Academy*, 20 March 1897, 332.
5 Rudyard Kipling, *Kim* (Harmondsworth: Penguin Books, 1987), p. 251.
6 Kipling, 'Private Learoyd's Story', in *Soldiers Three and In Black and White* (Harmondsworth: Penguin Books, 1993), p. 26.
7 Kipling, 'The God from the Machine', (1888) in *Soldiers Three and In Black and White*, op. cit., p. 16.

8 *The Times*, 7 July 1893, 3c.

9 Kipling, 'The Incarnation of Krishna Mulvaney', in *Life's Handicap* (Harmondsworth: Penguin Books, 1987), pp. 50–51.

10 It should be noted that Kim is often compared to the god Krishna by many critics: for example, Bart Moore-Gilbert, '"The Bhabhal of Tongues": Reading Kipling, Reading Bhabha', in Bart Moore-Gilbert (ed.), *Writing India 1757–1990* (Manchester: Manchester University Press, 1996), p. 129.

11 Kipling, *Kim*, op. cit., p. 177.

12 Kipling, 'The Incarnation of Krishna Mulvaney', op. cit., p. 46.

13 Kipling, *Kim*, op. cit., p. 223.

14 Ibid., p. 220.

15 Ibid., p. 239.

16 For a more detailed analysis of Kim's chee-chee accent, see Janet Montefiore, *Rudyard Kipling* (Plymouth: Northcote House, 2006), Chapter 6, 'Kim'.

17 Linda Dowling, *Language and Decadence in the Victorian Fin de Siècle* (Princeton: Princeton University Press, 1986), p. xv.

18 Ibid., p. 28.

19 Andrew Lang, 'Ballads', in *Encyclopaedia Britannica*, ninth edition, vol. 3 (1875), p. 285.

20 The word 'subaltern' was originally Gramsci's euphemism for the proletariat. In the postcolonial field it is used for the Others whose voices cannot be heard, since they have been deprived of the power of self-representation (David Lloyd, *Anomalous States: Irish Writing and the Post-Colonial Moment* (Dublin: Lilliput Press, 1993), p. 126).

21 Andrew Lang, 'Mr. Kipling's Stories', in *Essays in Little* (London: Henry & Co., 1891), pp. 198–9.

22 Kipling, 'The Man who would be King', in *Wee Willie Winkie* (Harmondsworth: Penguin Books, 1989), p. 224.

23 Charles Kingsley, *Charles Kingsley: His Letters and Memories of his Life, Edited by His Wife* (London: Kegan Paul, Trench & Co., 1888), p. 208.

24 In fact, many of Kipling's Irish characters have red hair. Kipling represents the Irish descendant Namgay Doola and his children with 'flaming red hair' in 'Namgay Doola' (1891; *Life's Handicap,* op. cit., p. 227). Judy Sheehy, who tries to seduce Mulvaney in 'The Courting of Dinah Shadd' (*Life's Handicap*), has hair 'that was like red snakes' and 'green cat's eyes' (p. 70). Jhansi McKenna in 'The Daughter of the Regiment' (*Plain Tales from the Hills* (Harmondsworth: Penguin Books, 1987)) also has 'all yellow freckles and red hair', (p. 185). In *Stalky and Co.* (1899; *The Complete Stalky & Co.* (Oxford: Oxford World's Classics, 1991)), an Irish boy, 'Paddy' Vernon, is also 'red-headed' (p. 170), and so is the Irish boy M'Turk, represented with hair of 'the dark mahogany red that goes with a certain temperament' (p. 11). In these cases, red hair represents the fiery temper and potential rebelliousness of the Irish, whereas the exemplary Irish couple, Mulvaney and Dinah Shadd are *not* marked with red hair.

25 For example, in 'The Daughter of the Regiment', the narrator proposes going to the parade ground 'under the stars' instead of listening to Mulvaney's story at the refreshment table (op. cit., pp. 185–6). 'In the Matter of the Private' and

'With the Main Guard' (*Soldiers Three and In Black and White*) also have a night-time setting.

26 Kipling, 'The God from the Machine', op. cit., p. 11.

27 M. M. Bakhtin, *The Dialogic Imagination, Four Essays, by M. M. Bakhtin*, edited by Michael Holquist and translated by Caryl Emerson and Michael Holquist (Austin: University of Texas Press, 1981), p. 431.

28 Kipling, 'The Three Musketeers', in *Plain Tales from the Hills*, op. cit., p. 88.

29 Ibid.

30 Ibid., p. 89.

31 Ibid., p. 88.

32 Ibid., p. 85; my italics.

33 Mae Gwendolyn Henderson, 'Speaking in Tongues: Dialogics, Dialectics and the Black Woman Writer's Literary Tradition', in Sidonie Smith and Julia Watson (eds.), *Women, Autobiography, Theory, A Reader* (London: University of Wisconsin Press, 1998), p. 344.

34 Michael Bernard-Donals, 'Knowing the Subaltern: Bakhtin, Carnival, and the Other Voice of the Human Sciences', in Michael Mayerfield Bell and Michael Gardiner (eds.) *Bakhtin and the Human Sciences* (London: Sage Publications, 1998), p. 124.

35 Robert Buchanan, 'The Voice of the Hooligan', *Contemporary Review* 76 (1899), repr. in Roger Lancelyn Green (ed.), Kipling: *The Critical Heritage* (London: Routledge & Kegan Paul, 1971), p. 241.

36 Ambreen Hai, in her 'On Truth and Lie in a Colonial Sense: Kipling's Tales of Tale-Telling', *ELH* 64:2 (Summer 1997), argues that Kipling is 'heavily self-conscious about his role as a colonial writer' (600) and suggests that he is well aware that he takes part in this silencing (622, n.15).

37 Kipling, *From Sea to Sea and Other Sketches: Letters of Travel* vol. 2, (London: Macmillan & Co., 1900), p. 125.

38 Kipling, 'The Three Musketeers', op. cit., p. 89.

39 Kipling, '"In Ambush"', in *The Complete Stalky & Co.*, op. cit., p. 35.

40 Ibid., p. 37.

41 Kipling, 'Private Learoyd's Story', op. cit., pp. 20–27.

42 Kipling, 'On Greenhow Hill', in *Life's Handicap*, op. cit., p. 79.

43 Ibid., p. 88.

44 Ibid., p. 93.

45 Kipling, 'My Lord the Elephant', in *Many Inventions* (London: Macmillan & Co., 1899), p. 61.

46 Ibid., p. 70.

47 Kipling, 'The Courting of Dinah Shadd', op. cit., p. 64.

48 Kipling, 'The Big Drunk Draf'', in *Soldiers Three and In Black and White*, op. cit., p. 30.

49 Ibid., p. 31.

50 Ibid., p. 30.

51 Ibid., p. 28; Kipling, 'Troopin'', in *The Complete Barrack-Room Ballads*, edited by Charles Carrington (London: Methuen & Co., 1973), pp. 61–2.

52 Kipling, 'The Big Drunk Draf'', op. cit., p. 28.

53 Ibid., p. 33.

54 Graham Pechey, 'On the Borders of Bakhtin: Dialogization, Decolonization', *Oxford Literary Review* 9:1–2 (1987), 64.
55 Kipling, 'With the Main Guard', op. cit., p. 48.
56 Kipling, 'The Incarnation of Krishna Mulvaney', op. cit., p. 32.
57 For a rough chronology of Mulvaney's life, see R. E. Harbord (ed.), *The Readers' Guide to Rudyard Kipling's Work*, vol. 1 (Canterbury: Gibbs & Sons Ltd, 1961), p. 10; see also Appendix B in Kipling's, *Soldiers Three and In Black and White*, op. cit., pp. 209–10.
58 Kipling, 'The Incarnation of Krishna Mulvaney', op. cit., p. 32.
59 P. J. Keating, *The Working Classes in Victorian Fiction* (London: Routledge & Kegan Paul, 1971), p. 143. See also Chapter 1 of this book, pp. 20–21.
60 Kipling, 'Black Jack' (1888), in *Soldiers Three and In Black and White*, op. cit., p. 74.
61 As F. V. F., in his article 'The Mavericks of "Kim"' (*Kipling Journal* 152 (December 1964)), points out, Father Victor in the Mavericks is described as 'the Roman Catholic Chaplain of the Irish contingent' (*Kim*, op. cit., p. 133), which suggests that the main body of the regiment is Protestant, of which the Reverend Arthur Bennett, 'the Church of England Chaplain of the regiment' (ibid., p. 130) is in charge (p. 9). Further evidence of this, according to F. V. F., is the existence of a Masonic Lodge in the Mavericks: 'Free Masonry was proscribed by the Roman Catholic Church and a Lodge would have been a constant cause of offence to the Catholics' (p. 9).
62 See the 'Notes' to *Soldiers Three and In Black and White*, op. cit., p. 177, n. 7.
63 Homer, *The Odyssey*, translated by E. V. Rieu (Harmondsworth: Penguin Books, 1991), p. 3.
64 Ibid., p. 127.
65 Ibid., p. 3.
66 Ibid., p. 125.
67 'Tiger! Tiger!' is the third of the seven stories of *The Jungle Book* (1894), while 'How Fear Came' is in *The Second Jungle Book*, published in 1895 (*The Jungle Books* (Oxford: Oxford World's Classics, 1992), pp. 48–66, 149–67).
68 Kipling, *Kim*, op. cit., p. 100.
69 Kipling, *The Complete Barrack-Room Ballads*, op. cit., p. 36.
70 It is worth noting that the idealization of the old days as a period free from violence and injustice was thought to be a common aspect of Irish nationalism. For example, Frances Power Cobbe, in her article 'The Fenian Idea' (*Atlantic Monthly* 17 (May 1866)), criticizes a 'popular Irish idea' (573) that Ireland, before being colonized by England, was 'an age of gold' (576), 'a grand era of universal prosperity and civilization' (575), in which every Irishman was 'not a labourer or carter, shoemaker or tailor, but the head of some ancient house, – Some O' or Mac, – living not in his own mud cabin, but in the handsome residence of some English gentleman whose estate was wrongly taken in "former times" from his – the labourer's or shoemaker's – ancestors' (574), an idea which helps perpetuate 'the tradition of imaginary wrongs' (577).
71 'The Black Mountain Expedition', *Illustrated London News*, 20 October 1888, 447.
72 Kipling, 'The Way Av Ut', *Pioneer*, 8 October 1888, repr. in Harbord (ed.), *The Readers' Guide to Rudyard Kipling's Work*, verse section, vol. 1 (Canterbury:

Messrs. Gibbs & Sons Ltd, 1969), p. 5226.

73 Ibid.

74 Ibid., p. 270.

75 Kipling, 'With the Main Guard', op. cit., p. 48; my italics.

76 In '"Love-O'-Women"', Mulvaney says, 'Faith, ivry time I go on prisoner's gyard in coort I wondher fwhy I was not where the pris'ner is. But the man I struk tuk it in fair fight, an' he had the good sinse not to die' (op. cit., p. 271). Also, in 'Black Jack', Mulvaney admits that he once 'nearly killed' one of the Black Irish [op. cit., p. 75].

77 Kipling, *The Complete Barrack-Room Ballads*, op. cit., pp. 36–7.

78 Kipling, 'Black Jack', op. cit., pp. 74–5.

79 Ibid., p. 75.

80 Bram Stoker, *Dracula*, edited by Nina Auerbach and David J. Skal (New York and London: Norton & Co., 1997), p. 316.

81 Much has already been written on how Stoker's Irishness is represented in *Dracula*. For example, Burton Hatlen argues that, though there are no Irish characters in the novel, his Irishness as Otherness is displaced onto the three outsiders, namely, Count Dracula, Quincey Morris and Van Helsing ('The Return of the Repressed/Oppressed in Bram Stoker's *Dracula*', *Minnesota Review* 15 (1980), 94). Stephen D. Arata suggests a way to read *Dracula* within the Anglo-Irish context, for Bram Stoker himself was a 'transplanted Irishman, one whose national allegiances were consciously split' ('The Occidental Tourist: *Dracula* and the Anxiety of Reverse Colonization', *Victorian Studies* 33 (Summer 1990), 633). Dracula's invasion of Britain can be read, according to Arata, not only as a manifestation of the 'seldom dormant fear of an Irish uprising' (633), but also as a good example of 'a reversal of Britain's imperial exploitations of "weaker" races, including the Irish' which is 'mirrored back as a kind of monstrosity' (634). See also, Michael Valdez Moses, 'The Irish Vampire: Dracula, Parnell, and the Troubled Dreams of Nationhood', *Journal X* 2:1 (Autumn 1997), 66–111, in which Moses argues that Stoker's vampire reflects the figure of Charles Stewart Parnell; and Susanne Hagemann, 'The Irishness of *Dracula*', in Winnifred M. Bogaards (ed.), *Literature of Region and Nation: Proceedings of the 6th International Literature of Region and Nation Conference, 2–7 August 1996* (Saint John, NB: Social Sciences and Humanities Research Council of Canada, with University of New Brunswick in Saint John, 1998), pp. 239–53, in which Hagemann suggests the possibility of reading the death of Dracula as a triumph of Irish nationalism, Count Dracula being a personification of England and Mina that of Ireland, which needs to be cleansed of the colonial violation.

82 Kipling, *Kim*, op. cit., p. 100.

83 Kipling, 'The Incarnation of Krishna Mulvaney', op. cit., pp. 39–40.

84 Ibid., p. 40.

85 Kipling, 'With the Main Guard', op. cit., p. 55.

86 Tim Watson, 'Indian and Irish Unrest in Kipling's *Kim*', in Laura Chrisman and Benita Parry (eds.), *Postcolonial Theory and Criticism* (Woodbridge, Suffolk: D. S. Brewer, 2000), p. 110.

87 Kipling, *Kim*, op. cit., p. 331.

88 Ibid., p. 332.
89 Hugh Haughton, 'Introduction', in Kipling, *Wee Willie Winkie*, op. cit., p. 428.
90 Kipling, 'The Last of the Stories', in *Wee Willie Winkie*, op. cit., p. 387.
91 Ibid., p. 375.
92 Ibid., p. 380.
93 Ibid., p. 381.
94 Ibid., p. 385.
95 Ibid., p. 386.
96 Ibid., p. 377.

Chapter 4. Shamrocks in the Veldt: Two Types of Aphasic Empire

1 Roman Jakobson, *Selected Writings, Volume 2: Word and Language* (The Hague: Mouton, 1971), p. 238.
2 Alfred Austin, *Songs of England* (London: Macmillan & Co., 1898), p. 7.
3 Ibid.
4 Ibid., p. 5.
5 Ibid., p. 36.
6 *Literature*, 7 May 1898 vol. 2, (New York: Arno Press, 1974), p. 526.
7 Ibid., 13 July 1901, vol. 9, p. 26.
8 Thomas Pinney (ed.), *The Letters of Rudyard Kipling*, vol. 3 (Iowa City: University of Iowa Press, 1996), p. 73.
9 Rudyard Kipling, 'Our Lady of the Snows', in *The Five Nations* (London: Methuen & Co., 1903), p. 87.
10 Kipling, 'The Young Queen', in *The Five Nations*, op. cit., pp. 100–103.
11 Julian Ralph, *War's Brighter Side: The Story of "The Friend" Newspaper Edited by the Correspondents with Lord Roberts's Forces, March–April 1900* (London: C. Arthur Pearson Ltd, 1900), p. 263.
12 Maud Gonne MacBride, *A Servant of the Queen: Reminiscences* (Suffolk: Boydell Press, 1983), p. 291.
13 C. Headlam (ed.), *The Milner Papers: South Africa, 1899–1905* (London: Cassell, 1931), pp. 29–30.
14 George Earle Buckle (ed.), *The Letters of Queen Victoria*, vol. 3 (London: John Murray, 1932), p. 457.
15 Jakobson, op. cit., p. 244.
16 Ibid., p. 251.
17 Ibid., p. 258.
18 William Whewell, 'The General Bearing of the Great Exhibition on the Progress of Art and Science', in W. Whewell et al., *Lectures on the Results of the Great Exhibition of 1851* (London: David Bogue, 1852), p. 14.
19 Ibid.
20 *The Friend*, 21 March 1900, cited in Ralph, op. cit., pp. 86–7. *The Friend* was edited by the special war correspondents of various newspapers (Julian Ralph of the *Daily Mail*, Perceval Landon of *The Times*, H. A Gwynne of Reuters) and by Rudyard Kipling, who willingly participated as sub-editor.
21 Ibid., p. 87.
22 *A Kipling Note Book* (New York: M. F. Mansfield & A. Wessels, 1899), pp. 49–50.

23 S. B. Cook, *Imperial Affinities: Nineteenth-Century Analogies and Exchanges Between India and Ireland* (New Delhi: Sage Publications, 1993), pp. 26–7.
24 Sigmund Freud, *The Interpretation of Dreams* (Harmondsworth: Penguin Books, 1991), pp. 417–19.
25 Pinney, op. cit., p. 87.
26 Ibid., p. 101.
27 Ralph, op. cit., p. 104. Kipling was not the only one who was reminded of his experience of India during the Boer War: Erskine Childers, when encountering the unpleasant smell of dead horses in the washing places, is also reminded of Kipling's description of 'a subtle and complex odour . . . of the great Indian Empire', adding that the 'simple and direct' smell of 'the great African Empire in this year of grace' is nothing like the subtle smell of Kipling's India. The contrast between the two smells perhaps suggests a discrepancy between the Empire's ideal (represented by Kipling's Indian Empire) and its reality, which the Irishman came to sense in Africa (*In the Ranks of the C.I.V.: A Narrative and Diary of Personal Experiences with the C.I.V. Battery (Honourable Artillery Company) in South Africa* (London: Smith, Elder & Co., 1901), p. 194).
28 Mohandas Karamchand Gandhi, *The Collected Works of Mahatma Gandhi*, vol. 3 (Ahmedabad: Navajivan Trust, 1960), p. 198.
29 Javed Majeed, *Ungoverned Imaginings: James Mill's The History of British India and Orientalism* (Oxford: Clarendon Press, 1992), p. 96. This passage can be found in Thomas Moore, *Lalla Rookh: An Oriental Romance* (London: Longmans, 1861), pp. xvii–xviii.
30 D. W. Cahill, *Important Letter from the Rev. D. W. Cahill, D.D.* (Dublin: J. F. Nugent, 1858), pp. 1–7: 'On the Defeat of the English in India, This Day, Saturday, 5 June 1858.'
31 Ibid., pp. 1–2: 'On the General Conditions of the Army in India, This Day, Saturday, 12 June 1858.'
32 Ibid., p. 7.
33 Ibid., p. 8.
34 Byron Farwell, *Queen Victoria's Little Wars* (London: Allen Lane, 1973), p. 180.
35 *Hansard*, 25 October 1899, 621.
36 Ibid., 7 February 1900, vol. 78, 831.
37 Ibid.
38 Michael J. F. McCarthy, *Five Years in Ireland, 1895–1900* (London: Simpkin, Marshall, Hamilton, Kent, 1901), p. 447.
39 J. B. Robinson, 'The South African Settlement', *Contemporary Review* 78 (October 1900), 461.
40 *Hansard*, 7 February 1900, 851.
41 Emanoel Lee, *To the Bitter End: A Photographic History of the Boer War 1899–1902* (Harmondsworth: Penguin Books, 1985), p. 53.
42 MacBride, *Servant of the Queen*, op. cit., p. 342.
43 Jakobson, op. cit., p. 248.
44 *Hansard*, 7 February 1900, 841.
45 Ibid., 850.
46 Ibid., 845.
47 *United Irishman*, 28 October 1899, 8.

48 It is interesting to note that *The Times History of the War in South Africa* represented two Irish brigades fighting for the Boer side as 'composed largely of Irish-Americans', and listed them among 'foreign' corps assisting the Boers – Dutch, German, French, American, Russian, Italian, etc. – making it clear that they were not rebels from within. (L. S. Amery (ed.), *The Times History of the War in South Africa, 1899–1902* vol. 2 (London: Sampson Low, Marston & Co., Ltd, 1902) p. 86).
49 *United Irishman*, 7 April 1900, 5.
50 Ibid., 17 March 1900, 7.
51 John Kelly (ed.), *The Collected Letters of W. B. Yeats* vol. 2 (Oxford: Clarendon Press, 1997), p. 503.
52 Letter from Maud Gonne to W. B. Yeats, 29 March 1900, in *The Gonne–Yeats Letters 1893–1938: Always Your Friend*, ed. Anna MacBride White and A. Norman Jeffares (London: Hutchinson, 1992), p. 73.
53 Janette Condon, 'The Patriotic Children's Treat: Irish Nationalism and Children's Culture at the Twilight of Empire', *Irish Studies Review* 8:2 (2000), 176.
54 *Black and White Budget*, 14 April 1900, 57.
55 *The Times*, 19 March 1900, 8.
56 Ibid. For an insight into Australia's enthusiasm for the Boer War, see Barbara R. Penny, 'Australia's Reactions to the Boer War – A Study in Colonial Imperialism', *Journal of British Studies* 7:1 (November 1967), 97–130.
57 Buckle, op. cit., p. 522.
58 Elizabeth Longford, *Victoria R.I.* (London: Weidenfeld & Nicolson, 1964), p. 555.
59 MacBride, *Servant of the Queen*, op. cit., p. 301.
60 *Hansard*, 4 April 1895, vol. 32, 909.
61 Ibid., 10 March 1896, vol. 33, 592.
62 Ibid., 13 February 1899, vol. 78, 667.
63 Buckle, op. cit., p. 501.
64 Ibid., p. 521.
65 *Black and White Budget*, 14 April 1900, 35.
66 Ibid., 36.
67 *Annual Register, A Review of Public Events at Home and Abroad, for the Year of 1900* (New York and Bombay: Longmans, 1901), p. 251.
68 *Irish Figaro*, 24 March 1900, 177.
69 *Academy* 58 (Jan–June 1900), 10 March 1900.
70 *The Times*, 19 March 1900, 8; V. C. Malherbe, *Eminent Victorians in South Africa* (Cape Town: Juta & Co. Ltd, 1972), p. 192.
71 Ralph, op. cit., p. 31.
72 Anonymous, 'The Wearin' o' the Green', *The New Oxford Book of Irish Verse* (Oxford: Oxford University Press, 1986), pp. 257–8.
73 *The Wearing of the Green (March 1900), Irish Air*, with new words by Alfred Perceval Graves, the music arranged by C. Villiers Stanford (London: Boosey & Co., 1900).
74 *By Order of the Queen: Song*, the words written by Isabel Sullivan, and set to the music of 'The Wearin' of the Green' by Alicia A. Needham (London: Novello & Co., Ltd, 1900).

75 *United Irishman*, 24 March 1900, 6.
76 Ibid., 17 March 1900, 5.
77 Ibid., 24 March 1900, 6.
78 Ibid., 17 March 1900, 7.
79 Kelly, op. cit., pp. 508–9.
80 Kipling, 'The Comprehension of Private Copper', in *Traffics and Discoveries* (Harmondsworth: Penguin Books, 1987), p. 147.
81 Kipling, 'Recessional', *The Five Nations*, op. cit., p. 215.
82 Kipling, 'The Sin of Witchcraft', *The Times*, 15 March 1900, 8.
83 Ibid.
84 Kipling, 'The Captive', in *Traffics and Discoveries*, op. cit., p. 39.
85 Ibid., p. 38.
86 Zigler reappears in Kipling's 'The Edge of the Evening' (1913), in *A Diversity of Creatures* (Harmondsworth: Penguin Books, 1987).
87 Kipling, 'The Captive', op. cit., p. 56.
88 Ibid., p. 38.
89 For the involvement of the United States in the Boer War, see, for example, Thomas J. Noer, *Briton, Boer and Yankee: the United States and South Africa, 1870–1914* (Kent, Ohio: Kent State University Press, 1978), Chapter 4, 'A British War for American Interests: The United States and the Boer War'.
90 Kipling, 'The Captive', op. cit., p. 47.
91 Kipling, 'The Sin of Witchcraft', op. cit.
92 'Mr. Kipling on Amnesty to Rebels', *The Times*, 3 February 1902, 10.
93 Kipling, 'The Science of Rebellion: A Tract for the Times. Specially Written for the Imperial South African Association', in *The Sussex Edition of the Complete Works in Prose and Verse of Rudyard Kipling*, vol. 30 (London: Macmillan & Co., 1938), p. 237.
94 Ibid., p. 233.
95 Ibid.
96 Ibid., p. 227.
97 Akbar S. Ahmed, 'Tribes and States in Central and South Asia', *Asian Affairs* 11:2 (June 1980), 160.
98 Kipling, 'The Science of Rebellion', op. cit., p. 236.
99 Rudyard Kipling, *Kim* (Harmondsworth: Penguin Books, 1987), p. 69.
100 Ibid., p. 70.
101 Ibid.
102 Akbar S. Ahmed, *Resistance and Control in Pakistan* (London and New York: Routledge, 1983), p. 174, n. 3.
103 Kipling, 'The Sin of Witchcraft', op. cit.
104 Kipling, 'Namgay Doola', in *Life's Handicap* (Harmondsworth: Penguin Books, 1987), p. 230.
105 Kipling, *Kim*, op. cit., pp. 132–4.
106 Ibid., p. 167.
107 Ibid., p. 84; my italics.
108 Ibid., p. 167.
109 Ibid.
110 Ibid., pp. 134–5.

111 Ibid., p. 192.
112 Ibid., p. 60.
113 Kipling, 'The Comprehension of Private Copper', op. cit., p. 147.
114 Ibid., p. 148.
115 Ibid., p. 145.
116 Ibid., p. 150.
117 Ibid., p. 145.
118 Ibid., p. 150.
119 For an excellent analysis of the Eurasian theme in 'The Comprehension of Private Copper', see C. A. Bodelsen, *Aspects of Kipling's Art* (Manchester: Manchester University Press, 1964), Chapter 4.
120 *The Irish World*, 4 December 1875, 4.

Chapter 5. Kim in South Africa

1 Rudyard Kipling, *Kim* (Harmondsworth: Penguin Books, 1987), p. 118.
2 A. Conan Doyle, *The Great Boer War* (London: Smith, Elder & Co., 1900), p. 1.
3 Paula M. Krebs, *Gender, Race, and the Writing of Empire: Public Discourse and the Boer War* (Cambridge: Cambridge University Press, 1999), p. 129.
4 Uys Krige (ed.) *Olive Schreiner: A Selection* (Cape Town: Oxford University Press, 1968), pp. 141–2.
5 Conan Doyle, op. cit., p. 4.
6 Byron Farwell, *The Great Boer War* (London: Allen Lane, 1977), p. 348.
7 C. Headlam (ed.), *The Milner Papers: South Africa, 1899–1905* (London: Cassell, 1931), p. 242.
8 Ibid.
9 Ibid., p. 243.
10 Ibid., p. 283.
11 Rudyard Kipling, 'A Burgher of the Free State', in *The Sussex Edition of the Complete Works in Prose and Verse of Rudyard Kipling*, vol. 30 (London: Macmillan & Co., 1938), p. 161.
12 Philip Holden, 'Halls of Mirrors: Mimicry and Ambivalence in Kipling's Boer War Short Stories', *ARIEL* 28:4 (October 1997), 102.
13 Ibid., p. 101.
14 Ibid., p. 97.
15 Ibid., p. 104.
16 Thomas Pinney (ed.), *The Letters of Rudyard Kipling*, vol. 3 (Iowa City: University of Iowa Press, 1990), p. 107.
17 Kipling, 'The Settler', in *The Five Nations* (London: Methuen & Co., 1903), p. 153.
18 Ibid.
19 Ibid., p. 154.
20 Arnold White, 'Concerning South African Settlers', *The Contemporary Review* 78 (November 1900), 670.
21 Charles W. Boyd (ed.), *Mr Chamberlain's Speeches*, 2 vols (London: Constable & Co. Ltd, 1914), vol. 2, p. 113.
22 Ibid., p. 114.

23 Ibid., p. 80. Here it may be appropriate to recall the speech of John Dillon in the House of Commons, in which he spoke for Ireland through the South African situation: 'When you have slaughtered a third of the whole population of the Transvaal, do you think the time will come to knit the two races together in harmony?' (*Hansard, 25 October 1899, fourth series*, vol. 77, 684).

24 Kipling, 'The Return', in *The Five Nations*, op. cit., p. 210.

25 Kipling, 'The Outsider', in *The Sussex Edition*, op. cit., vol. 30, p. 120.

26 Kipling, 'The Arrest of Lieutenant Golightly' (1886), in *Plain Tales from the Hills* (Hammondsworth: Penguin Books, 1987), p. 138. This story can be read as a good illustration of how one step out of the hill regions can instantly erode the Englishness of the Anglo-Indian, a point which I made in Chapter 2.

27 Kipling, 'The Outsider', op. cit., p. 123.

28 Ibid., pp. 124–5.

29 Kipling, 'Folly Bridge', in *The Sussex Edition*, op. cit., vol. 30, p. 101.

30 Ibid.

31 This episode might be based on Kipling's own experience, for, according to the *Academy*, 'Mr. Rudyard Kipling has been given a pass by Lord Roberts, enabling him to go wherever he pleases in South Africa' (10 March 1900).

32 Kipling, 'A Burgher of the Free State', op. cit., p. 144.

33 Krebs, op. cit., p. 166.

34 Ibid., p. 168.

35 Ibid., p. 169.

36 Kipling's letter to Charles Eliot Norton, 15 January 1900, in Pinney (ed.), *The Letters*, op. cit., p. 11.

37 Kipling, *Kim*, p. 139.

38 Bart Moore-Gilbert, '"The Bhabhal of Tongues": Reading Kipling, Reading Bhabha', in Bart Moore-Gilbert (ed.), *Writing India 1757–1990* (Manchester: Manchester University Press, 1996), p. 130. See also, Bart Moore-Gilbert, '"I am going to rewrite Kipling's *Kim*": Kipling and Postcolonialism', *Journal of Commonwealth Literature* 37 (2002), 39–58.

39 Don Randall, *Kipling's Imperial Boy: Adolescence and Cultural Hybridity* (Basingstoke: Palgrave, 2000), p. 16.

40 Ibid., p. 108.

41 Kipling, 'In the Rukh', in *Many Inventions* (London: Macmillan & Co., 1899), p. 201. 'In the Rukh' is the first story to be written for *The Jungle Books*, except possibly 'Mowgli's Brothers', completed in November 1892.

42 Kipling, 'Slaves of the Lamp, II', in *The Complete Stalky & Co.* (Oxford: Oxford World's Classics, 1991), pp. 287–8.

43 Kipling, 'Wee Willie Winkie' (1888), in *Wee Willie Winkie* (Harmondsworth: Penguin Books, 1988), pp. 255, 259.

44 Kipling, 'Mowgli's Brothers', in *The Jungle Books* (Oxford: Oxford World's Classics, 1992), p. 6.

45 G. F. Monkshood (W. J. Clarke) and George Gamble, *Rudyard Kipling: An Attempt at Appreciation*, third edition (London: Greening & Co., 1902), p. 268.

46 *The Times*, 6 October 1899, 8b.

47 Kipling's letter to Edward Lucas White, 11 November 1902, in Pinney, op. cit., p. 111.

48 Kipling, 'Red Dog', in *The Jungle Books*, op. cit., pp. 300–301. Mowgli's departure from the Jungle is narrated in 'The Spring Running', the last story of *The Jungle Books*.

49 Kipling, 'Slaves of the Lamp, II', op. cit., p. 283.

50 Kipling, 'Slaves of the Lamp, I', in *The Complete Stalky & Co.*, op. cit., pp. 54–71.

51 Kipling's letter to Margaret Burne-Jones, 28 November 1885–11 January 1886, in Thomas Pinney (ed.), *The Letters of Rudyard Kipling*, vol. 1 (Iowa City: University of Iowa Press, 1990), p. 100.

52 Edward W. Said, *Orientalism* (Harmondsworth: Penguin Books, 1995). For the art of quoting as a colonial strategy, see my article, 'Quotations and Boundaries: Kipling's *Stalky & Co.*' [Japanese], in Kazuhisa Takahashi and Makinori Hashimoto (eds.), *Rudyard Kipling* (Tokyo: Hakushosha, 2003), pp. 309–28.

53 Mark Kinkead-Weekes, 'Vision in Kipling's Novels', in Andrew Rutherford (ed.), *Kipling's Mind and Art* (Edinburgh: Oliver & Boyd, 1964), p. 217.

54 Gilles Deleuze and Félix Guattari, *A Thousand Plateaus: Capitalism and Schizophrenia*, translated with a foreword by Brian Massumi (London: Athlone Press, 1999), especially Chapter 10 on 'Becoming'.

55 Mahmood Mamdani, *When Does a Settler Become a Native?: Reflections of the Colonial Roots of Citizenship in Equatorial and South Africa, A. C. Jordan Professor of African Studies, Inaugural Lecture 13 May 1998* (Cape Town: University of Cape Town, 1998), p. 5.

56 Kipling, *Kim*, op. cit., p. 50.

57 Kipling, *With Number Three, Surgical & Medical, and New Poems; Also Letters from Julian Ralph, Charles E. Hands and Douglas Story* (Santiago de Chile: Hume & Co., 1900), p. 7; my italics.

58 R. E. Harbord (ed.), *The Readers' Guide to Rudyard Kipling's Work*, vol. 1 (Canterbury: Gibbs & Sons Ltd, 1961), p. 28.

59 Kipling, 'Lispeth', in *Plain Tales from the Hills*, op. cit., p. 33.

60 Ibid., p. 33.

61 Ibid., p. 34.

62 Ibid.

63 For the relation between the physical and social environment and the Victorian body, see, for example, Anthony S. Wohl, *Engendered Lives: Public Health in Victorian Britain* (London: Methuen, 1983).

64 Kipling, 'Lispeth', op. cit., p. 35.

65 Ibid., p. 36; my italics.

66 Ibid., p. 35.

67 Ibid.

68 Ibid., p. 36.

69 Ibid., p. 37.

70 Ibid.

71 Kipling, *Kim*, op. cit., p. 305.

72 Kipling, 'Namgay Doola', in *Life's Handicap* (Harmondsworth: Penguin Books, 1987), p. 228. It should be noted that Namgay Doola's wife is also a hill-woman, being a 'Thibetan' (p. 228).

73 Kipling, *Kim*, op. cit., p. 315.

74 Ibid., p. 313.
75 Ibid., p. 60.
76 Ibid., p. 315.
77 Kipling, 'Lispeth', op. cit., p. 37.
78 Kipling, *Kim*, op. cit., p. 315.
79 Kipling, 'Lispeth', op. cit., p. 33.
80 Kipling, *Kim*, op. cit., pp. 49–50.
81 In this respect, it is interesting to recall that Kim's father's regiment, the Mavericks, is elsewhere shown to have a long history of having fought as part of the British army: in 'The Mutiny of the Mavericks', the regimental colours, which the Mavericks 'keep long and guard . . . very sacredly' tell us the names of the important wars which the regiment fought for the British Empire: 'Vittoria, Salamanca, Toulouse, Waterloo, Moodkee, Ferozshah an' Sobraon . . . Inkermann, The Alma, Sebastopol' (*Life's Handicap*, op. cit., p. 183).
82 Kipling, *Kim*, op. cit., p. 68.
83 Ibid., p. 134.
84 Kipling, 'Lispeth', op. cit., p. 37.
85 Ibid.
86 Angus Wilson, *The Strange Ride of Rudyard Kipling: His Life and Works* (London: Secker & Warburg, 1977), p. 219.
87 Kipling, 'A Sahib's War', in *Traffics and Discoveries*, pp. 85–104.
88 Kipling, 'The Captive', in *Traffics and Discoveries*, op. cit., p. 53.
89 Kipling, 'Folly Bridge', op. cit.
90 Kipling, 'A Burgher of the Free State', op. cit., p. 183.
91 Ibid. p. 193.
92 C. A. Bodelsen, *Aspects of Kipling's Art* (Manchester: Manchester University Press, 1964), p. 155.
93 Ibid., pp. 159–60. Bodelsen, instead of dismissing the Eurasian motif as a digression, explains that it is 'a piece of daring symbolization' (p. 164) deliberately chosen by Kipling. He reminds the reader of the dispatch of Alfred Milner to Joseph Chamberlain, in which the former likens the position of the Uitlanders in the Transvaal to that of helots. Kipling, according to Bodelsen, by investing the renegade with the Eurasian accent and appearance, intends to show that the Uitlanders will actually degrade into an inferior race if they continue to be treated as such.
94 According to Catherine Wynne, *Kim* is a novel in which 'colonial and imperial converge to bolster the empire' (*The Colonial Conan Doyle: British Imperialism, Irish Nationalism, and the Gothic* (Westport: Greenwood Press, 2002), p. 5). Similarly, Joseph Lennon says, 'an Irishman in India is a free-floating signifier that Kipling could use to bolster imperialism' (*Irish Orientalism: A Literary and Intellectual History* (New York: Syracuse University Press, 2004), p. 281).
95 Kipling, 'A Sahibs' War', op. cit., p. 94.
96 Ibid.
97 Ibid.
98 Ibid., p. 92.
99 Kipling, *Kim*, op. cit., p. 174.

100 Kipling, 'A Sahib's War', op. cit., p. 92.
101 Ibid., p. 89.
102 Ibid., p. 103.
103 I wish to acknowledge the kind assistance of Dr Janet Montefiore, who pointed this out to me.
104 Kipling, 'A Sahib's War', op. cit., p. 104.
105 Ibid.
106 Percy Bysshe Shelley, 'Ozymandias' (1818), in Thomas Hutchinson (ed.), *Shelley: Poetical Works* (Oxford: Oxford University Press, 1971), p. 550.

Chapter 6. The Dynamite War of Analogies

1 Kipling's letter to H. A. Gwynne, 15 June 1907, in Thomas Pinney (ed.), *The Letters of Rudyard Kipling*, vol. 3 (Iowa City: University of Iowa Press, 1996), p. 241.
2 Peter Heehs, *The Bomb in Bengal: the Rise of Revolutionary Terrorism in India, 1900–1910* (Delhi: Oxford University Press, 1993), p. 63.
3 Thomas R. Metcalf, *Ideologies of the Raj* (Cambridge: Cambridge University Press, 1995), p. 200.
4 E. M. [Rudyard Kipling], 'Lord Ripon's Reverie', *Civil and Military Gazette*, 15 September 1884, repr. in R. E. Harbord (ed.), *The Readers' Guide to Rudyard Kipling's Work*, vol. 5 (Canterbury: Gibbs & Sons Ltd, 1969), p. 5063.
5 Sedition Committee 1918, *Report* (Calcutta: Superintendent Government Printing, India, 1918), p. 6. As for the 'Indian House' in London as the centre of the Indian nationalist movement, see also Valentine Chirol, *Indian Unrest* (London: Macmillan & Co., 1910), pp. 148–9; S. A. Wolpert, *Tilak and Gokhale: Revolution and Reform in the Making of Modern India* (Berkeley and Los Angeles: University of California Press, 1962), pp. 168–9.
6 See Anil Seal, *The Emergence of Indian Nationalism: Competition and Collaboration in the Later Nineteenth Century* (Cambridge: Cambridge University Press, 1968), p. 258; Narinder Kapur, *The Irish Raj: Illustrated Stories About Irish in India and Indians in Ireland* (Antrim: Greystone Press, 1997), p. 32.
7 *The Times*, 27 May 1880, 6c.
8 Maud Gonne MacBride, *A Servant of the Queen* (Woodbridge, Suffolk: Boydell Press, 1983), p. 259.
9 B. L. Grover, *A Documentary Study of British Policy towards Indian Nationalism 1885–1909* (Delhi: National Publications, 1967), p. 171.
10 Kipling, 'Trial by Judge', *Civil & Military Gazette*, 16 September 1885, in Harbord, op. cit., p. 5090.
11 Arthur Mee (ed.), *Popular Science* (London: Amalgamated Press, 1912–13), vol 4, p. 2402.
12 For example, Frank Hugh O'Donnell mentions Rossa as 'the O'Donovan Rossa of dagger and dynamite journalism' in his article 'Fenianism – Past and Present', *Contemporary Review* 43 (May 1883), 752.
13 As for contemporary accounts of dynamite outrages, see, for example, 'Crimes and Criminals: No. I. – Dynamite and Dynamiters', *Strand Magazine* 7 (February 1894), 119–32; Patrick J. P. Tynan, *The Irish National Invincibles and Their Times* (London: Chatham & Co., 1894), pp. 327–31.

14 In the *United Irishman*, the power of discourse was itself seen as being as powerful as dynamite, able to blast the British rule in Ireland. For example, Daniel O'Connell's book was called 'the Dynamite Book', which would make 'any man or woman of Irish blood . . . an apostle of dynamite, or of hell-fire, or any force that would strike the enemy of Ireland to her knees' (*United Irishman* (New York), 6 June 1885, 8).

15 Kipling, 'The Way Av Ut', *Pioneer*, 8 October 1888, and 'The Irish Conspiracy', *Pioneer*, 18 February 1889, both repr. in R. E. Harbord (ed.), *The Readers' Guide to Rudyard Kipling's Work*, vol. 1 (Canterbury: Gibbs & Sons Ltd, 1969), verse section, pp. 5226, 5256.

16 Kipling, 'The Mutiny of the Mavericks', in *Life's Handicap* (Harmondsworth: Penguin Books, 1987), p. 181.

17 Kipling, 'The Comprehension of Private Copper', in *Traffics and Discoveries* (Harmondsworth: Penguin Books, 1987), p. 151.

18 Kipling, *Kim* (Harmondsworth: Penguin Books, 1987), p. 70.

19 Kipling, 'On the City Wall', *Soldiers Three and In Black and White* (Harmondsworth: Penguin Books, 1993), pp. 157–8.

20 Kipling, *Kim*, op. cit., p. 204.

21 S. B. Cook, *Imperial Affinities: Nineteenth-Century Analogies and Exchanges Between India and Ireland* (New Delhi: Sage Publications, 1993), p. 79.

22 Ibid., p. 80.

23 Walter E. Houghton (ed.), *The Wellesley Index to Victorian Periodicals 1824–1900*, vol.1 (Toronto: University of Toronto Press, London: Routledge & Kegan Paul, 1966), pp. 286, 995.

24 Charles William McMinn, 'The Home Rule Movement in India and in Ireland: A Contrast', *Contemporary Review* 57 (January 1890), 78. He is also the author of *Famine Truths, – Half Truths, – Untruths* (Calcutta: Baptist Mission Press, 1902).

25 Ibid., p. 80.

26 Ibid., p. 78.

27 Ibid., p. 79.

28 Ibid., p. 78.

29 Ibid., p. 96.

30 Ibid.

31 Ibid., p. 79.

32 *India Office List for 1889* (London: Harrison & Sons, 1889), p. 159.

33 McMinn, 'The Home Rule Movement', op. cit., 81.

34 *The Times* , 22 January 1909, 7c.

35 Kipling's letter to Lord Kitchener, 6 November 1908, Pinney, op.cit., p. 343.

36 Ibid., p. 342.

37 Kipling's letter to Lord Curzon, 16 September 1902, Pinney, op. cit., p. 106. For the difference in representing the Indian Empire between the Delhi Darbar of 1903 and Kipling's *Kim*, see my article, 'The Writing on the Wall: The Commemoration of the Indian Mutiny in the Delhi Durbar, and Rudyard Kipling's 'The Little House at Arrah', *Interventions: International Journal of Postcolonial Studies*, 7:1 (2005), 84–96.

38 John Morley, 'The Government of Ireland: A Reply', *Nineteenth Century* 21:2 (February 1887), 319.

39 Ras Behari Ghose, 'Opening address, Twenty-second Indian National Congress, Calcutta, 26 December 1906', in *Report of the Twenty-First Indian National Congress*, quoted in Stephen E. Koss, *John Morley at the India Office, 1905–1910* (New Haven and London: Yale University Press, 1969), p. 8.

40 W. J. Johnston, 'Mr. Morley and Ireland', *Westminster Review* 165 (1906), 476.

41 John Morley's speeches in the House of Commons, 6 June 1907, *Hansard*, fourth series, vol. 175, 879–80.

42 'To Constituents', a speech made in Arbroath on 21 October 1907, in Viscount Morley, *Indian Speeches (1907–1909)* (London: Macmillan & Co., 1909), pp. 35–6.

43 For the accounts of the famines of 1896–7 and of 1899–1900, see, for example, B. M. Bhatia, *Famines in India: A Study in Some Aspects of the Economic History of India (1860–1965)* (London: Asia Publishing House, 1967), especially Chapter 9, 'Famines in India, 1896–1914'.

44 *The Times*, 7 June 1847, 3f. According to The *Bombay Times*, the sum subscribed towards the Irish and Scotch Relief Fund at Bombay amounted to £9,500, the total subscription throughout India amounting to nearly £26,000, within the short period of two months (20 May 1841).

45 *The Times*, 8 April 1861, 10f.

46 Ibid., 7 June 1847, 3f.

47 Mohandas Karamchand Gandhi, *The Collected Works of Mahatma Gandhi*, vol. 3 (Ahmedabad: Navajivan Trust, 1960), p. 152.

48 Maud Gonne, 'The Famine Queen', *United Irishman*, 7 April 1900, 5.

49 Ibid.

50 Maud Gonne, 'Her Subjects', *United Irishman*, 28 April 1900, 5.

51 Maud Gonne, 'India', *United Irishman*, 12 May 1900, 5.

52 Maud Gonne, 'The World's Justice', *United Irishman*, 25 August 1900, 6.

53 Maud Gonne, 'Signs of Hope', *United Irishman*, 13 January 1900, 5.

54 Maud Gonne, '"As India must be bled"', *United Irishman*, 14 July 1900, 6.

55 Ibid.

56 Ibid.

57 Thomas W. Laqueur ,'Bodies, Details, and the Humanitarian Narrative', in Lynn Hunt (ed.), *The New Cultural History* (Berkeley and Los Angeles: University of California Press, 1989), pp. 176–204.

58 Gonne, 'The World's Justice', op. cit., 6.

59 Gonne, 'Her Subjects', op. cit., 5. For the detailed account of Queen Victoria's popularity among her Irish subjects, see James H. Murphy, *Abject Loyalty: Nationalism and Monarchy in Ireland During the Reign of Queen Victoria* (Cork: Cork University Press, 2001).

60 Margaret Kelleher, *The Feminization of Famine: Expressions of the Inexpressible?* (Cork: Cork University Press, 1997), p. 2.

61 Antoinette Burton, *Burdens of History: British Feminists, Indian Women, and Imperial Culture, 1865–1915* (Chapel Hill and London: University of North Carolina Press, 1994).

62 Florence Nightingale, 'The People of India', *Nineteenth Century* 18 (August 1878), 193.

63 Kipling, 'William the Conqueror', in *The Day's Work* (Harmondsworth: Penguin

Books, 1988), pp. 157–89. Originally written for woman's magazines: *The Gentlewoman*, *The Ladies' Home Journal*.

64 Maud Gonne, 'What We Owe the Children', *United Irishman*, 7 July 1900, 5.

65 MacBride, *Servant of the Queen*, op. cit., p. 7.

66 *The Times*, 9 April 1900, 10a.

67 MacBride, *Servant of the Queen*, op. cit., p. 294.

68 Ibid., pp. 294–5.

69 George Earle Buckle (ed.), *The Letters of Queen Victoria*, third series, vol. 3, (London: John Murray, 1932), p. 524. There is an apparent confusion or manipulation in Gonne's narrative as to how many children actually attended the Queen's Treat and her Patriotic Children's Treat. In the *United Irishman* (7 July 1900, 5), Gonne mentions that 30,000 children attended her Patriotic Children's Treat, instead of the 20,000 she mentioned in her autobiography.

70 Gonne, 'What We Owe the Children', op. cit., 5.

71 Inghinidhe na hÉireann, *Second Annual Report: Session 1901–1902* (Dublin: Swan & Co., 1902), p. 2.

72 Maud Gonne, 'Ireland and the Children', *United Irishman*, 7 June 1902.

73 Maud Gonne, 'Famine in the West', *Irish Daily Independent*, 10 March 1898.

74 Gonne, 'The World's Justice', op. cit., 6.

75 Maud Gonne, 'Ireland and her Foreign Relations', *United Irishman*, 22 December 1900.

76 Kipling, 'On the Strength of a Likeness', in *Plain Tales from the Hills* (Harmondsworth: Penguin Books, 1987), pp. 254–9.

77 Sigmund Freud, 'The Uncanny', in *The Complete Psychological Works of Sigmund Freud*, edited by James Strachey (London: Hogarth Press, 1955), vol. 17, p. 233.

78 Ibid., p. 234.

79 Homi. K. Bhabha, 'Introduction', in Homi K.Bhabha (ed.), *Nation and Narration* (London and New York: Routledge, 1990), p. 2.

Conclusion

1 Ian Colvin, *The Life of General Dyer* (Edinburgh and London: William Blackwood & Sons, 1929), p. 12.

2 For Mulvaney's involvement in a row in 'Silver Street', see Chapter 3.

3 Colvin, op. cit., p. 126.

4 *Hansard*, 8 July 1920, fifth series, vol. 131, p. 1718.

5 Ibid., p. 1716.

6 Arthur Swinson, *Six Minutes to Sunset: The Story of General Dyer and the Amritsar Affair* (London: Peter Davies, 1964), p. 209.

7 Morton Cohen (ed.), *Rudyard Kipling to Rider Haggard: The Record of a Friendship* (London: Hutchinson & Co., 1965), p. 111.

8 Ibid., pp. 117–18.

9 Patrick Braybrooke, *Kipling and His Soldiers* (London: C. W. Daniel Co., 1926), p. 111.

10 Rudyard Kipling, *The Irish Guards in the Great War*, 2 vols. (Staplehurst, Kent: Spellmount, 1997).

11 J. M. S. Tompkins, *The Art of Rudyard Kipling* (London: Methuen & Co., 1959), p. 204.

12 Zohreh T. Sullivan, *Narratives of Empire: The Fictions of Rudyard Kipling* (Cambridge: Cambridge University Press, 1993), p. 47.
13 Edward W. Said, *Culture and Imperialism* (London: Vintage, 1994), p. 162.

Bibliography

Primary sources

Amery, L. S. (ed.), *The Times History of the War in South Africa, 1899–1902* vol. 2 (London: Sampson Low, Marston and Co, Ltd., 1902).

Annual Register, A Review of Public Events at Home and Abroad, for the Year of 1900 (New York and Bombay: Longmans, 1901).

Anonymous, 'Crimes and Criminals: No. I. – Dynamite and Dynamiters', *Strand Magazine* 7 (February 1894), 119–32.

Austin, Alfred, *Songs of England* (London: Macmillan & Co., 1898).

Boyd, Charles W. (ed.), *Mr Chamberlain's Speeches*, 2 vols. (London: Constable & Co. Ltd, 1914).

British Sessional Papers, House of Commons, 1857–8, VII, pt 1.

Buchanan, Robert, 'The Voice of the Hooligan', *Contemporary Review* 76 (December 1899), 774–89, repr. in Roger Lancelyn Green (ed.), *Kipling: The Critical Heritage* (London: Routledge & Kegan Paul, 1971), pp. 233–49.

Buckle, George Earle (ed.), *The Letters of Queen Victoria*, third series, vol. 3 (London: John Murray, 1932).

Cahill, D. W., *Important Letter from the Rev. D. W. Cahill, D.D.* (Dublin: J. F. Nugent, 1858).

Childers, Erskine, *In the Ranks of the C.I.V.: A Narrative and Diary of Personal Experiences with the C.I.V. Battery (Honourable Artillery Company) in South Africa* (London: Smith, Elder & Co., 1901).

Chirol, Valentine, *Indian Unrest* (London: Macmillan & Co., 1910).

Cobbe, Frances Power, 'The Fenian Idea', *Atlantic Monthly* 17 (May 1866), 573–7.

Colvin, Ian, *The Life of General Dyer* (Edinburgh and London: William Blackwood & Sons, 1929).

Darwin, Charles, *On the Origin of Species* (London: John Murray, 1859).

Doyle, A. Conan, *The Great Boer War* (London: Smith, Elder & Co., 1900).

Gandhi, Mohandas Karamchand, *The Collected Works of Mahatma Gandhi* (New Delhi: Publications Division, Ministry of Information and Broadcasting, Govt. of India, 1958–).

Graves, Alfred Perceval, *The Wearing of the Green (March 1900), Irish Air*, with new words by Alfred Perceval Graves, the music arranged by C. Villiers Stanford (London: Boosey & Co., 1900).

Grover, B. L., *A Documentary Study of British Policy Towards Indian Nationalism 1885–1909* (Delhi: National Publications, 1967).

Hamley, William, 'Ireland Our Reproach', *Blackwood's Edinburgh Magazine* 128 (December 1880), 775–92.

Hansard, Parliamentary Debates, third, fourth and fifth series.

Headlam, C. (ed.), *The Milner Papers: South Africa, 1899–1905* (London: Cassell, 1931).

Hill, Edmonia, 'Young Kipling', *Atlantic Monthly* 157 (1936), 406–15.

Homer, *The Odyssey*, translated by E. V. Rieu (Harmondsworth: Penguin Books, 1991).

India Office List for 1889 (London: Harrison & Sons, 1889).

Inghinidhe na hÉireann, *Second Annual Report: Session 1901–1902* (Dublin: Swan & Co., 1902)

Johnston, W. J., 'Mr. Morley and Ireland', *Westminster Review* 165 (May 1906), 476–80.

Kaye, John, *Kaye's and Malleson's History of the Indian Mutiny of 1857–8*, edited by Colonel Malleson, 6 vols. (1897–8) (Westport, Conn.: Greenwood Press, 1971).

Kelly, John (ed.), *The Collected Letters of W. B. Yeats*, vol. 2 (Oxford: Clarendon Press, 1997).

Kingsley, Charles, *Charles Kingsley: His Letters and Memories of His Life, Edited by His Wife* (London: Kegan Paul, Trench & Co., 1888).

Kipling, Rudyard, *Actions and Reactions* (London: Macmillan & Co., 1909).

—, *A Diversity of Creatures* (1917; Harmondsworth: Penguin Books, 1987).

—, *The Complete Barrack-Room Ballads* [1892], edited by Charles Carrington (London: Methuen & Co. Ltd, 1973).

—, *The Complete Stalky & Co.* (1929; Oxford: Oxford World's Classics, 1991).

—, *The Day's Work* (1898; Harmondsworth: Penguin Books, 1988).

—, *The Five Nations* (London: Methuen & Co., 1903).

—, *From Sea to Sea and Other Sketches: Letters of Travel*, 2 vols. (London: Macmillan & Co., 1900).

—, *The Irish Guards in the Great War, The First Battalion. Edited and Compiled from their Diaries and Papers by Rudyard Kipling*, with a foreword by George Webb, 2 vols. (1923; Staplehurst, Kent: Spellmount, 1997).

—, *The Jungle Books* (1894–5; Oxford: Oxford World's Classics, 1992).

—, *Kim* (1901; Harmondsworth: Penguin Books, 1987).

—, *A Kipling Note Book* (New York: M. F. Mansfield & A. Wessels, 1899).

—, *Land and Sea Tales for Scouts and Guides* (London: Macmillan & Co., 1923).

—, *Life's Handicap* (1891; Harmondsworth: Penguin Books, 1987).

—, *Many Inventions* (1893; London: Macmillan & Co., 1899).

—, *Plain Tales from the Hills* (1888/9; Harmondsworth: Penguin Books, 1987).

—, *Soldiers Three and In Black and White* (1888; Harmondsworth: Penguin Books, 1993).

—, *Something of Myself: For My Friends Known and Unknown* (1936; Harmondsworth: Penguin Books, 1977).

—, *The Sussex Edition of the Complete Works in Prose and Verse of Rudyard Kipling*, vol. 30 (London: Macmillan & Co., 1938).

—, *Traffics and Discoveries* (1904; Harmondsworth: Penguin Books, 1987).

—, *Wee Willie Winkie* (1888; Harmondsworth: Penguin Books, 1988).

—, *With Number Three, Surgical & Medical, and New Poems; Also Letters from Julian Ralph, Charles E. Hands and Douglas Story* (Santiago de Chile: Hume & Co., 1900).

Kipling, Rudyard and Wolcott Balestier, *The Naulakha: A Story of West and East* (London: Macmillan & Co., 1892).

Krige, Uys (ed.), *Olive Schreiner: A Selection* (Cape Town: Oxford University Press, 1968).

Lang, Andrew, 'Ballads' in *Encyclopaedia Britannica*, ninth edition, vol. 3 (1875), pp. 283–5.

—, *Essays in Little* (London: Henry & Co., 1891).

Lee-Warner, William, *The Life of the Marquis of Dalhousie K.T.*, 2 vols. (1904; Shannon: Irish University Press, 1972).

Lenin, V. I., *Imperialism: The Highest Stage of Capitalism: A Popular Outline* (1917; Moscow: Foreign Languages Publishing House, 1970).

Literature vol.2 [1898], vol. 9 [1901]. (London: *The Times*, 1897–1902; repr. New York: Arno Press, 1974)

MacBride, Maud Gonne, *Maud Gonne's Irish Nationalist Writings: 1895–1946*, edited and introduced by Karen Steele (Dublin: Irish Academic Press, 2004).

—, *A Servant of the Queen: Reminiscences* (1938; Suffolk: Boydell Press, 1983).

McCarthy, Michael J. F., *Five Years in Ireland, 1895–1900* (London: Simpkin, Marshall, Hamilton, Kent, 1901).

McMinn, Charles William, *Famine Truths, – Half Truths, – Untruths* (Calcutta: Baptist Mission Press, 1902).

—, 'The Home Rule Movement in India and in Ireland: A Contrast', *Contemporary Review* 57 (January 1890), 78–97.

Maugham, W. Somerset, *The Complete Short Stories of W. Somerset Maugham*, 3 vols. (London: Heinemann, 1951).

Mee, Arthur (ed.), *Popular Science*, 7 vols. (London: Amalgamated Press, 1912–13).

Monkshood, G. F. (W. J. Clark) and George Gamble, *Rudyard Kipling: An Attempt at Appreciation*, third edition (London: Greening & Co., 1902).

Moore, Thomas, *Irish Melodies* (London: Longmans, 1849).

—, *Lalla Rookh: An Oriental Romance* (1817; London: Longmans, 1861).

Morley, John, 'The Government of Ireland: A Reply', *Nineteenth Century* 21:1 (January 1887), 19–39; 21:2 (February 1887), 301–20.

—, *Indian Speeches (1907–1909)* (London: Macmillan & Co., 1909).

Müller, F. Max, *Chips from a German Workshop*, 3 vols. (London: Longmans, Green & Co., 1880).

Nightingale, Florence, 'The People of India', *Nineteenth Century* 18 (August 1878), 193–221.

O'Donnell, Frank Hugh, 'Fenianism – Past and Present', *Contemporary Review* 43 (May 1883), 747–66.

Oliphant, Margaret, ''Tis Sixty Years Since', *Blackwood's Edinburgh Magazine* 161 (May 1897), 599–624.

Pinney, Thomas (ed.), *Kipling's India: Uncollected Sketches 1884–88* (Basingstoke: Macmillan, 1986).

—, (ed.), *The Letters of Rudyard Kipling*, 6 vols. (Iowa City: University of Iowa Press, 1990–99).

Ralph, Julian, *War's Brighter Side: The Story of "The Friend" Newspaper Edited by the Correspondents with Lord Roberts's Forces, March–April 1900* (London: C. Arthur Pearson Ltd, 1900).

Roberts, F. S. R., *Forty-One Years in India, from Subaltern to Commander-in-Chief* , 2 vols. (1897; London: Macmillan & Co., 1902).

Robinson, E. Kay, 'Rudyard Kipling in India', *Pearson's Magazine* 1 (June 1896), 657–62.

Robinson, J. B., 'The South African Settlement', *Contemporary Review* 78 (October 1900), 457–67.

Russell, William Howard, 'The Climate and the Work', *Cornhill Magazine* 6 (August 1862), 241–57.

—, *My Indian Mutiny Diary* [1860], edited with an essay on the Mutiny and its consequences by Michael Edwardes (New York: Kraus Reprint Co., 1970).

Sedition Committee 1918, *Report* (Calcutta: Superintendent Government Printing, India, 1918).

Stoker, Bram, *Dracula* [1897], edited by Nina Auerbach and David J. Skal (New York and London: Norton & Co., 1997).

Sullivan, Alexander Martin, 'Why Send More Irish Out of Ireland?', *Nineteenth Century* 14 (July 1883), 131–44.

Sullivan, Isabel, *By Order of the Queen: Song*, the words written by Isabel Sullivan, and set to the music of 'The Wearin' of the Green' by Alicia A. Needham (London: Novello & Co., Ltd, 1900).

Tone, Theobald Wolfe, *Memoirs of Theobald Wolfe Tone*, edited by William Theobald Wolfe Tone, 2 vols. (London: Henry Colburn, 1827).

Whewell, William, 'The General Bearing of the Great Exhibition on the Progress of Art and Science', in W. Whewell et al., *Lectures on the Results of the Great Exhibition of 1851* (London: David Bogue, 1852), pp. 1–34.

White, Anna MacBride and A. Norman Jeffares (eds.), *The Gonne–Yeats Letters 1893–1938: Always Your Friend* (London: Hutchinson, 1992).

White, Arnold, 'Concerning South African Settlers', *Contemporary Review* 78 (November 1900), 669–75.

Yule, Henry and A. C. Burnell, *Hobson-Jobson: A Glossary of Colloquial Anglo-Indian Words and Phrases, and of Kindred Terms, Etymological, Historical, Geographical and Discursive*, second edition [1903], edited by William Crooke, with a new foreword by Anthony Burgess (London: Routledge & Kegan Paul, 1986).

Newspapers and periodicals

Academy.

Black and White Budget.

Bombay Times.

Illustrated London News.

Irish Figaro.

Irish World.

Judy, or The London Serio-Comic Journal.

Punch, or The London Charivari.

The Times.

United Irishman (Dublin).

United Irishman (New York).

Secondary sources

Ahmed, Akbar S., *Resistance and Control in Pakistan* (London and New York: Routledge, 1983).

—, 'Tribes and States in Central and South Asia', *Asian Affairs* 11:2 (June 1980), 152–68.

Allen, Charles (ed.), *Plain Tales from the Raj* (London: Futura Publications, 1975).

Anderson, Benedict, *Imagined Communities: Reflections on the Origin and Spread of Nationalism*, revised edition (London and New York: Verso, 1991).

—, *The Spectre of Comparisons: Nationalism, South Asia and the World* (London and New York: Verso, 1998).

Anderson, N. F., '"Mother Besant" and Indian National Politics', *Journal of Imperial and Commonwealth History* 30:3 (September 2002), 27–54.

Anderson, Warwick, 'Climates of Opinion: Acclimatization in Nineteenth-Century France and England', *Victorian Studies* 35:2 (Winter 1992), 135–57.

Arata, Stephen D., 'The Occidental Tourist: *Dracula* and the Anxiety of Reverse Colonization', *Victorian Studies* 33 (Summer 1990), 621–45.

Arnold, David, *Colonizing the Body: State Medicine and Epidemic Disease in Nineteenth-Century India* (Berkeley: University of California Press, 1993).

Babington, Anthony, *The Devil to Pay: The Mutiny of the Connaught Rangers, India, July, 1920* (London: Leo Cooper, 1991).

Bailin, Miriam, *The Sickroom in Victorian Fiction: The Art of Being Ill* (Cambridge: Cambridge University Press, 1994).

Bakhtin, M. M., *The Dialogic Imagination, Four Essays by M. M. Bakhtin*, edited by Michael Holquist and translated by Caryl Emerson and Michael Holquist (Austin: University of Texas Press, 1981).

Barrell, John, *The Infection of Thomas de Quincey: A Psychopathology of Imperialism* (New Haven and London: Yale University Press, 1991).

Bartley, J. O., 'The Development of a Stock Character', *Modern Language Review* 37 (1942), 438–47.

Bayly, C. A., *Empire and Information: Intelligence Gathering and Social Communication in India, 1780–1870* (Cambridge: Cambridge University Press, 1996).

Bernard-Donals, Michael, 'Knowing the Subaltern: Bakhtin, Carnival, and the Other Voice of the Human Sciences', in Michael Mayerfield Bell and Michael Gardiner (eds.), *Bakhtin and the Human Sciences* (London: Sage Publications, 1998), pp. 112–27.

Bhabha, Homi K. (ed.), *Nation and Narration* (London and New York: Routledge, 1990).

Bhatia, B. M., *Famines in India: A Study in Some Aspects of the Economic History of India (1860–1965)* (London: Asia Publishing House, 1967).

Bodelsen, C. A., *Aspects of Kipling's Art* (Manchester: Manchester University Press, 1964).

Boehmer, Elleke, *Empire, the National, and the Postcolonial, 1890–1920: Resistance in Interaction* (Oxford: Oxford University Press, 2002).

Brasted, Howard, 'Indian Nationalist Development and the Influence of Irish Home Rule, 1870–1886', *Modern Asian Studies* 14:1 (1980), 37–63.

Braybrooke, Patrick, *Kipling and His Soldiers* (London: C. W. Daniel Co., 1926).

Buettner, Elizabeth, 'From Somebodies to Nobodies: Britons Returning Home from India', in Martin Daunton and Bernhard Rieger (eds.), *Meanings of Modernity: Britain from the Late-Victorian Era to World War II* (New York: Berg Publishers, 2001), pp. 221–40.

Burton, Antoinette, *Burdens of History: British Feminists, Indian Women, and Imperial Culture, 1865–1915* (Chapel Hill and London: University of North Carolina Press, 1994).

Candy, Catherine, 'Margaret Cousins's Occult Feminism in Ireland and India, 1878–1954', in Mary Cullen and Maria Luddy (eds.), *Female Activists: Irish Women and Change, 1900–1960* (Dublin: Woodfield Press, 2001).

—, 'Relating Feminisms, Nationalisms and Imperialisms: Ireland, India and Margaret Cousins's Sexual Politics', *Women's History Review* 3:4 (1994), 581–94.

Carey, James W., *Communication as Culture: Essays on Media and Society* (Boston, Mass.: Unwin Hyman, 1989).

Carrington, Charles, *Rudyard Kipling: His Life and Work* (London: Macmillan & Co., 1955).

Carroll, Clare and Patricia King (eds.), *Ireland and Postcolonial Theory* (Cork: Cork University Press, 2003)

Cohen, Morton (ed.), *Rudyard Kipling to Rider Haggard: The Record of a Friendship* (London: Hutchinson & Co., 1965).

Condon, Janette, 'The Patriotic Children's Treat: Irish Nationalism and Children's Culture at the Twilight of Empire', *Irish Studies Review* 8:2 (2000), 167–78.

Cook, S. B., *Imperial Affinities: Nineteenth-Century Analogies and Exchanges Between India and Ireland* (New Delhi: Sage Publications, 1993).

—, 'The Irish Raj: Social Origins and Careers of Irishmen in the Indian Civil Service, 1855–1914', *Journal of Social History* 20:3 (1987), 507–29.

Curtis, L. Perry, Jr., *Apes and Angels: The Irishman in Victorian Caricature* (Newton Abbot, Devon: David & Charles, 1971).

Deleuze, Gilles and Félix Guattari, *A Thousand Plateaus: Capitalism and Schizophrenia*, translated with a foreword by Brian Massumi [1980] (London: Athlone Press, 1999).

Derrida, Jacques, 'Hospitality', translated by Barry Stocker and Forbes Morlock, *Angelaki* 5:3 (December 2000), 3–18.

Dowling, Linda, *Language and Decadence in the Victorian Fin de Siècle* (Princeton: Princeton University Press, 1986).

Eagan, Catherine M., '"White," if "Not Quite": Irish Whiteness in the Nineteenth-Century Irish-American Novel', *Éire-Ireland: A Journal of Irish Studies* 36:1–2 (Spring–Summer 2001), 66–81.

Edmond, Rod, *Affairs of the Hearth: Victorian Poetry And Domestic Narrative* (London: Routledge, 1988).

Farwell, Byron, *The Great Boer War* (London: Allen Lane, 1977).

—, *Queen Victoria's Little Wars* (London: Allen Lane, 1973).

Fenwick, J. H., 'Soldiers Three', in Andrew Rutherford (ed.), *Kipling's Mind and Art* (Edinburgh: Oliver & Boyd, 1964), pp. 235–54.

Fraser, T. G., 'Ireland and India', in Keith Jeffery (ed.), *'An Irish Empire'?: Aspects of Ireland and the British Empire* (Manchester and New York: Manchester University Press, 1996), pp. 77–93.

Freud, Sigmund, *The Complete Psychological Works of Sigmund Freud*, edited by James Strachey vol.17 (London: Hogarth Press, 1955).

—, *The Interpretation of Dreams* (1900; Harmondsworth: Penguin Books, 1991).

F. V. F., 'The Mavericks of "Kim"', *Kipling Journal* 152 (December 1964), 9–10.

Gerould, Katherine Fullerton, 'The Man Who Made Mulvaney', *Harper's Monthly Magazine* 172 (1936), 531–8.

Gibbons, Luke, 'Race Against Time: Racial Discourse and Irish History', *Oxford Literary Review* 13:1–2 (1991), 95–117.

Gorman, Mel, 'Sir William O'Shaughnessy, Lord Dalhousie, and the Establishment of the Telegraph System in India', *Technology and Culture* 12 (October 1971), 581–601.

Hagemann, Susanne, 'The Irishness of *Dracula*,' in Winnifred M. Bogaards (ed.), *Literature of Region and Nation: Proceedings of the 6th International Literature of Region and Nation Conference, 2–7 August 1996* (Saint John, NB: Social Sciences and Humanities Research Council of Canada, with University of New Brunswick in Saint John, 1998), pp. 239–53.

Hai, Ambreen, 'On Truth and Lie in a Colonial Sense: Kipling's Tales of Tale-Telling', *ELH* 64:2 (Summer 1997), 599–625.

Hanham, H. J., 'Religion and Nationality in the Mid-Victorian Army', in M. R. D. Foot (ed.), *War and Society: Historical Essays in Honour and Memory of J. R. Western, 1928–1971* (London : Elek, 1973), pp. 159–181.

Harbord, R. E. (ed.), *The Readers' Guide to Rudyard Kipling's Work*, 8 vols. (Canterbury: Gibbs & Sons Ltd, 1961–72).

Harrison, James, 'Kipling's Jungle Eden', in Harold Orel (ed.), *Critical Essays on Rudyard Kipling* (Boston, Mass.: G. K. Hall & Co., 1989), pp. 77–92.

Hatlen, Burton, 'The Return of the Repressed/Oppressed in Bram Stoker's *Dracula*', *Minnesota Review* 15 (1980), 80–97.

Heehs, Peter, *The Bomb in Bengal: The Rise of Revolutionary Terrorism in India, 1900–1910* (Delhi: Oxford University Press, 1993).

Henderson, Mae Gwendolyn, 'Speaking in Tongues: Dialogics, Dialectics and the Black Woman Writer's Literary Tradition', in Sidonie Smith and Julia Watson (eds.), *Women, Autobiography, Theory, A Reader* (London: University of Wisconsin Press, 1998), pp. 343–51.

Hoffenberg, Peter H., *An Empire Display: English, Indian, and Australian Exhibitions from the Crystal Palace to the Great War* (Berkeley: University of California Press, 2001).

Holden, Philip, 'Halls of Mirrors: Mimicry and Ambivalence in Kipling's Boer War Short Stories', *ARIEL* 28:4 (October 1997), 91–109.

Holmes, Michael and Denis Holmes (eds.), *Ireland and India: Connections, Comparisons, Contrasts* (Dublin: Folens, 1997).

Hopper, Glenn and Colin Graham (eds.), *Irish and Postcolonial Writing: History, Theory, and Practice* (New York: Palgrave Macmillan, 2002).

Houghton, Walter E., *The Victorian Frame of Mind, 1830–70* (New Haven: Yale University Press, 1957).

—, (ed.), *The Wellesley Index to Victorian Periodicals 1824–1900*, 5 vols. (Toronto: University of Toronto Press, London: Routledge & Kegan Paul, 1966–89).

Howe, Stephen, *Ireland and Empire: Colonial Legacies in Irish History and Culture* (Oxford: Oxford University Press, 2002).

Hubel, Teresa, 'Tommy Atkins in India: Class Conflict and the British Raj', *Kunapipi* 22:1 (2000), 95–105.

Hutchins, Francis G., *The Illusion of Permanence: British Imperialism in India* (Princeton: Princeton University Press, 1967).

Hutchinson, Thomas (ed.), *Shelley: Poetical Works* (Oxford: Oxford University Press, 1971).

Hyman, Ronald, *Empire and Sexuality: The British Experience* (Manchester and New York: Manchester University Press, 1990).

Innes, C. L., 'Orientalism and Celticism', in Glenn Hopper and Colin Graham (eds.), *Irish and Postcolonial Writing: History, Theory, and Practice* (New York: Palgrave Macmillan, 2002), pp. 142–56.

Jakobson, Roman, *Selected Writings, Volume 2: Word and Language* (The Hague: Mouton, 1971).

James, Lawrence, *Mutiny: In the British and Commonwealth Forces, 1797–1956* (London: Buchan & Enright, 1987).

JanMohamed, Abdul R., 'Worldliness-without-World, Homelessness-as-Home: Toward a Definition of the Specular Border Intellectual', in Jessica Munns and Gita Rajan (eds.), *A Cultural Studies Reader: History, Theory, Practice* (London and New York: Longman, 1995), pp. 442–62.

Jeffery, Keith (ed.), *'An Irish Empire'?: Aspects of Ireland and the British Empire* (Manchester and New York: Manchester University Press, 1996).

Kapur, Narinder, *The Irish Raj: Illustrated Stories About Irish in India and Indians in Ireland* (Antrim: Greystone Press, 1997).

Karsten, Peter, 'Irish Soldiers in the British Army, 1792–1922: Suborned or Subordinate?', *Journal of Social History* 17 (Fall 1983), 31–64.

Keating, P. J., *The Working Classes in Victorian Fiction* (London: Routledge & Kegan Paul, 1971).

Kelleher, Margaret, *The Feminization of Famine: Expressions of the Inexpressible?* (Cork: Cork University Press, 1997).

Kennedy, Dane, *The Magic Mountains: Hill Stations and the British Raj* (Berkeley: University of California Press, 1996).

—, 'The Perils of the Midday Sun: Climatic Anxieties in the Colonial Tropics', in John M. Mackenzie (ed.), *Imperialism and the Natural World* (Manchester: Manchester University Press, 1990), pp. 118–40.

Kiberd, Declan, 'The Fall of the Stage Irishman', *Genre* 12 (1979), 451–72.

—, *Inventing Ireland* (London: Jonathan Cape, 1995).

Koss, Stephen E., *John Morley at the India Office, 1905–1910* (New Haven and London: Yale University Press, 1969).

Krebs, Paula M., *Gender, Race, and the Writing of Empire: Public Discourse and the Boer War* (Cambridge: Cambridge University Press, 1999).

Laqueur, Thomas W., 'Bodies, Details, and the Humanitarian Narrative', in Lynn Hunt (ed.), *The New Cultural History* (Berkeley and Los Angeles: University of California Press, 1989), pp. 176–204.

Lee, Emanoel, *To the Bitter End: A Photographic History of the Boer War 1899–1902* (Harmondsworth: Penguin Books, 1985).

Lennon, Joseph, *Irish Orientalism: A Literary and Intellectual History* (New York: Syracuse University Press, 2004).

—, 'Writing Across Empire: W. B. Yeats and Rabindranath Tagore', in Patrick Colm Hogan and Lalita Pandit (eds.), *Rabindranath Tagore: Universality and Tradition* (Madison, NJ: Fairleigh Dickinson University Press, 2003), pp. 213–29.

Lloyd, David, 'After History: Historicism and Postcolonial Studies', in Clare Carroll and Patricia King (eds.), *Ireland and Postcolonial Theory* (Cork: Cork University Press, 2003) pp. 46–62.

—, *Anomalous States: Irish Writing and the Post-Colonial Moment* (Dublin: Lilliput Press, 1993).

Longford, Elizabeth, *Victoria R.I.* (London: Weidenfeld & Nicolson, 1964).

MacRaild, Donald M., *Irish Migrants in Modern Britain: 1750–1922* (London: Macmillan, 1999).

Majeed, Javed, *Ungoverned Imaginings: James Mill's The History of British India and Orientalism* (Oxford: Clarendon Press, 1992).

Malherbe, V. C., *Eminent Victorians in South Africa* (Cape Town: Juta & Co. Ltd, 1972).

Mallett, Phillip, *Rudyard Kipling: A Literary Life* (Basingstoke and New York: Palgrave Macmillan, 2003).

Mamdani, Mahmood, *When Does a Settler Become a Native?: Reflections of the Colonial Roots of Citizenship in Equatorial and South Africa, A. C. Jordan Professor of African Studies, Inaugural Lecture, 13 May 1998* (Cape Town: University of Cape Town, 1998).

Metcalf, Thomas R., *Ideologies of the Raj* (Cambridge: Cambridge University Press, 1995).

Montefiore, Janet, 'Day and Night in Kipling', *Essays in Criticism* 27 (October 1977), 299–314.

—, *Rudyard Kipling* (Plymouth: Northcote House, 2006).

Moore-Gilbert, Bart, '"The Bhabhal of Tongues": Reading Kipling, Reading Bhabha', in Bart Moore-Gilbert (ed.), *Writing India 1757–1990* (Manchester: Manchester University Press, 1996), pp. 111–38.

—, '"I am going to rewrite Kipling's *Kim*": Kipling and Postcolonialism', *Journal of Commonwealth Literature* 37 (2002), 39–58.

Morey, Peter, *Fictions of India: Narrative and Power* (Edinburgh: Edinburgh University Press, 2000).

Moses, Michael Valdez, 'The Irish Vampire: Dracula, Parnell, and the Troubled Dreams of Nationhood', *Journal X* 2:1 (Autumn 1997), 66–111.

Moss, Robert F., *Rudyard Kipling and the Fiction of Adolescence* (London: Macmillan, 1982).

Mukherjee, J., 'The Relevance of the Irish Aspect in Rudyard Kipling's *Kim*', *Literary Criterion* 22:4 (1987), 41–5.

Murphy, James H., *Abject Loyalty: Nationalism and Monarchy in Ireland During the Reign of Queen Victoria* (Cork: Cork University Press, 2001).

Murphy, J. J. W., 'Kipling and the Irish Soldier in India', *Kipling Journal* 168 (December 1968), 20–25; 169 (March 1969), 20–22; 170 (June 1969), 10–14.

Nagai, Kaori, 'Quotations and Boundaries: Kipling's *Stalky & Co.*' [Japanese], in Kazuhisa Takahashi and Makinori Hashimoto (eds.), *Rudyard Kipling* (Tokyo: Hakushosha, 2003), pp. 309–28.

—, 'The Writing on the Wall: The Commemoration of the Indian Mutiny in the

Delhi Durbar, and Rudyard Kipling's 'The Little House at Arrah', *Interventions: International Journal of Postcolonial Studies* 7:1 (2005), 84–96.

Naik, M. K., *Mirror on the Wall: Images of India and the Englishman in Anglo-Indian Fiction* (New Delhi: Sterling Publishers, 1991).

Nair, Rukmini Bhaya, 'The Pedigree of the White Stallion', in Marshall Brown (ed.), *The Use of Literary History* (Durham, NC, and London: Duke University Press, 1995), pp. 159–86.

Netzer, Nancy, 'Picturing an Exhibition: James Mahony's Watercolors of the Irish Industrial Exhibitions of 1853', in Adele M. Dalsimer (ed.), *Visualizing Ireland: National Identity and the Pictorial Tradition* (Boston, Mass.: Faber & Faber, 1993), pp. 88–98.

Noer, Thomas J., *Briton, Boer and Yankee: The United States and South Africa, 1870–1914* (Kent, Ohio: Kent State University Press, 1978).

Pechey, Graham, 'On the Borders of Bakhtin: Dialogization, Decolonization', *Oxford Literary Review* 9:1–2 (1987), 59–84.

Pedley, Colin, 'Blake's Tiger and the Discourse of Natural History', *Blake: An Illustrated Quarterly* 24:1 (Summer 1990), 238–46.

Philip, Kavita, 'English Mud: Towards a Critical Cultural Studies of Colonial Science', *Cultural Studies* 12:3 (July 1998), 300–331.

Pittock, Murrat G. H., *Celtic Identity and the British Image* (Manchester: Manchester University Press, 1999).

Quinn, Antoinette, 'Cathleen ni Houlihan Writes Back: Maud Gonne and Irish Nationalist Theatre', in Anthony Bradley and Maryann Gialanella Vaaliulis (eds.), *Gender and Sexuality in Modern Ireland* (Amherst: University of Massachusetts Press, 1997), pp. 39–59.

Randall, Don, *Kipling's Imperial Boy: Adolescence and Cultural Hybridity* (Basingstoke: Palgrave, 2000).

Rao, K. Bhaskara, *Rudyard Kipling's India* (Norman: University of Oklahoma Press, 1967).

Richards, Thomas, *The Imperial Archive: Knowledge and the Fantasy of the Empire* (London and New York: Verso, 1993).

Rutherford, Andrew (ed.), *Kipling's Mind and Art* (Edinburgh: Oliver & Boyd, 1964).

Said, Edward W., *Culture and Imperialism* (1993; London: Vintage, 1994).

—, *Orientalism* (1978; Harmondsworth: Penguin Books, 1995).

Sandison, Alan, 'Kipling: The Artist and the Empire', in Andrew Rutherford (ed.), *Kipling's Mind and Art* (Edinburgh: Oliver & Boyd, 1964), pp. 146–67.

Scheerer, Constance, 'The Lost Paradise of Rudyard Kipling', in Harold Bloom (ed.), *Rudyard Kipling's* Kim, (New York: Chelsea House Publishers, 1987), pp. 75–85.

Seal, Anil, *The Emergence of Indian Nationalism: Competition and Collaboration in the Later Nineteenth Century* (Cambridge: Cambridge University Press, 1968).

Short, K. R. M., *The Dynamite War: Irish-American Bombers in Victorian Britain* (Dublin: Gill & Macmillan, 1979).

Silvestri, Michael S., 'The "Sinn Fein of India": Irish Nationalism and the Policing of Revolutionary Terrorism in Bengal, 1905–1939', *Journal of British Studies* 39 (October 2000), 454–86.

Spivak, Gayatri Chakravorty, 'The Burden of English', in Carol A. Breckenridge and

Peter van der Veer (eds.), *Orientalism and the Postcolonial Predicament: Perspectives on South Asia* (Philadelphia: University of Pennsylvania Press, 1993), pp. 134–57.

Stephen, Leslie and Sidney Lee (eds.), *Dictionary of National Biography*, 22 vols. (London: Oxford University Press, 1959–60).

Sullivan, Zohreh T., *Narratives of Empire: The Fictions of Rudyard Kipling* (Cambridge: Cambridge University Press, 1993).

Swift, Roger and Sheridan Gilley (eds.), *The Irish in Victorian Britain: The Local Dimension* (Dublin: Four Courts Press, 1999).

Swinson, Arthur, *Six Minutes to Sunset: The Story of General Dyer and the Amritsar Affair* (London: Peter Davies, 1964).

Tompkins, J. M. S., *The Art of Rudyard Kipling* (London: Methuen & Co., 1959).

Trudgill, Eric, *Madonnas and Magdalens: The Origins and Development of Victorian Sexual Attitudes* (London: Heinemann, 1976).

Tucker, Irene, 'International Whiggery', *Victorian Studies* 45:4 (Summer 2003), 687–97.

Tynan, Patrick J. P., *The Irish National Invincibles and Their Times* (London: Chatham & Co., 1894).

Viola, Andre, 'Empire of the Senses or a Sense of Empire? The Imaginary and the Symbolic in Kipling's *Kim*', *ARIEL* 28:2 (April 1997), 159–72.

Virilio, Paul, *Open Sky*, translated by Julie Rose (London: Verso, 1997).

—, *Speed and Politics: An Essay on Dromology*, translated by Mark Polizzotti (New York: Semiotext(e), 1986).

Viswanathan, Gauri, 'Ireland, India, and the Poetics of Internationalism', *Journal of World History* 15:1 (March 2004), 7–30.

—, 'Spirituality, Internationalism and Decolonization: James Cousins, the "Irish Poet from India"', in Clare Carroll and Patricia King (eds.), *Ireland and Postcolonial Theory* (Cork: Cork University Press, 2003), pp. 158–76.

Watson, Tim, 'Indian and Irish Unrest in Kipling's *Kim*', in Laura Chrisman and Benita Parry (eds.), *Postcolonial Theory and Criticism* (Woodbridge, Suffolk: D. S. Brewer, 2000), pp. 95–113.

Wegner, Phillip E., '"Life as He Would Have It": The Invention of India in Kipling's *Kim*', *Cultural Critique* 26 (Winter 1993–4), 129–59.

Wilson, Angus, *The Strange Ride of Rudyard Kipling: His Life and Works* (London: Secker & Warburg, 1977).

Wohl, Anthony S., *Engendered Lives: Public Health in Victorian Britain* (London: Methuen, 1983).

Wolpert, S. A., *Tilak and Gokhale: Revolution and Reform in the Making of Modern India* (Berkeley and Los Angeles: University of California Press, 1962).

Young, Robert J. C., *Colonial Desire: Hybridity in Theory, Culture and Race* (London: Routledge, 1995).

Index